First published in Great Britain in 2004.

This book is dedicated to the people of Uplyme past, present and future.

British Library Cataloguing-in-Publication Data.
A CIP record for this title is available from the British Library.

ISBN 1 84114 335 9

HALSGROVE

Halsgrove House
Lower Moor Way
Tiverton, Devon EX16 6SS
Tel: 01884 243242
Fax: 01884 243325
email: sales@halsgrove.com
website: www.halsgrove.co.uk

Frontispiece photograph: *The Black Dog immediately after its rebuilding in 1916.
The photographer was standing on the Devon/Dorset boundary looking at the first and last building in Devon.*

Printed and bound by CPI Bath Press, Bath.

Acknowledgments

The authors are grateful to the following for permission to use their pictures, memoirs and memorabilia in this history:

The 1st Lym Valley Scout Group, The British Museum, Jo Draper and the Lyme Regis Philpott Museum, Axminster Museum, The Society of Antiquaries, The West Country Studies Library, *Pulman's Weekly News*, Muriel Arber, Derek Baker, Les Berry, Pat Carroll, Will Crabbe, Fred Day, Beryl Denham, Jane Edwards, Thelma Finnemore, Sandra Furzey, Neil Goldsworthy, Violet Gosling, Stan Gudge, Marion Hellier, Molly Matthews, Laurence Masters, David Mostyn, June Moulding, Adrian Pearson, Jennie Pearson, Jim Purvis, Penny Randerson, Violet Raymond, Diana Shervington, Bill Simpson, Fred Smith, Wendy Smith, Kathy Summers, Imogen Thomas, Mark Thomas, Bill Tivenan, Lyn White, John Wood, Edna Woodman, Paula Wyon-Brown, Frederick Warne & Co.

Lane End Farm in 1926. In front of their home stand the Wyatt family with, left to right: *Queenie, Millie, Florence and Nelly.*

At Granny's

Granny has an old thatched cottage
In an Uplyme lane
With rambling roses twining round
The little window pane.

This is where the children love
To spend their holiday,
Running wild around the woods
And romping in the hay.

They like to go up to the farm
To fetch the milk for tea;
They love to watch the honey hives
And climb the apple trees,

To feed the chickens and to look
For fresh eggs in the nest
And walk to church across the mead
Dressed in their Sunday best.

Then when supper's cleared away
To climb the twisty stairs
And kneel beside their small, white beds
To say their evening prayers.

To lie and watch the candlelight
Make shadows on the wall.
A holiday at Granny's home
Is greatest fun of all.

George Furzey
(1905–80)

Contents

Uplyme from Knoll Hill in 1908. Mrs Ethelston's School is in the foreground. In the background Whalley Lane boasts only two houses, Hilltop on the left and Higher Fold on the right, with the railway line running below it.

The main street of Uplyme in 1937. On the right at the corner of Gore Lane is Eddy Wheadon's butcher's shop with a tearoom (formerly a cycle shop) beyond. It was owned by Anne Ostick who called it Anne's Pantry. Behind the wall on the right in the foreground was Uplyme's Post Office at that time. Out of sight to the left of the car is the village stores (the Post Office in 2003) run by Miss Brewer.

Chapter 1

A BRIEF HISTORY OF THE PARISH OF UPLYME

The earliest known picture of our village, c.1800, with the church and Court Hall Farm sheltering beneath Knoll Hill. The hedge in the foreground marks the present main road (B3162) through the village. The field in the foreground, then the property of the Church, is the cricket field in 2003.

The parish of Uplyme is one of the largest in Devon. Ask anyone who has beaten the bounds by walking round the 16 miles of its boundary. Not only is it the last parish in the Diocese of Exeter (or the first), it also contains a number of scattered hamlets – Holcombe, Harcombe, Cannington, Yawl, Ware, Shapwick, Happy Valley, Rocombe, Cathole, Amherst, Hunters Cross, Trinity Hill, St Mary's, Whitty Down, Rhode Hill, Woodhouse, Carswell and Burrowshot, to name but 18!

The little River Lym rises at the top of the parish, runs down to the sea and gives its name not only to our village, but also to the adjacent town in Dorset and the whole of a vast bay which stretches from Portland to Start Point. In 1284 Edward I gave a royal charter to Lyme, making it Lyme Regis. Before that the village and the port, umbilically joined by the cord of the Lym, were known as Upper Lyme (or Uplyme) and Netherlym-supra-mare or Lower Lyme on sea. To this day people in Lyme Regis may refer to Uplyme as 't'other Lyme!'

If you look at the back of your left hand, you can easily imagine that you are gazing at a simple relief map of Uplyme. Your little finger is Shapwick Hill, your second finger Woodhouse Hill, your middle finger Knoll Hill, your index finger Springhead and your thumb Rhode Hill. Then between your five fingers lie four combes, or 'bottoms' as we call them. Starting on the left we have the first bottom containing Happy Valley, Shapwick Valley, Holcombe Valley and Cannington. The second bottom, up which runs the main road, is Yawl Bottom, the third one is Rocombe Bottom and the final one is Harcombe Bottom. Of course the middle of the back of your hand is where the Post Office and shop are, with Church Street leading up to the church and Mrs Ethelston's Primary School.

Man has chosen to live in this green and pleasant place since prehistoric times. He has left behind him relics of his occupation from the Stone Age onwards. From the Domesday Book and from other sources it appears that Uplyme consisted of an estate of 1,008 acres, valued at £4. In the year AD740 Cynewulf, King of Wessex, gave the manor of Uplyme to the Abbey and Convent of St Mary of Glastonbury. Aethelstan, the first King of all England and King Alfred's grandson, confirmed this gift in AD937 and included the advowson or patronage of the church. Uplyme was the only estate held by that monastery in Devon at the time of the Domesday survey in AD1086. On 18 May 1239, the estate of Lahale (now known as Yawl) within the manor of Uplyme was also given to the monastery at Glastonbury by Sir William Mohun, knight.

In 1368 Nicholas Pinnocke bestowed on the monks a virgate of land (approximately 30 acres) with the office of Beadle of Uplyme, and the reversion of a tenement, then occupied by John Wotton and Iditha his wife. In 1330 King Edward III granted the monastery the right of free warrenage in Uplyme. In the Domesday Book Uplyme is described as belonging to Glastonbury, a situation which lasted until the Dissolution of the Monasteries in 1536. The estate was valued then at £33.0s.3d. In that year the Drakes of Musbury, rich landowners, bought the manor and advowson and held it until 1775. Uplyme's patronage had changed hands only once in 1,000 years.

In the sixteenth century the people of Uplyme possessed the right of pasture for their sheep on the common called Wolcomb's Down (Wooly Hill) and Rocombs-hed (Trinity Hill). Shapwick was, at the time of the Domesday survey in 1086, in the hundred (or district) of Axminster. In 1249 it was the estate of Henry de Burton and Mabel his wife. They sold it on 14 May 1249 to Newenham Abbey near Axminster for 30 marks of silver. Shapwick did not become part of the parish of Uplyme until 1884.

The Civil War brought misery to Uplyme in the seventeenth century. In 1644, for six long weeks, Royalist troops unsuccessfully besieged Lyme Regis, a Parliamentarian stronghold. Many troops were billeted in Uplyme, especially in the church, which had to be extensively restored after the war. The churchwardens' accounts for 1649 show that the church roof, glass and pews had to be completely restored – an expensive business for the rector, Revd Edmund Hunt, and his Parochial Church Council.

Meanwhile, over at Musbury the widowed Lady Drake, a Parliamentary supporter, was forced to flee from her house, which was set on fire. Hostilities over, she offered a home to her daughter who had married a Royalist captain called Winston Churchill. Their son, the future famous Duke of Marlborough (victor at Blenheim and owner of Blenheim Palace), was born at Musbury in 1650, a grandson to the patron of Uplyme church.

On 11 June 1685 the Duke of Monmouth landed at Lyme Regis, where he spent three days before marching through Uplyme on 15 June, heading north to his bloody and ignominious defeat at the Battle of Sedgemoor. Nemesis followed. At Court Hall Farm, a very ancient building abutting the churchyard, there is a chair which is said to be that on which Judge Jeffreys of Bloody Assizes fame once sat. At the Exeter, Dorchester and Taunton Assizes Judge Jeffreys sentenced 12 local rebels to be hanged, drawn and quartered on what is now called Monmouth Beach in Lyme Regis. Amongst 13 persons executed at Bridport

Uplyme from the railway line in the 1920s above Gore Lane. The Havering is the house to the right of the church, Mrs Ethelston's School is on the left. Note the absence of houses between the B3165 road and Knoll Hill.

Uplyme, in around 1900, from Springhead, before the railway was built

on 11 September 1685 was G. Collier of 'Uplime'. 'The heads and quarters of these persons to be fixed where the King shall appoint.' To the north of Uplyme there used to stand a gibbet on which mangled limbs of executed rebels were displayed. To this day the road is still called Red Lane, a gory reminder of a savage age.

In 1811 Sweetman built a bridge over the River Lym at the bottom of Springhead Road, and the new main road up to Hunters Lodge opened in 1832. Hunters Lodge itself, the most northern building in Uplyme, was rebuilt in 1850. Jane Austen came down through Uplyme, which she described as 'a cheerful village.' On Christmas Day, 1839, the cliffs collapsed, creating in the Undercliff the Landslip which crowds came to admire and wonder at, including the newly crowned Queen Victoria herself.

William and Dorothy Wordsworth set up their first home at Racedown in the vale of Marshwood in 1795. One day Dorothy told William to ride down to the Cobb and order a cart-load of sea coal for the winter. William did as he was told by his sister. He ambled along on his horse through Marshwood, down through Uplyme, doubtless composing poetry all the way, until he tethered his horse on the Cobb. He ordered the coal which cost him 24 shillings and walked back to his home at Racedown. 'Did you get the coal?' asked Dorothy. 'Yes,' replied William. 'Good,' said Dorothy, 'and where's the horse?' Poets can be a trifle absent-minded! That's why they write good poetry.

In the middle of a boiling hot summer's day in the 1850s, some people were taking liquid refreshment outside Hunters Lodge Inn. As they sat there quietly enjoying their tankards of ale, they noticed a man running as if for a wager, much distressed by his efforts and the heat of the day. As he came up from the Charmouth direction, he touched a chord to which their hearts responded. When he managed to pant out, 'Race, gem'men, Devon 'gainst Dorset,' a seat was provided for him and refreshments bountifully afforded. As soon as 'Devon' had adequately refreshed himself with liberal quantities of ale speedily quaffed, he set off again in the general direction of Axminster to the cheers and encouragement of the onlookers. It was not long before they saw 'Dorset' coming up with an attendant, both greatly distressed. Bets were offered and taken on 'Devon' winning the race. But when

'Dorset' could regain his breath and make enquiries for the thief, the party were considerably mortified to find that these pursuers were in fact the constables of Charmouth in pursuit of a man who had been seen robbing a gentleman's garden!

Thereafter Uplyme reverts to its placid and undramatic existence with only the occasional blip or natural disaster. In 1881 there was a great snowstorm. On Whit Sunday in 1890 a cloudburst turned the River Lym into a raging torrent which flooded the village. The Black Dog burnt down in 1905 and, not to be outdone, the Talbot Arms had fires on two successive Thursdays in 1926. In 1922 the first council-houses were built in Whalley Lane. The old Rectory became the Devon Hotel in 1934 with a new Rectory being built in Rhode Lane. A bomb fell on Uplyme in 1941 with very little effect, Frank Hutchings, in the house that was hit, at the time sleeping peacefully through the disturbance! Uplyme acquired a new and much-loved Village Hall in 1923 that lasted 70 years until the new, handsome Village Hall was opened in 1994. Despite vigorous opposition Wickens won their appeal to build 27 houses in the centre of the village. Now Wykeham Homes have transformed Barnes Meadow from a large and rather unkempt field, the home of dormice and badgers, into 41 'luxurious homes, quintessentially English, in a setting beyond compare', to quote from the builder's glossy brochure. The badgers and the dormice have long since departed to make way for newcomers. Whilst we regret the passing of the mammals, we welcome the newcomers, of course. Come to think of it, most of us are 'newcomers'. Few can claim to be of families that have lived in the village for generations.

Uplyme is in an Area of Outstanding Natural Beauty. It stretches from Hunters Lodge in the north, almost 700 feet above sea level all the way down to Pinhay Bay and Seven Rock Point on the coastline, part of Lyme Bay. The coast from Poole to Exmouth has been declared a World Heritage Site. So now Uplyme can modestly say that it is on a par with the Grand Canyon or the Pyramids of Giza. If the builders say we live in 'a setting beyond compare', who are we to disagree with them?

Looking down Uplyme's main street in 1921, called Rectory Road on this postcard; on the right the high wall concealed the Rectory from inquisitive eyes. At the far end stands Bert Simmonds' smithy – Bert was so popular that he started to shoe horses at daybreak.

9

Above: *Map of Uplyme in 1827 made from an actual survey by C. & J. Greenwood. Note that there is no main road through Yawl, here mistakenly called Yatt.*

Right: *John Turner (father of Joe) in 1910 at Woodhouse Fields with Fatty and Patty. The three Prescott sisters came from a Lancashire family that had made its money in coal. They moved to Woodhouse in 1904, bringing John Turner with them as a groom. One of the sisters, Miss Alice Prescott, carved the handsome panels in the porch of the Parish Church.*

Chapter 2

THEN & NOW

A COMPARISON BETWEEN UPLYME IN 1851 AND 2001.

What was Uplyme like 150 years ago? Let's see what *White's Directory of Devonshire* says for 1850:

UPLYME, a large scattered village, is pleasantly situated at the most eastern extremity of Devon, only about a mile N.W. of the town and sea-port of Lyme-Regis, in Dorsetshire. Its parish is a suburb of that town, and comprises 3149 acres. 2 roods. 5 perches. of land with 50 acres of water. The Manor was anciently held by Glastonbury Abbey, and afterwards passed to the Drake and Tucker families. The Hon. Sir John Talbot, K.C.B., Admiral of the Red, is now lord of the manor and owner of a great part of the parish. He has a handsome seat here called Rhode Hill House. Robert Bourchier Wrey, Esq., of Ware Cliff House; James Davidson, Esq., and the Rev. C.W. Ethelston, M.A., have estates in the parish. The latter is also patron and incumbent of the Rectory, valued in K.B. at £20. 8s. 11½d., and in 1831 at £386. The glebe is 35 acres, and the Rectory House is a handsome residence, which was enlarged and much improved in 1838, when the tithes were commuted for £461. The Church (St. Peter and St. Paul) is an ancient structure, with a remarkably low tower.

So much for the large, scattered village of 1850. In the early-twenty-first century in Uplyme there are 633 houses with approximately 1,500 people living in them. Contrast that with 150 years previously. The 1851 census reveals that there were 107 houses with a population of 583 (244 males, 339 females). The population of Uplyme has trebled in a century and a half whilst the housing has increased sixfold.

In 1850 what were the occupations in Uplyme, how many farms were there, who was doing what, and was it fundamentally the same village as the one we know today, or was it radically different?

In 1850 Uplyme was predominantly an agricultural community with the vast majority of men employed as agricultural labourers. There were 29 farms in Uplyme: Underhill Farm, Yawl Farm, Cathole Farm, Amherst Farm, Valley Farm, Perhams Farm, Court Hall Farm, Lower Holcombe Farm, West Hill Farm, Penn Croft Farm, Higher Holcombe Farm, Hook Farm, Hill Farm, Shapwick Grange Farm, Ware Farm, Home Farm, Hunters Cross Farm, Upper Mill Farm, Beech Farm, Hillside Farm, Harcombe Farm, Lane End Farm, Cannington Farm, Hoyton Farm, Woolcombe Farm, Thirty-Acre Farm, Winter's Farm, Carswell Farm and Coombehayes Farm. In 2003 there are no more than three.

What else has changed since 1850? Well, for starters, a new main road was built in 1832 up through Yawl. 'A number of narrow lanes which meandered aimlessly from Hunters Lodge to Uplyme were cut through and straightened.' (Wanklyn) – that means that the old main road (Springhead Road) was no longer the main thoroughfare. It also ensured that after 1945 ribbon development would ensue all the way from the Talbot Arms up to Yawl.

Francis Bickley in *Where Dorset Meets Devon* (1911) describes Uplyme as 'a pretty scattered village with some fine chestnut trees.' So all the commentators agree that Uplyme is scattered. That is its main feature and chief attraction. It has a centre of sorts but there are also numerous outlying hamlets or suburbs – Holcombe, Harcombe, Rocombe, Shapwick, Carswell, Cannington, Yawl, St Mary's, Trinity Hill, Woodhouse Hill, Newcastle, Springhead, Ware, Burrowshot and others. As for the chestnut trees, they have mostly gone. But there are some fine ones at the top of Tapper's Knapp and one was planted in 1965 on the green outside the church as a memorial to Sir Winston Churchill. Happily it is flourishing in 2004 and offers shade to the Uplyme Stone.

Bickley continues by saying:

Uplyme Church is worth visiting, if only for the pretty lane in which it stands. This makes a pleasant change from the main road and its hedges seem to contain finer blackberries than are to be found elsewhere in the neighbourhood.

Alas, this no longer seems to be the case – blackberries in Pound Lane are conspicuous by their absence. Bickley has this to say about Yawl:

[It is] a place, for all its tiny body, with a soul. The balcony-like nature of the road is very striking. For a mile or more this one runs above the charming hollow known as Yawl Bottom, through which meanders the

Above: *Thomas Hardy, in his poem 'In Time of the Breaking of Nations', speaks of the unchanging face of the English countryside, sadly no longer true. Happily John Quick at his horse's head with a team of haymakers in 1917 on Lower Holcombe Farm evokes the golden past.*

Below: *Harcombe Bottom.*

Right: *The Smithy at the end of Venlake.*

upper waters of the familiar Buddle [Bickley's name for the River Lym]. *Opposite lie the clad slopes of Woodhouse Hill and further to the north the greater height and barer summit of Trinity Hill. These bottoms, green cups moulded among the hills, are characteristic of the neighbourhood. On the other side of the road, not hidden from view is Rocombe Bottom with Knoll Hill and Yawl Hill at either end; and divided from that by Whitty Hill is Harcombe Bottom, the fairest of them all. One can wander about these pleasant places at will, for there are many lanes and footpaths there and many hills worth climbing. Shapwick Hill, Trinity Hill, Rhode Hill and the rest. Any of them offer to show you, at the price of a little breath, this varied and verdant country mapped beneath you. This is praise indeed and well merited. Uplyme's chief glory is its landscape, not its architecture.*

But it is time to introduce some of the characters who were living in this verdant place called Uplyme in 1850. In 1851, besides all those farmers, there were some landed gentry and clergy. In the Rectory resided Revd Charles Wickstead Ethelston and his wife Anne. They had many servants living with them – a butler called William South, a coachman called Moses Gale, a footman called Francis Newberry, Maryanne Clarke who was the house-keeper, Elizabeth Stuart the upper housemaid, Maryanne Swayne the housemaid and Charlotte Hitchcock who was the under-cook. Ethelston, on a stipend of £450 a year with a free residence and 35 acres of glebe land, employed seven servants.

Sir John Talbot Esq. up at Rhode House was lord of the manor. The census described him as a landed proprietor who had two sons, Reginald and Neill, and three daughters, Laura, Julia and Kitty. He too had a bevy of servants. Elizabeth Croker was the housekeeper, Mary Vincent the lady's maid, Jane Gave the cook, Elizabeth Seward a housemaid, Eliza Hodder another housemaid, Sarah Brown a dairy-maid, Mary Eldon a kitchenmaid, with William Clark and Alfred Tucker as footmen. That's inside Rhode House – outside Sir John employed Chris Fowler as a lime burner and 16 labourers to manage the estate and farm 130 acres.

Then there was Albert William Beetham Esq. He was a Fellow of the Royal Society, a barrister, the Recorder of Dartmouth and a Justice of the Peace for Middlesex and the Tower Hamlets. Obviously an important man, much of his working life was spent away from Uplyme.

What were the shops like in 1851? In Uplyme in 2003 we have one shop, the Post Office, although until recently we had three. In 1851 there were at a conservative estimate nearly 20 places in Uplyme where one could buy various products. For example, because people did a great deal of walking in those days and shoes were at a premium, John Cox, John Hoare and William Woolcott all made shoes for

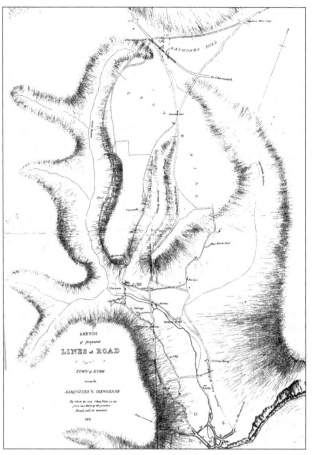

The 1821 map of Uplyme.

the community. It is difficult to envisage three shoemakers making a living in Uplyme in the twenty-first century. There were three grocers – Robert Matthews, John Mountstephen (who was also an ironmonger) and Job H. Fowler (still a popular name in the village in 2003), who was a draper, grocer and sub-postmaster. Letters from Lyme Regis arrived at 8.40a.m. and were dispatched at 4.55p.m. One wonders whether there has been any significant postal improvement in 150 years. William Lane was a poulterer, Thomas Harding a butcher and John Salter a baker. Richard Dean and James Welsman were blacksmiths, Henry Butcher a wheelwright, and John Hill a saddler and harness maker. Uplyme in those days needed three carpenters – John Butcher, John Lockyear and Job Moore. Alice Deane, Simeon S. Swain and Robert Hoare were shopkeepers, while Mrs Mary Ann Moore made dresses and John Larcombe was a tailor. Charles Randle was the landlord of the Talbot Arms, James Brockway that of Hunters Lodge and Mrs Gabriel Hilliar kept The Black Dog. Henry Webb was appropriately a webbing manufacturer. John Long of Hook called himself a dairyman, John Edwards a miller and John Lockyear a builder. John Adams was the schoolmaster, and William Marshall the parish clerk.

The 1851 census reveals that there were also a carter, painter, gardener, chiropodist, wool packer, governess, mason, driver of mineral waters, market

Whalley Lane, at the top of the picture, and the village in 1930 from above the church and school. Work on the new council-houses started in 1922. The houses were built in groups of six, every three houses sharing an outside toilet and cistern, a system which persisted until the 1950s.

gardener, monthly nurse, laundry assistant, seam-stress, cordwainer and a scholar. Oh yes, and let's not forget, there was Mary Gosling who was living on parish relief.

Jane Austen is not the only visitor who came to and admired Uplyme in those days. Let us introduce Emily Smith (whose daughter married Jack Thomas' grandfather). She was the wife of Revd Reginald Smith, rector of West Stafford near Dorchester. In 1852 Emily Smith had a week's holiday in Lyme with her family and kept a diary, recording:

Tuesday, 31 August, 1852. Lyme Regis. At 10, bidding adieu to our 5 dear ones, and taking Emily Anna with us, also Mary and Richard, we started on our expedition to Lyme. We got a leader [an extra horse to help their own horse, Mr George, up the hills] at Dorchester in the Antelope, and passed by Long Bredy and Askerswell, with distant views of fine shaped hills, to Bridport, where we baited two hours [i.e. fed and watered the horses], taking luncheon with Mr Templar and went up to Down Hall, a nice old place with views of the harbour. Then we went on by Chideock Hill and charming country, through pretty Charmouth to Lyme, so full of dear associations, by 4 o'clock. We met with a kind welcome from Mrs Ames at her pretty house up the hill leading to Uplyme.

Emily and her family stayed in Poulett House, built in 1735, which is the Alexandra Hotel at the time of writing. On their first full day in Lyme, Wednesday, 1 September, they went to inspect the Landslip at Dowland Cliffs:

... a most wonderful thing and full of bold and picturesque scenery, washed by the sea, the land having regularly descended from a height of 400 feet towards the sea some years since. We descended it by a most steep path and were charmed with it.

Thursday, 2 September, 1852. I walked after breakfast to see Mrs England and buy specimens [i.e. fossils]. Emily Anna bathed. At half past 12 we drove to Uplyme and called on the Ethelstones and saw their fine new dining room and pretty place with such a charming valley around. Then we called on Mrs Ames and drove to Pinney House [Pinhay House, as it is called in 2003, is just outside the boundary of Uplyme, in the parish of Rousdon]. Mr John Ames, a sick bachelor of great taste and an exquisite artist who admitted us to his studio, gave us luncheon and showed us his house, yet unfinished, like an Italian Villa, and then his lovely grounds of great extent, occupying the coast where are Pinney and Whiteland Cliffs, with old landslips, roads and paths cut amid the rocks, lovely old trees foreign and native. We clambered up to the Chapel Rock, and had a splendid walk with every variety of cliff, woodland and marine scenery.

On another occasion Emily walked after dinner:

... up to Uplyme and distributed tracts and sat in a cottage in Devonshire, just over the border! We went beyond Uplyme to Woodhouse, the sweet rural retreat of Mr Rhodes who is absent, and we looked about and saw many rare and fine plants. The situation, walks and views are lovely. We all walked back and saw Uplyme church, then by Middle Mill Fields and home by 7. Then tea.

Chapter 3
THE POST OFFICE

In the early 1600s Uplyme's mail, what there was of it, most likely came via Axminster to where it arrived from Crewkerne by horseback. If so there were early difficulties that would affect the Uplyme mail. In 1673 the Crewkerne postmaster, Mr John Bonnhill, was instructed to arrange for Axminster's (and thus Uplyme's) mail to be taken by a rider. It is not known why he acted thus, but Bonnhill refused to do this on a regular basis; perhaps it was not for personal but economic reasons. And it was not until his resignation that the new postmaster at Crewkerne, Mr Greenway, began sending mail to Axminster regularly.

However, the service was still far from satisfactory. But, after pressure from merchants and the upper classes, a move was made to change the mail coach run that took the London–Exeter mail via Salisbury, Crewkerne and, bypassing Axminster, to Honiton via Yarcombe. The new and easier coach route that opened in October 1785 would be via Salisbury, Blandford, Dorchester, Bridport, Axminster, and Honiton and Exeter. The Lyme Regis (and Uplyme) mail was offloaded at Bridport, from where it was sent to Lyme Regis and delivered by a foot post who collected outgoing letters at a receiving house in the village. As the name suggests, a receiving house was a place where mail was handed in for collection by the foot post.

Since the eighteenth century there had been a charge of one penny to cover the cost of the journey from the receiving house to the Post Office and the letter was usually, but not always, hand stamped to show that the penny had been paid. Not unnaturally, the local system which Uplyme came under was called the Lyme Regis Penny Post. It was not unique to Lyme Regis, almost every small town that had a

A Victorian letter-box in Yawl.

Post Office served its smaller neighbours. Thus, there was an Ashford Penny Post, an Ashburton Penny Post and so on.

Many people confuse the Penny Post with the universal postal system introduced in May 1840 because of the Penny Black stamp that was introduced at the same time – certainly until at least 1998 *The New Oxford Dictionary of English* did so. Sir Rowland Hill's new postal arrangement did not herald in a universal penny charge on letters, only on the first weight step; heavy letters cost more.

Uplyme's mail either reached or left Lyme Regis by four different types of posts – London letters, country letters, cross-post letters and bye-letters. The first group is self explanatory, letters that went direct to or from the capital. Country letters passed through London on their way to their final destination, say Uplyme via Lyme Regis to Norwich. As the name suggests, a cross post was one that went 'across country' and did not touch London on its way from one provincial town to another, Dorchester–Bristol, Exeter–Cardiff and many others. Bye-letters travelled along the main coach runs without getting as far as London, from Uplyme again via Lyme Regis say, to Salisbury or Andover.

Once the letter arrived at Lyme Regis from Uplyme, the distance it had to travel decided the cost of conveying it to its final destination. Before the introduction of the Universal Post and the postage stamp the charges were considerable, although the rate tended to be lowered for longer distances. Thus, although a letter from Lyme Regis to Dorchester cost about five pence ($2^1/_4$p), one to London was only ten pence.

Where Uplyme's receiving house was is not

Uplyme Devon.
TO BE PEREMPTORILY SOLD BY AUCTION,
At the *Hotel*, in *Lyme Regis*, on TUESDAY, the 9th
day of DECEMBER 1823, at two o'clock in the af
ternoon, either together or in lots.

THE Fee-Simple of a Compact and
desirable ESTATE, situate in the above pa
rish, comprising a Farm House, and Outbuildings
recently erected and about 53 acres of excellent
Arable, Meadow, and Pasture Land, distant about
one mile from Lyme, and adjoining the Turnpike
Road leading from thence to Sidmouth, tenanted
by Mr. John Newbery, for a term of which eight
years is unexpired.
Also, four Newly-Built COTTAGES, with Gar
dens adjoining, situate near to the above Estate,
and to the road leading from Uplyme to Sidmouth.
For viewing the property, apply to the said JOHN
NEWBERY, and for further particulars to Mr.
BARNES, Solicitor, Exeter : or to Mr. HINGESTON,
Solicitor, Lyme.

Uplyme has always been a desirable place to live.

known, although it is claimed that the earliest known Post Office was in a house between the present Post Office (in 2004) and the Talbot Arms. Perhaps Uplyme did not have a receiving house at first and its inhabitants took their mail to Lyme Regis. But certainly by 1840 it would have had a receiving house and by 1856 the sub-postmaster was Job Ezekiah Fowler who was a general shopkeeper, which suggests that the sub-office was by the New Inn. The letters for the village arrived there at 8.30 in the morning. Fowler was succeeded by Frederick Saunders as postmaster towards the end of the nineteenth century and, by 1906, Uplyme was receiving three deliveries a day; they were at 0800, 1315 and 1545, with a Sunday delivery at 0800. Outgoing letters went to Lyme Regis at 1110, 1255 and 1740, 1840 and 2200, and at 1710 on Sundays. The timing of the outgoing mail was determined by the timetable of the newly constructed Lyme Regis branch line, although much of it would go by road to Bridport. It was at that time that the first wall box appeared in the village at Yawl, where it was cleared at 0900 and 1620, but not on Sundays.

In the 1930s, when Mrs Stephens was the post-mistress, the Post Office moved to the house behind the telephone box opposite the Talbot Arms. Then it moved a few yards away into Venlake Lane where Mrs Stephens had a purpose-built office incorporated into her new home. When Mrs Stephens retired, the Post Office moved to its present home.

That a postman's life is not always an easy one, what with dog bites and the public complaining about the service, can perhaps best be illustrated by an incident in 1903, at a time when the Axminster and Lyme Regis mail was carried by a mail cart from Chard. One day this cart was going towards Axminster when, near Coaxden Cross, one of the horses suddenly pulled up, seemingly lame. An examination revealed that the poor horse had a broken leg

and it had to be put down. Mr Stapleforth, the Uplyme man contracted to supply the Post Office with its horses, was told about his horse's mishap and rushed to Axminster Post Office, then still in Chard Street (it moved to Trinity Square around 1908) to check on the situation. While he was inside his own horse bolted, dragging the cart with it for some distance before the vehicle overturned. Happily the horse was unscathed; the only damage done was a broken wing on the cart.

A later breed of Uplyme residents will remember Henry Stapleforth, a son of the above Mr Stapleforth we would think, and by his time the horse-drawn carts in the family transport business had been replaced by taxis. Henry was one of Uplyme's characters whose driving often gave cause for concern to his passengers.

LOCAL NEWSPAPERS

Residents of the village have been able to read two local papers for almost a century and a half; the first being *The Bridport News*, launched in 1855 by William Charles Frost, and soon renamed *The Bridport News, Dorchester, Lyme and Beaminster Chronicle*. It returned to its former name and, after including Lyme Regis (and Uplyme) among its contents, brought out a *Lyme Regis News* edition, which naturally covers our village.

It was first produced in West Street, Bridport, where the four pages were printed on a Columbia hand-fed press. It stayed in the Frost family's hands until 1962 when William Frost's grandson, Wilfred Frost, sold it to the Berrows Group. At that time the paper moved to its present East Street address but was actually printed at Salisbury and, later, Taunton. Today it is part of News Comm Plc and printed on state-of-the-art machinery at Weymouth.

Our other local weekly newspaper is *Pulman's Weekly News* which was first published in 1857 by George Philip Rigney Pulman, the eldest son of Philip and Ann (née Rigney) Pulman, who was born in Axminster on 21 February 1819. Philip Pulman, the son of a Colyton blacksmith, was a watchmaker who lived in Lyme Street in a red-brick house on the corner of Lyme Street and George Street, which is known at the time of writing as Pulman's House. Mr Barrow Pulman sold the house in 1920 to a Mr Vince. George Pulman is best known to the present genera-tion for his publication, *The Book of the Axe*, which was first published in parts in 1844–45 and later as a book. It is both a history of the parishes that flank the river and a piscatorial guide. In all there were four editions and, around the 1960s, a facsimile edition was also brought out.

In 1848 he moved to Crewkerne where he lived for 30 years, and where he had acquired a printing and stationery business. There was no low-cost newspaper in the Axminster-Chard-Lyme Regis area at the time, although *The Bridport News* was first published in 1855 at a cost of a penny. All the other newspapers, published at Yeovil, Taunton, Dorchester and Exeter, cost around four pence. In an attempt to fill the void, Pulman first published his *Pulman's Weekly News* in 1857 at a cost of 1¹/₂d. An instant success, it was often said 'It must be true, it was in Pulman's.' It was acquired by the *Western Gazette* group and then bought by Tindle Newspapers Ltd of Farnham in Surrey in 1996 and, appropriately, published in South Street, Axminster, not much more than a stone's throw from the house in which George Pulman was born.

Because of his failing health, he sold the paper and his printing business in 1878 and retired to Uplyme where he died on 3 February 1880, aged 60; he was buried in Axminster four days later. In the 1 January 1901 edition of *Pulman's Weekly News*, the last link with the Pulman family was broken when the report of the death of George Pulman's widow, Mrs Pulman, was given. She had died at Shepherd's Bush, London, on Christmas Day, 1900, at the age of 78. She left a son, Mr W.G. Pulman, a solicitor of Lutterworth, and a married daughter, Mrs H. Franklin of Barnes. Two years after her death, Hermitage House, the family home in Uplyme, was destroyed by fire.

The body of the deceased arrived at Axminster by train at 1.13p.m. and the vicar, Revd A. Newman, conducted the service in St Mary's Church. Remarkably, the 86-year-old Mr T.N. Webber, the man who played the 'Dead March' in Saul when the coffin entered and left the church, had been the organist at the church since 1835 when he took over from none other than George Pulman himself. A nice touch was that Mrs Pulman had been one of his pupils.

Uplyme's *Parish Magazine* is delivered to every house in the village and it is always a welcome sight on the doormat, not least because it covers the secular life of Uplyme as well as the spiritual. Inside you will find the doings of everything in the village from the Parish Church and its associated bodies, such as the Mothers' Union, down to the Parish Council, the cricket and football clubs, the WI and the Horticultural Society.

Also available in the parish is the *Midweek Herald*, a free newspaper first published in the very early 1980s by Jimmy Hall, the proprietor of the *Sidmouth Herald*. The first edition of the paper was brought out by Philip Evans, now the editor of *Pulman's Weekly News*. Today the Archant Devon Group, which was formerly Community Media Ltd, owns the *Midweek Herald*.

The 1949 Uplyme Official Guide.

The Uplyme parish magazine.

The Old Mill in 1900, one of nine mills on the River Lym between its source near Hunters Lodge and the sea at Lyme Regis. It is the last building in the parish, the bridge in the foreground being part of the Devon/Dorset boundary.

Right: *The bridge over the River Lym in Springhead Road.*

Left: *Little Pig Robinson crosses the bridge over the River Lym with Middle Mill, the last house in Devon, visible in the background. Behind Little Pig Robinson lies Devon, in front Dorset. The illustration is from* The Tale of Little Pig Robinson *by Beatrix Potter* (COPYRIGHT FREDERICK WARNE & CO, 1930, 2002. REPRODUCED BY PERMISSION OF FREDERICK WARNE & CO).

Chapter 4

THE OLD MILL

By David Mostyn

It is the first (or last) house in Devon. It is also known as Upper Middle Mill, or The Old Mill, Lyme Regis (even though it is in Devon!). Others call it Higher Mill, Uplyme. At any rate, call it what you will, it has been in my family's ownership since 1815. Neither I nor Mark, my second son, and his wife Jane, who own it, know very much about its early history. It does not feature in any archives of the Lyme Regis Museum nor in any military account of the Civil War siege of Lyme Regis or the Monmouth Rebellion.

What do we know about this Grade II listed historic building? It is a water-mill with an overshot wheel. That is, the water goes over the top of the wheel, filling its buckets and thus turning it.

The water from the River Lym was directed down the mill leat whose line can be clearly seen at the bottom of the steep bank below the footpath. The foundations of the dam, long since collapsed, are visible just downstream from Bill and Carole Halden's Honeysuckle Cottage in Mill Lane.

Having gone over the wheel the water rejoins the Lym at the bottom of the mill garden. Reputedly, the mill is fourteenth century in origin, a fact which was confirmed a few years ago. A heritage mill expert told me that he thought the thatch over the granary at the wheel end of the mill was the original fourteenth-century thatch!

Some time ago, when the thatch was being patched, the thatcher told Jane that one interior strut was broken. He said it would save a great deal of time and reed if someone could get a ladder up inside and slide a new one in – a five-minute job. As I climbed higher into the roof I found that my body, particularly my bare arms, was covered in scratches. By the time I had got down the ladder and cleaned up, my arms had swollen up and I was feeling very ill. I went straight home, had a brandy and collapsed shivering and flu-like into a chair, feeling very sorry for myself. Half an hour later, by sheer coincidence, my good friend Dr Andy Llewelyn breezed in, purely on a social matter, and stopped dead. 'What on earth's the matter with you, David?' So I told him what had happened and jokingly asked him if he knew anything about bubonic plague. To my

astonishment he turned on his heels and left the room, saying over his shoulder, 'Only one thing and that is I shook hands with you, so I am going to wash them straight away!' By next day it was all over and I was as right as rain. How we have laughed over that incident ever since.

The Old Mill, unlike many mills in Lyme which made flax or cloth, was a flour and bakery mill. All the interior works are still *in situ* in the kitchen and the granary above, except for one grindstone which is on the terrace at White Ley, being used as a table, but it is promised back to the mill whenever it is wanted.

The bakery with its 14-foot oven is the building opposite the mill's front door. The mill and bakery were certainly working until just before the First World War, because a man once asked me if he could look into the bakery as he remembered being sent there as a young lad to buy two loaves for 2d. (tuppence old money – 1p new money!). Presumably it all ceased to function when the dam collapsed, whenever that was.

In 1964 when I came here, Jim White, his wife and his brother-in-law Walter lived there. Jim was the estate woodman and an absolute master craftsman. I once saw him in the course of one day, using only a cross-cut saw, wedges, sledge hammer and a bill-hook, cut and split a fallen chestnut tree into four gateposts and 100 fencing stakes.

All the downstairs of the mill is built into the hill behind. The back wall has an outer and inner wall with a man-sized passageway which drains into the millpond, thus keeping the inner wall dry.

When I inherited the place, the mill-wheel had virtually collapsed. Although I was determined to restore it, it was some time before I could find a wheelwright to do the job. Meanwhile, I got Jim White to cut out and season the necessary oak and elm from the estate. Eventually I heard of Mr Gapper of Sector near Axminster, who might do the job. I rang him one evening and asked whether he would take it on. There was a long pause before his reply, to the extent that I asked him if he was still there. 'Aye,' he replied, 'I'm just putting on my gumboots. I'll be with you in ten minutes.' It transpired that Mr Gapper, then in his early 70s and about to retire, had started his apprenticeship 60 years previously making a mill-wheel and was keen to end his craftsmanship as he had begun it. It took him a year working in the evenings, using his father's old tools and the wood which Jim White had prepared.

Eventually the great day arrived. It was finished. By now a lot of people were taking quite an interest in the project, including West Country TV. They did a short programme on it, but of course with no mill leat there was no water. They wanted to see the mill working. So I had to persuade our local fire brigade to come and pump up water from the River Lym over the wheel. As it started turning apace, we all cheered and celebrated with much beer. The next day was the day of reckoning when I had to ask Mr Gapper what I owed him for a year's work and a 12-foot wheel. He beamed from ear to ear and said, 'I've so enjoyed doing it; it has made my day and capped my career. Shall we say £100, sir?' I could not believe it. I was expecting at least ten times more, even in 1968.

Sadly, Jim White had died at the end of 1967 and so never saw his wood at work in the wheel. We did try holiday letting but soon realised that the mill needed the daily, loving care and attention of a resident. Thereafter, for the next 20 years, we had a number of Lyme families as tenants; the longest tenancy, lasting from 1978 to 1984, were the Murphys who had been proprietors of the Cobb Arms.

In 1995 John Murphy, under the pseudonym of Neville Attwood, wrote a book of memoirs, *Mainly in the Country*, about half of which are stories of life at The Old Mill. The only other book which features the mill is Beatrix Potter's *Little Pig Robinson*, in which appears a pen-and-ink drawing of the mill. Apparently she was staying in Lyme when she wrote it. Then in 1989, when Mark and Jane were married, they took over the mill and have done wonders to it.

Legend has it that an underground passage goes all the way from the mill to Court Hall Farm and the church, used by smugglers. But it's a legend of course. The main route from Lyme to its hinterland was down Tapper's Knapp, up Springhead Road and over Uplyme Hill. However, it appears that the smugglers' route was along the Lym Valley to Middle Mill, thence up Rhode Hill and on to Penn via Harcombe. Mark and Jane who live at the mill say they have seen Rattenbury wandering by on a stormy evening more than once. On another occasion they watched a cart and laden packhorses with smuggled goods pass by their house. And they hadn't been drinking!

The Old Mill

Chapter 5

ANTIQUITIES

A Roman pillar, 2 feet 10 inches high, found at the villa.

THE ROMAN VILLA

Higher Holcombe Farm lies west of the main village of Uplyme, 350 feet above sea level and a mile from the sea. On the south and west sides the farm is surrounded by hills rising to nearly 600 feet which afford some protection for its fields from the fierce Atlantic gales. The soil is greensand overlaid with clay and flints.

The field above Higher Holcombe Farm was called Church Field by the villagers, because the ruined Roman bathhouse with its three apses sitting there gave a superficial appearance of a small chapel. These Roman remains were lost to posterity when, as an aged parishioner named Mansfield remembered, hundreds of cart-loads of worked stone were taken for the building of a farmhouse by farmer Gay early in the nineteenth century.

In 1852 a ploughman struck something hard as his coulter uncovered a foreign element. Excavation by archaeologists revealed that it was a very fine geometrical mosaic pavement of Romano-British origin dating from the second or third century AD.

In 1880 another dig on the same site produced an octagonal plunge bath. Then in 1969, with the full cooperation of the owner of Higher Holcombe Farm, Mr L.J. Denning, the Devon Archaeological Society mounted an emergency excavation which lasted three years. The Roman villa they unearthed is one of only four in Devon, the others being at Seaton, Membury and Budleigh Salterton. This magnificent villa was found to be just over 250 feet long and 42 feet broad. The site was probably occupied for the

first four centuries AD. A pattern of increasing prosperity was indicated by all the additions made to the house, culminating in an elaborate octagonal bathhouse, one of the finest yet to be found in Britain. The room is 11 feet wide and around it, on all eight sides, are seats projecting seven inches from the walls, two feet ten inches high, tesselated in front and capped with neat slabs of blue lias. The floor is laid with tesserae of pale fawn colour. The bathhouse was littered with the shells of edible snails. Picture the scene – your decadent Roman sybarite landowner (Maximus Magificus) is lounging in his exotic bathhouse eating the latest delicacy, snails.

For more than 200 years from the second century AD the villa was expanded with the addition of more and more rooms painted a rich pink, until there was a line of no fewer than 14 rooms with a pillared verandah running the whole length, connected to the octagonal bathhouse with its eight surrounding rooms. The villa was probably abandoned towards the end of the fourth century, as the latest coin found on the site was that of the Roman Emperor Valentinian I (AD367–75).

During the 1969 excavations many objects were brought to light, including pieces of fourth-century pottery, some earlier Samian ware (both plain and decorated), glass beads, window glass and fragments of glass bottles. There were iron tools, a cleaver or

Part of a geometrical mosaic pavement of the Romano-British villa uncovered in 1852 at Higher Holcombe Farm. (COPYRIGHT, THE SOCIETY OF ANTIQUARIES.)

The octagonal plunge bath, part of a Romano-British villa which was uncovered in 1852 at Higher Holcombe Farm. (COPYRIGHT, THE SOCIETY OF ANTIQUARIES.)

knife, and many hexagonal lias roofing tiles, some of which still had nails in place. Also found were bronze studs, a bone hairpin and a small bone spoon. These finds can be seen in the Rougemont House Museum in Exeter.

THE HOLCOMBE MIRROR AND OTHER ANTIQUITIES

Archaeologists discovered in the 1969 dig that there was a pre-Roman settlement consisting of four huts, three furnaces for producing iron and an enclosure directly beneath the Roman villa above Higher

Holcombe Farm. The diet of the inhabitants included wild boar, ox, pig, horse, woodcock, song- and mistle thrush, salmon and bream – what one might call a mixed diet.

Some time in the first half of the first century AD an Iron-Age inhabitant of the settlement at Higher Holcombe dropped a bronze mirror on the floor of his wattle-and-daub thatched dwelling. And there the mirror lay forgotten and undisturbed for 19 centuries. The Holcombe Mirror, which now resides proudly in the British Museum (there is an excellent copy of it in the Lyme Regis Museum) is a magnificent addition to the series of decorated mirrors, 16 in all, peculiar to southern Britain. In size, complexity of design and subtlety of decoration of the mirror plate and the handle, it is as good as the acknowledged masterpieces found at Birdlip in Gloucestershire and Desborough in Northamptonshire. It is unique in being recovered from an Iron-Age settlement and is both large and heavy. Nearly 15 inches long from rim to handle, and ten and a half inches wide, it weighs nearly three pounds. The mirror plate consists of a thin sheet of bronze. What could the Iron-Age lady see when she looked at herself in the darkly reflecting surface of the mirror, kept polished by gentle scouring with wood ash? Perhaps it would have been like looking at oneself in a modern brass or copper plate, providing a softened image, a little indistinct.

But the true glory of the mirror lies in its highly decorated back and elegant handle. The engraved design of the Holcombe Mirror back was probably set out with the aid of a compass, producing a fine

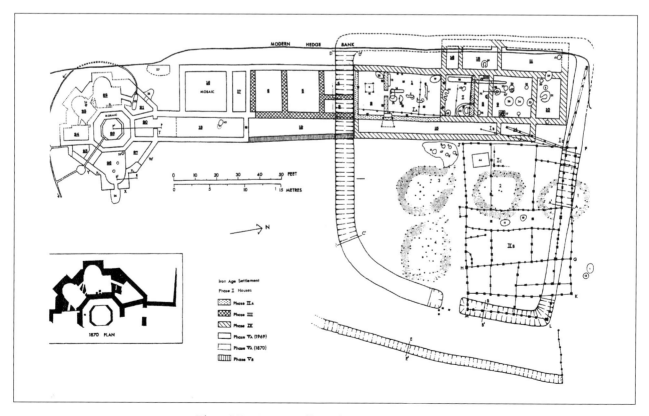

Plan of the Roman villa and Iron-Age settlement.

Left: *The design on the back of the Holcombe Mirror.*

Right: *A five-million-year-old shark's tooth, found in Whalley Lane and now in Seaton Museum.*

scratched line on the surface of the plate. The craftsman would then deepen the outline by engraving and chasing the patterning. What he produced is a double lyre pattern with a small light shield at the centre with a crescent tail. The handle, which is five and a half inches long, was perhaps intended to be uppermost, suspended by the terminal loop from a hook in the centre of the hut where it would hang as a status symbol for the wealthy owner. Looked at in this way, the trumpet scrolls and studs seem to be a feline face with bulging red eyes, rounded ears and nostrils. These elusive images are a recognised feature of Celtic art.

The Roman villa has long been covered over. Grass now grows where once a splendid tesselated pavement stood. And underneath that pavement, a hole in the ground produced a very precious artefact which we can all admire to this day. What is certain is that the Holcombe Mirror on display in the British Museum in Room 22 is a wonderful example of Celtic craftsmanship.

The mirror was not the only antiquity found in the parish. In 1817 a man was digging a hole for a gatepost in an Uplyme field near Gore Lane. He was in the immediate neighbourhood of a branch of the Ikeneld Way which may, with great probability, be assigned to the early British period. The Ikeneld Way, or Icening Street or Ickling Dyke, derives its name from the country of the Iceni. The road begins on the coast of Norfolk and comes west, dividing several times. One branch goes through Dorchester, over Eggardon, through Loders, to the eastern entrance of Bridport and thence through Chideock and Morcombelake to Charmouth, where it runs into Devon. In Gore Lane the man was digging the hole. Imagine his surprise when he turned up a golden ornament or utensil in the form of a rod. It was about 14 inches long and more than an eighth of an inch in diameter, except towards the ends, where it gradually increased in size. It was finished like the top of a ramrod. It was without ornament of any sort and in quality it was better than standard gold. It was flexible and weighed about two ounces. The man who found it took it to a watchmaker in Axminster who, unaware of its intrinsic value, consigned it to the melting-pot. From similar gold relics found in other parts of the country, we may conjecture that the object

dug up in Uplyme was perhaps a British ornament called a 'torque'. Judging by its size, it would have been suitable for a child and was purely ornamental, to be worn about the neck or for supporting part of the dress. Another theory is that it could conceivably have been a golden wand for use by Druid priests in their mysterious and ancient rites. In that case the Uplyme find was a verge (still carried by vergers in cathedrals), a wand of office and symbol of government and administration (such as the Black Rod in the Houses of Parliament).

Again in a field called Holcombe Bottom in Uplyme, some time in the early-nineteenth century, a man employed to remove a large heap of stones discovered an earthen vessel containing a large number of Roman coins, which he took to Exeter and sold.

In 1818, about half a mile east of Hunters Lodge on the Bridport Road near Greenway Head, 22 silver coins were found under a heap of stones. They were identified as belonging to the first and second centuries AD.

Who knows what today's budding archaeologists, armed with the latest metal detectors, may find in Uplyme's fields? In *The Mayor of Casterbridge* Thomas Hardy wrote:

Casterbridge announced old Rome in every street, alley, and precinct. It looked Roman, bespoke the art of Rome, concealed dead men of Rome. It was impossible to dig more than a foot or two deep about the fields or gardens without coming upon some tall soldier or other of the Empire, who had lain there in his silent unobtrusive rest for a space of fifteen hundred years.

What was true for Casterbridge (aka Dorchester) may well be the case in Uplyme.

Imogen Thomas and Lyn White look at the site of the Roman villa in Chapel Field overlooking the viaduct.

A painting of an original photograph of the 'Lyme Billy' after passing under Uplyme's Gore Lane Bridge on its way to Lyme Regis. The engine (30583) is one of three Adams Tanks used on the line in the 1950s.

Right: *Cannington Viaduct, one of the first concrete constructions, nearing completion in 1902. The viaduct's 90-foot height required an aerial railway, known colloquially as a Blondin, to carry the cement.*

Right: *When the L&SWR took over the line, men posted at each end of the viaduct to watch for any movement when trains crossed were removed, but an Uplyme man, Sid Baker, was retained to measure the height of the damaged arch for many years to ensure there was no further sinking.*

Left: *An Axminster-bound train crossing Cannington Viaduct in 1930. The subsidence under one of the arches, on the left, meant that a jack arch had to be built to support it. Loom Cottage is in the fore-ground with Cannington Farm peeping through the arches.*

Chapter 6

GETTING ABOUT

RAILWAYS

The railway might have been late in reaching Lyme Regis (its branch line has to be one of the last ever built in England), but, when it did, the delay led to the opening-day jollifications held at both Axminster and Lyme Regis stations on 24 August 1903 being all the more enjoyable.

At 12.30p.m. the Axminster Parish Council, under its chairman Mr Pitfield-Chapple, assembled at the Council Room and, headed by the Pride of the Axe Band, marched in state to the railway station to receive the civil representatives of Lyme Regis who had arrived by the second passenger-carrying train to leave the Lyme terminus (at 12.25p.m.) that day which (a foretaste of things to come, what with leaves and the wrong kind of snow) was late. That same evening, six hours later at the most, the following day's edition (25 August) of *Pulman's Weekly News* was on sale in Uplyme and carried a full account of all of the historic moments.

The previous Friday Major Druitt, RE, one of the Board of Trade inspectors, had carried out the final inspection of the line. He left Lyme Regis Station at ten o'clock. With his party in an inspection coach and bogey compo, with two engines (734 and 735) which were driven by Mr S. Dyer (Yeovil) and Mr W. Lailley (Exeter), the gallant Major inspected every point, bridge, and especially the Cannington Viaduct in

Uplyme, the safety of which had been much doubted, and about which so much gossip had been heard. For nearly an hour it was severely tested and examined and in the end it was found to be safe. The inspecting party then left to arrive at the Axminster end of the line just before two o'clock, where Major Druitt announced that the whole of the line was to his satisfaction.

Pulman's Weekly News told its readers that the opening of the line by the Lyme Regis Light Railway Company would be:

A distinct boon to the little borough of Lyme Regis, which has hitherto not been connected with the outside world by any railway, and to the villages of Uplyme, Rousdon and Combpyne. Previously the nearest station had been at Axminster, some 5½ miles distant, which was reached by a [horse-drawn] bus service, several buses going to and fro each day.

At first the six trains that ran each day left Lyme Regis at 0940, 1225, 1410, 1650, 1810 and 2005, but soon the Lyme Regis Town Council were demanding more. The fare to Combpyne from Axminster was 4½d. (barely 2p) and from Axminster to Lyme 6½d., both third class. A ticket from Lyme Regis to Waterloo cost 12s.7d. (63p).

Lyme's civic party were wise to travel on the second train – the first train that day had departed at 0940 in pouring rain that had left the bunting, flags

The view from Chapel Field of the viaduct. (LYN WHITE)

and flowers looking a little the worse for wear. The train, its engine also decorated with flags and bunting, consisted of seven coaches and was in the charge of Inspector Chamberlain of Exeter and seen off by the new stationmaster, Mr Ely from Poole; the stationmaster at Combpyne was Mr Greenslade of Exeter.

The driver of the first train out of Lyme Regis was Mr S. Dwyer of Yeovil and it was crowded with passengers. Many others hoping for their own little niche in the town's history, that of being able to tell their grandchildren 'I rode on the first train out of Lyme Regis', were unable to get a seat and had to watch those who were more fortunate (or arrived earlier) depart to the sound of much cheering and exploding fog signals.

This train reached the prettily decorated Axminster Station dead on time at 1005, where it was greeted by more fog signals and hundreds more cheering people. Again packed with passengers, it started its return journey to Lyme Regis at 1045.

After the civic parties clasped hands on Axminster Station's up platform when train number two arrived at Axminster, they were entertained in the waiting-room by Mr Ball, the stationmaster. Both parties then took the train back to Lyme Regis for the official celebrations which were held at the Royal Lion Hotel, where 150 of the great and good of Axminster, Lyme Regis and the Lyme Regis Light Railway Company, not forgetting Colonel Williams (MP for West Dorset) and Sir John Kennaway (MP for Honiton), tucked in with gusto.

The children were not forgotten. After their betters had junketed at The Royal Lion, they were entertained with sports on the sands and then tucked in on their own account to tea.

That first train to Lyme Regis carried 137 passengers, or at least 137 tickets were sold, according to the half-yearly meeting of the company. But the second train attracted around 350 paying customers plus, of course, the civic parties of both towns. This meeting dwelt at some length on the delay in the opening of the line, much of which had been caused by heavy rains which hindered the workmen, to

Springhead Road, Uplyme, in 1949.
The bridge was built in 1811.

such an extent that, at one stage, 250 extra workers were drafted in to unsuccessfully try to get the project back on schedule.

The first breakdown followed four days later. The 1318 train left Axminster as usual but, about two miles out, one of the cylinders of the engine broke and the train had to return to Axminster. Another light engine was quickly brought up from Exmouth Junction and, after a slight delay while they changed engines at Axminster, the train set out again.

A later generation of the good people of Uplyme often asked the question 'Why no station at Uplyme?' Those that did would cite either end of Whalley Lane as being the ideal positions for a station or, at least, a halt. But at the time fields surrounded the top end of Whalley Lane, and a walk to catch a train there would have taken longer than that of going to the station at Lyme Regis. A halt at the lower end near the New Inn would have been a couple of smoke puffs away from that same Lyme Station and was a no-goer from the start.

But the branch line did leave its mark on the village. Tucked away out of sight of almost all the village is the 230-yard-long Cannington Viaduct that takes the line over the steep Cannington valley. It is one of the earliest examples of a major concrete construction in the South of England (the Axe Bridge between Seaton and Axmouth that was built in 1877 is said to be the first in the entire country). It was the cause for considerable concern soon after it was built when its extreme weight led to the number-one pier and west abutment sinking into the sandy foundations. A jack arch had to be built to prop it and stop any more sinking. Flag men were posted at each end of the viaduct to watch for any movement when trains crossed over (with only 12 a day it must have been a boring sort of life) but no movement was ever recorded and, when the L&SWR took over the line, the men were removed. But an Uplyme man, Sid Baker, was still retained to measure (check) the height of that particular arch for many years to ensure there was no further sinking *(see p24)*.

The bridge that took the Lyme Regis branch line over the lower end of Whalley Lane. Although the line closed in 1965 and the track was removed soon afterwards, it was not until the early 1990s that this bridge was demolished.

Looking down on the village and the viaduct from Springhead Road. (IMOGEN THOMAS)

Sadly Dr Beeching removed much of the rest of the line when his infamous 'axe' changed our English railways forever. The line was closed to goods traffic in February 1964 and to all other traffic 13 months later. In 1967 the track was lifted and, the odd bridge excepted, all that remains of the famous old Bluebell Line is the lonely viaduct with its jack arch. And even that received the final insult when BR offered it for sale for just one pound. There were no takers.

In 2002 a public meeting was held at Axminster with a view to reopening the line. At the time of writing nothing has come of the idea and, with much of the trackbed in private hands, several cuttings filled in, and no possibility of reaching Lyme Regis or entering Axminster Station, there is not much hope of there ever being any progress.

COACHES AND CARRIERS

Today the ubiquitous motor car clogs every road around Uplyme and Lyme Regis; ever-increasing-in-size lorries join them, both needing more and more roads, which, in turn, need more and more tarmac due to the constantly increasing usage. It was not always so. Once man had to use real horsepower for his transportation needs. Indeed the horse, far more than its canine cousin, was man's real friend.

The horse was always around of course. For centuries it pulled the plough. For centuries it was the dominant factor on the battlefield, at least until the English archers showed the French two fingers at Poitiers, Crecy and Agincourt. Even then the myth of its invincibility persisted until the Colonel Blimps of the First World War were introduced to the machine-gun, which showed scant respect to man or his mount.

But it was not until after the turn of the twentieth century that *equus caballus* began to be replaced by the internal combustion engine on the roads of England where, since time immemorial, it had kept the country's commerce moving. Long before the beginning of the nineteenth century a network of carrying routes criss-crossed England. Hardly any town, village or hamlet was not served by at least one route, some by several. They carried the lifeblood of the nation's commerce along its arteries and veins. And even if town A was not directly connected with town B, a transfer could be made at town C that was.

The coaching services were integral to the carrying counterpart in so much that, although the coaches connected the larger towns and the villages along that line, the carrier and his cart fed the village passengers into it, as well as acting as the first local bus service. One other service the carrier provided was unintentional; but the driver did become the means of transportation of the news – and gossip.

Naturally, Uplyme had its own local services as well as connections with the wider world beyond. In 1830 the Royal Mail, on its way from Exeter to London, left the George Hotel at Axminster (all coaches used the George) every day at 12.30p.m. going via Uplyme, Lyme Regis, Bridport, Dorchester, Blandford and Salisbury. Forty-five minutes later the 'down' coach that had travelled in the opposite direction left for Exeter. There were other non-mail coaches of course. One, the Celerity, using the same route as the mail, passed through Uplyme around 7p.m.

Two coaches travelled the coast road to Southampton. The Portsmouth carried on to the town whose name it bore, leaving Axminster on Monday, Wednesday and Friday mornings at nine. It went to Blandford before turning south for Southampton. The Southampton went to the town of that name on the same days as the Portsmouth. As it

William Marchant holding Bobby in 1880 in the stables at St Mary's, where he was gamekeeper between 1860 and 1880. He was the father of Sidney Marchant (killed on New Year's Day, 1949, whilst working on the Lyme Regis branch line as a ganger). William's grandson, Stan Marchant, still lives in Uplyme in 2003.

Jim Copp, who operated a milk round from Middle Mill Farm, is seen here in 1930 beside his horse. Reg Irish is the little boy on the float, supervised by his mother, Mrs Violet Irish.

The metal road above Middle Mill. It is along here that Monmouth's men marched to the Battle of Sedgemoor.

left Axminster at the same time and travelled along the same road (certainly as far as Blandford) as the Portsmouth, one cannot but suspect there was often a touch of rivalry between them, although the mind boggles at the suggestion of two coaches racing neck-and-neck through Uplyme.

Those were the coaches, the Rolls Royces of their age. More down-to-earth, the carrier and his cart plodded the roads and lanes carrying much more commerce than it did passengers. Day in, day out, week in, week out, summer and winter, sunshine and rain, year in, year out, they followed their route.

Thomas Hardy was talking of the unending cycle of England's agricultural year when he wrote 'Yet this will go onward the same tho' dynasties pass.' If the uncomprehending English labourers were capable of such thoughts, they would have said the same about the carrier. But he would have been just as wrong as Hardy had been about farming. The seeds of Britain's modern farming ways had already been sown. The farm labourer's year was bound in time-honoured chapters that dictated the time for ploughing, sewing, reaping, lambing, hay, the time for this and the time for that. That was slowly changing.

The carrier's cart would resist the horseless carriage for almost another 100 years but, in 1830, the railway age was already five years old. The Iron Horse had arrived. But not yet in East Devon, where the carrier still held sway and would survive until after the First World War when thousands of redundant Army lorries became available at knock-down prices and the carriers at last plodded into history.

Two carriers who ran a short-haul service from Axminster to Lyme Regis served Uplyme. Giles Gill,

who operated out of The Bell in Axminster, did the route once a week (on Mondays), and William Edwards (also from The Bell) on Mondays and Fridays. Goods from Lyme Regis and Uplyme for the long-haul routes were transferred at Axminster where The Bell catered for much of the carrier trade.

William Edwards' Bristol cart left from there on Mondays and Fridays, as did Robert Jefford for Chard on Monday, and Henry French for Exeter on Wednesdays and Saturdays. From Honiton Street, T. Russell & Co operated a similar service on Tuesdays. Before anyone asks, we can only suppose that Honiton Street was another name for some part of Axminster beyond West Street or Anchor Hill.

There were other services. Robert Gill did the Beaminster run, leaving Back Lane on Tuesdays. Giles Gill called in at Axminster on his way from Kilmington to Bridport. Both went there direct. And, on Wednesdays and Saturdays, and in harness this time, Giles and Robert Gill were also bound for Exeter. It made for a crowded road westwards out of Axminster. Also heading for Exeter, T. Russell & Co operated a daily service and Woolcott & King ran one a week on Thursdays. And it was by these many carriers that Uplyme's long-haul goods travelled.

ROADS

Upyme's main street, the B3165 that runs from Lyme Regis to Crewkerne, originally turned right at Tapper's Knapp and went up to the main trunk road (A35) via Rocombe. There was obviously a track serving the farms at Yawl and other places but nothing else that was fit for traffic until around 1832 when the Raymond's Hill–Uplyme road was cut. Which rather does away with the legend that a highwayman was hanged on a gibbet beside the crossroads at Hunters Lodge. Public executions at crossroads had been done away with long before 1832 and, if a highwayman was hanged in that area, which is highly unlikely, it would

Church Street in 1923 with Winne Start, later Winnie Cawley. Just out of the picture on the left is Myrtle Cottage, which used to be the Village School until Mrs Ethelston's was built.

Left: *Springhead Road with the bridge over the River Lym built in 1811. Mill Lane leads off to the right with The Roost, formerly Waterside Cottage, beyond.*

Below: *Church Street in 1904, when it was the heart of the village. Barely visible in the background, Knapp Cottage was a smithy, once the home of a Mr Sansom and later Richard Dean, builder of the Talbot Arms in 1860. Church Cottage on the left, one of the oldest houses in Uplyme, was where Stephanie Gudge lived. Just below is Hacker's Mead where the village used to hold its fêtes and club days. The tree in Hacker's Mead and those on the right at the entrance to the Glen are sadly long since gone.*

The Talbot Arms on the left in 1918, seen from what is at the time of writing the football field. The orchard behind the football field has long since been grubbed out and forms part of Venlake. Homebury (Goldenhome), top right, was one of the few houses in Gore Lane at that time.

have been at the spot where Green Lane crosses the main A35 and becomes Red Lane.

The cutting of the new road from the Talbot Arms area to the A35 at Hunters Lodge was carried out by the Axminster Turnpike Trust which was responsible for the maintenance of the roads from Penn Inn (near Charmouth Tunnel) to Mount Pleasant above Honiton. The steep hill from Waterside to the top of Whitty Down was proving too much for the horse-drawn coaches and carts of the time and the new B3165 came into being.

But the village lies within a triangle of roads that are older than the village itself. To the north is the Ickneld Way, the ancient British road that the Romans took over. To the south is a branch of the Ickneld Way that, in all probability, was cut to connect the main-stream Roman world with the little port at Seaton and the stone at Beer. This branch left its parent at the top of modern Charmouth and ran, via Clappentail, Rousdon, Colyford, Sidford and Newton Poppleford, before rejoining the main Ickneld Way outside Isca (Exeter). It ran arrow-straight out of Durnovaria (Dorchester), following the A35 trunk road as far as Winterbourne Abbas. From there its path is less certain, around Bridport, which it skirted to the north. It rejoins the A35 to the west of Bridport and, via Chideock, Morecombelake, Stonebarrow, Charmouth and Colway Lane, enters our story below Lyme Regis golf course and runs more or less parallel to Uplyme's coastline.

The main Ickneld Way is Uplyme's parish boundary from the Devon-Dorset boundary at Green Lane as far as Trinity Hill, where it wanders away to cross a field before running down Woodbury Lane and across the River Axe and on to Exeter via Honiton.

The northern arm is crossed in the Hunters Lodge area by the Ridgeway, one of Britain's oldest roads, and one along which the Phoenician trade entered the country. It ran from the Wash southwards and crossed the Thames at Goring. It kept going west to enter our story at Lamberts Castle and then ran along the now B3165, before crossing the Roman road, probably via Pidgeon's Lane, to go across Trinity Hill

and through the two lodges of what became Allhallows School to Axmouth. There it reached the sea after running through the middle of what is now the Axe Cliff Golf Club's first fairway.

Its age is uncertain. But, if the evidence hinted at by the right-angled turn it makes at Charton to run towards Axmouth is added to the fact that the straight north–south line of the road also runs the few yards on to the edge of the cliffs, it is possible that before the seas broke through to create the English Channel some 7,000 years ago, the Ridgeway ran on to Gaul.

The Romans apart, the Saxons laid down most of the country's road system. Where two landowners' property met, each would more than likely erect a hedge and it was between many of these double hedges that people walked. In time they became public paths and then lanes and roads. This is the reason why today in many parts of Devon you will suddenly come across a lane that starts and ends without a reason. They are parts of ancient Saxon roads that have survived a later removal of one of its hedges in the interests of increasing the size of a field. Several neighbouring fields were shaped to give each one access to a pond or a stream – a reason for the often bewildering twisting and turnings of our hedges. Or a hedge was planned to include a large boulder or tree stump rather than face the work necessary to remove them when woodlands were being cleared. This in turn also gave way to 'the rolling English drunkard and his rolling English road.'

Uplyme is no exception. Apart from the new road to Hunters Lodge and a few new housing estates, almost every road in the parish has been there since our Saxon forebears laid them down. And most likely all were there before Alfred the Great died in 901. Most of them bear names given to them by the Saxons who usually made sure those names could be recognised.

Crogg Lane.

Left: *Gore Lane looking towards the Crossways in the 1930s.*

Right: *In 1930 Hope Cottages on the right were demolished and rebuilt further back from the road. On the left is Fuller's shop, the village Post Office in Edwardian times and later a general stores. Note the handsome gas standard on the left.*

Left: *The junction of Gore Lane and Venlake, called Cross Corner here, in 1908.*

Right: *Mr and Mrs Charlie Stocker (née Fisher) on their wedding day in 1922 outside Loom Cottage. They were one of the first couples to go to an Uplyme wedding by motor car. The Model T Ford (Y 2948) which belonged to Henry Stapleford was the second car in Uplyme. Loom Cottage was the home of the Fishers for five generations. The discovery of flax in the roof suggests that cloth was once woven there.*

Chapter 7

GEOGRAPHY

THE UPLYME WALK

In Devon one is spoilt for choice when it comes to walks. Wherever you go, finger-posts invite you to try yet another footpath with glorious views in all directions. East Devon is no exception and Uplyme is blessed with 38 official footpaths which enable the hardened hiker or casual walker out for an undemanding stroll to explore its extraordinarily rich and diverse scenery. For the horse riders too there are four bridleways in the parish.

Southern England is unique in possessing the East Devon Way and the South West Way, which stretches from Poole Harbour all the way to Land's End and up the coast of the Bristol Channel as far as Minehead, nearly 400 miles in length. In 1992 East Devon District Council created an inland walk from Uplyme to Exmouth, a distance of 38^1/$_2$ miles. This walk, intended as an alternative to the coastal path, is called the East Devon Way. If you start at Exmouth, you climb past A La Ronde over Woodbury Common and up to Woodbury Castle, with fine views of Dartmoor, Exmoor and the Quantocks. From there the path runs up and down dales, across the

View of the village, the church and Knoll Hill from where Barnes Meadow stands at the time of writing.

RSPB nature reserve at Aylesbeare, rising 700 feet up Fire Beacon Hill, dipping down for the rivers Otter, Sid, Axe and finally the Lym. From this route spring four circular loops or local walks. They are the Commons, Sweetcombe, the Axe Valley and the Uplyme Walk.

With its excellent network of public rights of way, affording the walker outstanding views in a beautiful landscape, the Uplyme Walk of about four easy miles was planned to give maximum variety and enjoyment. At a moderate pace, it should take an hour and a half, or maybe two hours if the going is very gentle.

The logo of the East Devon Way is a foxglove and this marks signs on the Uplyme Walk, together with a yellow arrow.

Start the Uplyme Walk at the Village Hall where there is an excellent map on a stone in the car park. Go up to the church opposite the Village Hall. A short walk past the church brings you to the road north up to Carswell Farm with a lovely view of Rocombe Bottom to the right. At the farm, footpath 74 skirts Knoll Hill with its superb views of the village, and descends through woodland to Yawl, one of Uplyme's many hamlets. Cross the B3165 (carefully), pass the Victorian postbox and go down Cathole Lane. After a few hundred yards, turn left at a finger-post and walk along a pretty valley, past Cathole Farm to the right and a small lake to the left. When the path enters woodland, it widens into a track, passes one or two houses and emerges into a field with a glimpse of Woodhouse Hill to the left and an arboretum to the right with fine conifers and deciduous specimens. Cross Woodhouse Lane, over a stile and follow the footpath, bearing slightly left across the field going down to Lower Holcombe Farm. Pause halfway across to admire Shapwick Hill with its tumuli on the right and a distant prospect to the left of the flat top of Golden Cap, the highest point on the South Coast (618 feet or 191 metres). The path then continues over a stile at the bottom and goes a short distance towards the viaduct (93 feet high, 206 feet long). On your right there is a wet meadow replete with orchids, yellow flag and other traditional flowers. It was just beyond here that the Romans built their villa, no longer visible.

Turn left just before Loom Cottage and follow the path along Horseman's Hill until you reach a red-brick

Above: *The Village Hall, cricket field, church, Mrs Ethelston's and Knoll Hill, painted by Jane Edwards.*

Right: *A glimpse of Dorset from Uplyme – Golden Cap and Chesil Beach.*

This aerial view shows St Peter and St Paul standing cheek by jowl with Court Hall Farm with Mrs Ethelston's School at the top. The five barns in the foreground which date from at least the sixteenth century are Grade II listed buildings.

house in Cuckoo Lane. Here there is an exceptional view of the whole village with its hills, woods and scattered houses. It is a breathtaking panorama. In front of the house there is a stile and a path which leads diagonally down to Venlake and back across Wadley Hill and the King George V cricket field to the Village Hall. Mission accomplished.

THE UPLYME STONE

Back in 1989 Devon County Council promoted a Devon village-sign competition. Urged on by Christine Case, Beryl Denham, the late Lexie Sumner and Terry Sweeney, the Parish Council decided to enter. The full creative talent of Mrs Ethelston's Primary School was enlisted. It became a project in their craft, design and technology department.

William Howe and James Marsh, both aged nine, drew the winning design which they intended to be sculpted in wood. But Woodroffe's design department pointed out that wood might not last very long. They suggested that it should be carved in stone.

The services of Ham Hill Quarry were enlisted. Saul Harvey quarried out a piece of honey-coloured, oolitic limestone of the Jurassic period, approximately 180 million years old. The stone was richly textured and subtly grained.

Saul's mother, Eva Harvey, carved four animals on the three-sided stone, on each face of which the name of 'Uplyme' proudly reads. Facing the church there is an owl and a rabbit; towards the sea there is a squirrel; and looking up the valley is a hedgehog. Their eyes, ears, noses and paws have been picked out in varnish.

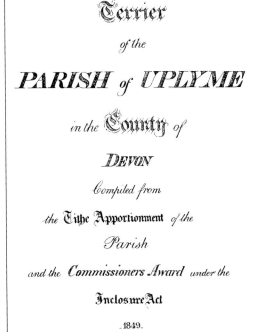

The three-sided stone has been set in the triangular piece of grass opposite the church. It is here that the Horticultural Society planted a chestnut tree in 1965 to commemorate the life of Sir Winston Churchill. There is also a seat 'in memory of Keith H.J. Honeybun, Clerk to Uplyme Parish Council, 1950 to 1969.'

So, just below our church, underneath a spreading chestnut tree, there meet the memories of a devoted local man and a great national statesman in the company of three British mammals and a nocturnal bird.

In the competition Uplyme's sign was highly commended and won £150. Uplyme shared third place with Shaugh Prior. The Uplyme village sign is most unusual, eye-catching and artistic.

WHAT'S IN A NAME?
By Imogen Thomas

One of Sir David Mostyn's prized possessions is a handsome leather bound book entitled *The Terrier*. It was made during Admiral Sir John Talbot's (1768–1851) tenure as the lord of the manor. In it is inscribed, in beautiful copperplate writing, the names of all the landowners of the parish and the occupants of each parcel of land, together with the amount they were to pay to the rector in tithes for the church to distribute for the good of the inhabitants of the parish. This latter included allotments for repair of the turnpike road, the recreation of the inhabitants and the chapel and school. Small individual amounts would also have been given to vagrants to speed them on their way and to the elderly and poor of the parish.

This book gives a vivid picture of the structure of the community. The largest landowner by far was Sir John Talbot himself who had nearly 100 tenants living on or farming parcels of his land. Revd Charles Wickstead Ethelston, the rector, a rich man himself whose wealth came from his wife, owned 35 acres. There were a dozen others who owned between 50 and 200 acres. The parish was intensively farmed. The fields are listed as arable, meadow, orchard, plantation, pasture and coppice, giving a picture of activity everywhere. Those who didn't come into the category of farmer frequently had a smallholding to grow vegetables for the family and a plot on which to keep the house cow, some hens and a pig. Some of these fields sound distinctly unattractive. Poor Close, Barren Hayes, Rough Meadow, Stony Close, Yonder Cold Harbour and Poison Close all look unpromising. Reading through, one gets a picture of the way of life. To take one holding at random here is William Moore, tenant of John Clarke, who is listed as occupying Lionel's Plot, Yonder Mead, Bog Plot, House, Garden and Yard, Pit Orchard, Orchard Mead, Garden Plot and Benjy's Plot – nine acres in all, just enough to keep his family fed throughout the year with maybe a little extra produce to sell. These nine acres were rated at £2.3s.0d. to be paid annually to the rector.

The names of the fields are informative too. Some are straightforward and describe their shape: Square Close, Wedge Close, Round Close, Little Three-cornered Close, Snipe Bill Plot and Sickle Field. Others are more descriptive: Runaway Close, Lovers'

THE UPLYME STONE

This chestnut tree which is thriving stands beside the Uplyme Stone in front of the church. It was planted in 1965 in memory of Sir Winston Churchill.
(PHOTOS COURTESY OF MARK THOMAS)

Walk, Calves' Plot, Lapwing Meadow, Badgers' Glory and Cathole Meadow (where a polecat lived). Mary Hodder had Petticoat Close (was that where she hung them out to dry, or did it come from the shape?) and Lionel Hodder had Quacks Close (where, presumably, he kept ducks). The most beautiful name is Heaven's Gate, where, having climbed the hill, suddenly the whole sky opens up before one. Hodder is still a local name of course and there are many other familiar names in the book such as Hellier, Collier, Gear, Loveridge, Larcombe, Gosling, Gay, Hayball, Case, Austin, Case, Denning, Stocker, Govier and Gage. By far the most numerous entry is Fowler. Because the book lists only landlords and occupiers, there are few women's names given, but from the men's names, one gets a general picture of the village being inhabited by good solid English names such as William, John and James, plus a sprinkling of Biblical names. The Fowlers, for example, included John, James, Job, Eli, William, Charles, Stephen, Simeon, Benjamin, Uriah and Charity. Other Biblical names listed include Reuben, Abel, Noah and Caleb.

The name of the village is obvious. Before 1284, when Lyme became Lyme Regis, the two places straddling the county border were known sometimes as Nether Lyme and Up Lyme (we were recently identified by a Lyme man as coming from 't'other Lyme'). Combe is the Celtic word for valley, so Harcombe is the valley where the hares played; Holcombe is a hollow or deep valley, and Rocombe probably a rocky valley. Lea or ley is a clearing and thence a field, so Wadley is a field where woad was grown. Hay was a field enclosed by hedges, but when most names were passed on by word of mouth, spellings changed so that Penhay easily became Pinney. Ton is a settlement (later becoming town), so Cannington is where the Cannings, a family name, lived. Because sleech comes from the Old English word for mud, we can deduce that Sleech Wood was muddy. Gor is the Old English word for dirt; Gore Lane was either described as a dirt track or possibly ran up beside a gore-shaped or long triangular field. Pound Lane was where the village pound, an enclosure in which straying animals were impounded, would have been. Shapwick meant sheep farm. Ware comes from war, meaning watch or guard, hence wary, aware and beware. It got this name from the lookout and beacon on Ware cliffs. Crogg Lane most probably came from the Old English word 'crok', a bend, from which we get crooked. Smoky Hole might be where the charcoal burners worked. The Ven in Venlake alludes to a fen, so that it means a boggy place. Whalley Lane probably comes from a person's name. What about Jericho? Well, it is very likely that was a joke. The name was used for a far-off place just as we now might say Timbuktu. And Yawl? Now there's a problem. Molly Matthews, author of *Place

Names of the English-Speaking World, has no idea of its origin but suggests that it is Old English or earlier. Let Shakespeare have the final word on the subject: 'What's in a name? That which we call a rose. By any other name would smell as sweet.'

THE UPLYME MAP

It all started in 1985. An environmental arts group calling itself Common Ground had the bright idea of sponsoring a Parish Maps Project which was launched nationally in 1987. The purpose of making a parish map is to show each other and those with power what we value and care about in our localities, and to become actively involved in the protection of those things. By displaying the map in a public place there is a better chance that the things which local people value will not only be recognised and enjoyed by others, but also respected and conserved.

In Uplyme the plan was enthusiastically taken up by the late Lexie Sumner. She enthused and was determined to do it before Lyme Regis beat Uplyme to it. 'Lyme Regis is always upstaging us,' she said, 'we'll show 'em!' Lexie was the driving force behind the scheme. She it was who found artists, put plans in place, got pictures drawn and galvanised the community into doing all sorts of research projects. When illness handicapped her, the map was driven forward for several years by Cynthia Herbert, the map group coordinator. A number of Uplyme folk did the research needed for the map which gives so much fascinating history about the parish. There are notes on the Roman villa, Thomas Whitty and his carpets, Amherst Farm with its trout lakes, Springhead Road and Jane Austen, Harcombe House with its azaleas from Laos, Church Acre, Court Hall Farm and its alleged association with Judge Jeffreys, Waterside Cloth Factory and the Undercliff.

All over the map the text tells us that there are numerous animals and birds to be seen. Up at Shapwick live the badgers, owls, bats and house martins. On Donkey Green you may see kestrels, rabbits, woodpigeons and flycatchers; above Whalley Lane the goldcrests fly, the roe-deer graze and the badgers burrow; whilst below Cathole Farm we are informed that frogs may be found. There is a delightful border around the map, drawn and painted by Christine Case, now Christine Hill. Along the bottom she has painted some of Uplyme's more prominent buildings – the church, of course, Mrs Ethelston's School, the Middle Mill, the old cricket pavilion, and the toll-gate cottage at the top of Tapper's Knapp. Mischievously, between the buildings, peep out a fox, a hedgehog, a hare and a field mouse. At the top of the map flies a barn owl, some seagulls, a pair of magpies and a buzzard. On the left-hand border a steam engine puffs under the viaduct, and there are badgers, an adder, a rainbow trout, a fritillary and an ammonite. On the right-hand

Left: A design by Jennie Pearson for a tea towel sold in aid of the new Village Hall. At the top are Mrs Ethelston's and the church. Below is the top of Tapper's Knapp at the top of Springhead Road. Below that is the Talbot Arms, the county boundary sign, a water trough and various flowers. The tea towel was very successful and sold in large numbers.

side one can see a deer peeping out from conifers, a moorhen, a frog, a grasshopper, an orange-tip butterfly and a brown trout. Finally, all round the border the artist has drawn flowers, amongst them violets, bluebells, orchids, foxgloves, irises, primroses, clover, arum lilies, wild strawberries, honeysuckle, dog roses and blackberries.

Christine at the time was a freelance designer and part-time teacher at Symondsbury Art School, as well as being a full-time mother of three young children. Later she became Head of Art at Colyton Grammar School. She remembers vividly the process and problems of producing the Uplyme Parish Map:

Quite honestly I had never considered the whole parish of Uplyme before. It was a place I took my children to school in, a place I drove through, always admiring the trees as I went, but really I took its beauty and character for granted as I think we often do in a place that is familiar. It is not until changes occur that we notice; but often it is too late. So, if nothing else, here was a good reason to make a map, something that simply through awareness would jolt people out of lazy complacency to an appreciation of what they have on their doorstep and a need to preserve it.

Lexie Sumner had seen a brief television mention about the project. Through her the seed had been planted in Uplyme. She contacted a number of people in the parish and got us all together in the Village Hall. We decided on the best wall for the display of the map and made a plan as to how information was to be collected about the area. Little red memo books were issued to the 'scouts' who agreed to collect information about their immediate area, write down what they felt or knew, and read or talk to other people. We duplicated a questionnaire for the local shops and schools. While this network of information collecting was going on, I was looking at enlarged Ordnance Survey maps of the

parish and trying to decide how the finished map would look. I can remember feeling slightly panicky at this stage, not quite knowing what I was doing and feeling overawed at the task I had undertaken. Beyond a vague idea that the 'map' part should be in the middle with some sort of decorative and informative border around the outside, I hadn't a clue what it would look like.

After another meeting at the Village Hall and the return of collected information, the map began to gel. Suddenly it grew in size because it felt right to have it as big as the wall allowed. With my friend Sally Hargraves, an artist living in Monkton Wyld, we planned the final map. Very conveniently our interests fell into two areas. We agreed that we did not want it to look like a coloured OS map. It was to have depth and the feeling of looking down on the five valleys, joined in the middle at the village. We were not concerned with pinpointing every house and lane on the map — although most would be there, some would disappear behind the hills. Sally and I taped together pieces of paper and we began to draw the rough draft. Although OS maps are useful reference, they do not give the 'feel' of the area. We made journeys to the far-flung corners of the parish, all the while taking photographs, looking and remembering every detail so we could record them. During that planning stage of getting the map to look right, we wished many times for a pair of wings. How much easier it would have been to look down on the parish as a whole and take one all-encompassing photograph. Life not being like that, we made collages of photographs until the whole area had been covered.

My spare room became the map's room. No visitors for nine months, a 6ft x 5ft lodger instead. Gradually the room also filled with papers, reference books and magazines, tracings, notations, drawings and maps. This map became part of the household, demanding attention, exciting but draining me of energy. In many ways it was like a fourth child. I felt proud of it but resented the demands it made upon me. On the kitchen floor we stuck the paper on to a piece of half-inch plywood — a task that took a whole evening. After that Sally and I began the finished artwork. She painted the map we had prepared. With the help of the information in the memo books, I began drawing the border. Using references to the flora, fauna and buildings in those books, it became apparent what should be featured.

As with the paper, Lexie again did the telephoning round. She it was who found the inks that we needed, and a good range of colours and (most important) 'fade-fast'. We were all set to go. Sally and I worked whenever we were free, seldom at the same time, often late into the night. Drawings and yet more drawings, then transferring the drawings on to the artwork, painting. It took a long time. Next we needed a calligrapher. Lexie approached a professional living locally who quoted an astronomical sum. But ours was a project done for love, not money. A local schoolgirl, just 17 years old, Clare Dell, daughter of the vicar of Lyme Regis and a pupil at the Woodroffe School, was known to have a fair hand. Lexie asked her and she said 'yes'. Poor Clare, what a brave girl she was to put pen to map after all the colour work had been done! Of course, before Clare could do anything, we had to decide what went where. It wasn't easy. What do you put in, what do you leave out from the information collected by the map group? More meetings.

Whilst all this artwork was going on, Lexie, our coordinator, was making endless phone calls. She managed to get us a grant from the Amenities and Countryside Committee of Devon County Council. This was quite a breakthrough. The local Village Hall committee gave us a sum towards the cost of the frame. A sympathetic local building firm took on the rest of the costs of making the frame from a locally grown ash tree felled in 1985. Lexan, a perspex, replaced the glass. Nine months after that seed had been planted, completion was in sight. What a relief! Finally, it was out of my spare room and hung on the Village Hall wall. I must admit that there was a gap in my household. The fourth child had grown up and left home.

Of course the poster of the map had become another major facet of the project, one that has taken organisation by Lexie and energy from Pat Whitehead, Adrian Pearson and others for distribution and sales. It has certainly been a success. To date, we have handed several thousand pounds to projects in the parish. And still the map sells.

The Uplyme parish map is a living exemplum of the quotation at the foot of the map. The group's motto, taken from a tablet at Fairford Church in Gloucestershire, is 'Greatness is to take the common things of life and walk truly among them.'

On 16 May 1987 the Uplyme Map was unveiled, one of the first in all of England to be completed. It was an instant success. Copies were produced and sold at the Post Office where, up to 2003, more than 2,000 replicas have been sold. From the proceeds £1,200 has been given to the Village Hall, and contributions made towards the Ware Cliff Appeal, a local wildlife meadow (Hacker's Mead) and the Uplyme Stone. The map itself, in all its glory, hangs in the foyer of the Village Hall where it is frequently admired. In 1996 at an exhibition of parish maps in the Barbican in the City of London, the Uplyme Map took pride of place to be admired by one and all.

Sue Clifford, a director of Common Ground, whose offices are in Shaftesbury, Dorset, is ecstatic about its impact on others: 'It was the first map to be printed and it influenced others. It was so clever to get a bird's eye view of the village. I have used it endlessly in talks I have given.'

After the Barbican the Uplyme Map was shown in the Environment Centre in Bath along with other West of England maps, the Brewhouse Theatre in Taunton, and then at the Queen Street Museum in Exeter. Copies have been deposited at the British Library and the Bodleian Library. Village after village in Devon, Dorset and Cornwall has followed Uplyme's pioneering lead in producing a village map. Noticed by the national press, discussed on 'Woman's Hour' and illustrated in magazines, it has generated interest, admiration and plagiarism.

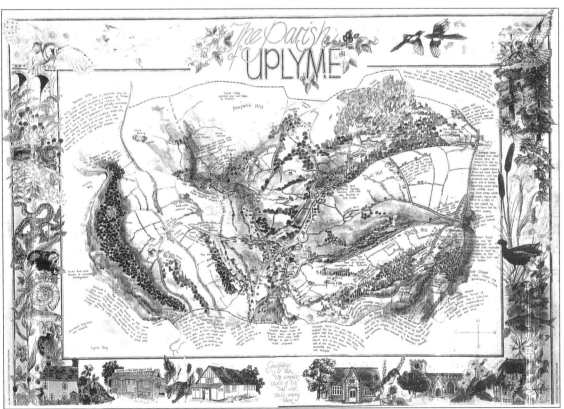

The Uplyme map.

On the front of the gallery is the Royal coat of arms, which signifies the union between Church and State. It was presented by Mrs Mence to celebrate the coronation of Queen Elizabeth II, replacing an earlier version.

Revd Alex James Bestic and his choir in 1946.

Chapter 8

RELIGION

ST PETER AND ST PAUL'S CHURCH, UPLYME

Uplyme in the county of Devon is the last (but by no means the least) parish in the Archdeaconry and Diocese of Exeter and in the Rural Deanery of Honiton. A church has stood on its little hill in the centre of the village for at least 12 centuries. Here, villagers have climbed the steep, flagged path through the well-kept churchyard, past the ancient and massive yew tree, up to the porch to worship.

From the sturdy fourteenth-century tower flutters the flag of St George on Sundays. The handsome clock, wound by Alex Jacks, which tells the village the time, was presented in 1846 by Mrs Peel, Mr Ethelston's mother-in-law. Pevsner was somewhat dismissive of the tower, which is a mere 47 feet high ('medieval w tower, battlemented, with square NE stair-turret'). But from the top the view is incomparable. One can see all the village and the landscape, with its folds, uplands, valleys or bottoms, and to the east a tantalising glimpse of the sea and distant Portland. A broad arrow of the Ordnance Survey at the foot of the porch indicates that the tower is a triangulation point used in map-making. There is a fine gargoyle on the south-east corner of the tower, said to represent a demon devouring Judas Iscariot whose feet can just be seen about to vanish in the devil's jaws!

In the porch there is a statue in Beer stone of St Peter (1953), to whom the church is dedicated. On the door is a crucifix taken from a German dugout in the First World War and placed there in 1919. The oak panels with their elaborate details were beautifully carved from old beams in the church by Mrs Alice Cartwright (née Prescott). The emblems on the west side are symbolic of St Paul and on the east of St Peter, the two saints to whom the church is dedicated.

There have been bells in the tower from at least 1557. It has a peal of six bells, set in the key of G. The six in the tower at the time of writing were cast and hung in 1805, then rehung in 1906 and 1959. The tenor bell weighs 12 cwt. The bells are inscribed as follows:

1. *When I begin, let all strike. T.B. f.1805.*
2. *T.B. f.1805.*
3. *Thomas Bilbie, Cullompton, cast us all in the year of Our Lord 1805.*
4. *Rev. N. Veere Rector, W.D. Patterson & S. Gage, Churchwardens. Bilbie fecit, 1805.*
5. *God preserve the Church & King. WDP & SG, CW. T. Bilbie, Cullompton, fecit 1805*
6. *Rev. Nicholas Veere rector. William Drewe Patterson & Samuel Gage Churchwardens Bilbie fecit 1805.*

Note for non-Latin readers: fecit or just f means 'he made it.' In other words, Thomas Bilbie cast the bells. Patterson and Gage were the churchwardens, or CW, at the time.

Uplyme's bells ring out for the births of princes, the coronations of monarchs, the 100th birthdays of villagers and the late Queen Mother, for most weddings, and, of course, to call the village to worship. Was the first ring of the newly hung bells, we wonder, on 21 October 1805, to celebrate Nelson's glorious victory at the Battle of Trafalgar?

The captain of the tower at the time of writing is June Moulding, who has been faithfully ringing since 1950 when she was instructed by her grandfather, Arthur Start. The bells used to be rung from a gallery in the tower, but in 1876 a major restoration of the interior of the church at the west end was carried out. Since then, the bell-ringers have rung the six bells from the floor of the tower.

Inside, the church is both warm and welcoming. Both the nave and the chancel have a wagon-roof, painted with gold stars on a blue background. The beams are ornamented with gilt bosses. Anyone who

Stuart Worth preaching his last sermon as rector of Uplyme.

The pulpit.

loses interest in a long sermon may start to count the number of stars on the ceiling. There are 18 in each section. Few have the mathematical skill or patience to arrive at the correct total.

Almost all the furnishings date from a major refurbishment paid for by the Ethelston family in 1876 and carried out by G.L. Bather of Shrewsbury. The Jacobean double-decker reading desk was removed. The handsome pulpit (made in the year of Shakespeare's death, 1616) was re-sited without its sounding-board. The woodwork of the reading desk and the sounding-board were at first put in the loft of the Rectory stable, where Mr Egerton and his groom cut off the huge wooden dome of the sounding-board, which was badly worm-eaten. When Revd Parke became rector in 1883 he had the woodwork of the desk put round the large fireplace of the study in the Rectory, where it can be seen to this day (it is the reception office of the Devon Hotel at the time of writing). In 1927 another rector, Revd J.H. Scott, found the canopy of the pulpit, part of which was badly worm-eaten, and had it made into a table for the vestry. It now resides upstairs in the gallery. It was Mrs Parke who paid for its restoration. Revd Ethelston poured his money (or to be more precise, his wife's money) into the church. In 1867 he tore down the medieval oak rood-screen and erected in its place a chancel screen which is made of stone, with Perpendicular tracery, but is otherwise undistinguished. Small heraldic coloured shields at the top represent the Province of Canterbury, the sword and keys of the Diocese of Exeter, the monogram of Chi and Rho (being the first two letters of the Greek word Khristos, or Christ), the crossed keys of St Peter and the sword of St Paul.

The nave is divided from the north aisle by two columns and two half-columns, which are octagonal with plain moulded capitals supporting three pointed arches on square bases of unusual shape. Cresswell, in her *Notes on Devon Churches* (1920), dates these columns to the end of the fourteenth or early-fifteenth century.

At a meeting held on 28 May 1826 it was agreed that:

... proper arrangements be made for the erection of a gallery in the North part of the church, by a Committee composed of Revd C.W. Ethelston, Sir John Talbot and B.A. Wrey Esq, the Churchwardens and the Overseers.

And that they be empowered by the Parishioners to carry it into execution in any manner they may think proper.

This was signed by 20 parishioners (one parishioner who shall be nameless was unable to sign his name but made a cross). The churchwardens were William Boon and Thomas Gay.

The gallery in the north aisle was duly erected in 1827. One enormous oak beam supports the front of it. Parishioners of a nervous disposition seldom venture up there. On the front of the gallery is the Royal coat of arms, which signifies the union between Church and State. It was presented by Mrs Mence to replace an earlier version.

The north aisle has a memorial oak screen dividing it off from the organ chamber and vestry. Three books live here – one a book of benefactors of the church since 1900; one a book of all those who have been cremated; and the third a list of all those buried in the churchyard and the new cemetery. The books of benefactors and those cremated have been beautifully inscribed by Iris Cox, a professional calligrapher and artist. A member of the Society of Scribes and Illuminators, she has been beautifying Uplyme church since the late 1970s.

On a jamb of the west window in the tower can be seen marks scratched by the choirboys when they used to sing in the gallery at the west end. The oldest graffiti are an 'anchor of hope' and a bishop's mitre with the date 1595. On a column at the back of the church can be seen the elegant (though reprehensible) carvings of: '1603, ROBERT HORE, JOHN JONES, 1601'.

In the tower stands the Gothic font, which Cresswell called 'meretricious'. It was given in 1921 by the family of the late Revd A.W. Parke, for 30 years rector of Uplyme. Standing discreetly in a corner of the tower is a small octagonal font which is perhaps our original Norman or even Saxon font. It is plain but very beautiful. It was restored in 1996 in memory of Lady Edith Fortescue Blair Cox (1888–1992).

In the chancel stand the choir stalls, where there is some seventeenth-century panelling. The decorated reredos behind the altar, with its statues of St Peter and St Paul on either side of Christ the King

The nave.

enthroned, was given in 1943 by Mrs Williams in memory of her mother, Hilda Parke, widow of Revd A.W. Parke. The communion rails were given by Stuart Pears in 1952.

The organ was rebuilt at the sole expense of the Prescott family of Woodhouse. The present organ was built by Percy Daniel in 1965 and cleaned and overhauled in 1986.

None of the windows are very remarkable. The stained-glass window above the altar in the east end was given in 1854 to commemorate the death of Anne Ethelston, wife of the rector, in whose name stands the church school next to the church. The most distinguished stained-glass window is the Parke window in the south wall, in which Hardman depicts the empty tomb. The charming Selby window of 1976 in the north aisle shows the nativity scene. The newest windows are in the north aisle, designed and paid for by Colin Cameron in memory of his wife, Meryl, who sang in the choir and died in 1995. The windows strikingly portray events in the life of Uplyme's two patron saints, St Peter and St Paul.

Also in the north aisle is an illuminated wall cabinet displaying two glass etchings by Laurence Whistler, the distinguished glass engraver who lived in Lyme Regis. The etchings record the tragic deaths of two young girls, Clare and Sarah Baxter. One diamond pane shows Amherst Lodge where the two girls lived, the other Uplyme church.

There are one or two interesting memorials in the church. One above the main door is to William Alfray, described at his death in 1827 as the oldest Lieutenant in the Royal Navy:

His character was never impeached either as a gentleman, an officer or seaman. Under divine providence he had the fortunate means of saving two of his Majesty's ships and a cutter at different times from destruction by fire an [sic] water with their crews in all about 400 men.

The Saxon font in Uplyme church.

The bell-ringers get ready to ring for matins. June Moulding, captain of the tower, stands on the left, ready to call the changes. Stuart Worth is on the right.

It is said that three weeks before his death, he had his grave dug which he inspected to ensure it was up to his high standards!

Two of the oldest tablets in the church, both brass, record in verse the dangers of childbirth. Elizabeth, wife of Revd Charles Hutton, 'died in childbed' on 2 July 1683, aged 21. Buried in the chancel, Elizabeth Hutton is Uplyme's earliest inhabitant of any grave. This is what her grieving husband wrote:

Adieu my better part, fair, chaste and good,
Snatched from the world ere by it understood.
God knew thy sacred piety and love
And now rewards it openly above.

Another brass records the death on 12 September 1703 of Grace Hutton, the rector's second wife who died aged 36 and is buried with three of her sons who all died in infancy. This time Charles Hutton wrote:

Here lye three children by their mother's side,
The fourth at Moreton where he lived and died,
The branches thus lopped off, the tree at last
So quickly overthrown by a strong blast,
The mother went to heav'n to see her babes in haste.

This tablet also commemorates Grace's grandmother, Grace Jones, widow of John Jones of Cannington. In a heroic couplet worthy of Alexander Pope himself, her merits are extolled: 'Wee'l not presume her vertues to relate, A theme for angells well to celebrate.'

One of John Jones' descendants was a beautiful young girl called Sarah Andrew. The novelist Henry Fielding courted and attempted to abduct her. Perhaps he used this incident when he published his famous novel *Tom Jones* (1749), in which Tom Jones pursues the adorable but unattainable Sophia Western all the way from the West Country up to London.

The communion plate is of no special interest, but a plain paten bearing the London hallmark 1685 is worthy of mention. It is inscribed 'Uplyme 1685'.

Left: *A gargoyle busy devouring Judas Iscariot.*

Below: *Uplyme church drawn by Molly Matthews. This drawing was used on all church stationery until the entrance was changed in 2003.*

Mrs Seale, the rector's wife, and George Tucker, the sexton of Uplyme church, in 1959. They were inspecting the re-cast bells before they were re-hung. These bells were rung for the first time on 18 July 1959 by a team which included June Moulding, captain of the tower in 2003.

Outside the church, in the tidy and dignified churchyard, there lie 'where heaves the turf in many a mouldering heap, our rude forefathers', as Thomas Gray put it, 'each in his narrow cell'. There are 622 bodies buried in the churchyard and 86 cremation slabs. In the cemetery are a further 562 names. The ages range from one day to 102 years! There are no fewer than seven centenarians, showing that Uplyme is a healthy place in which to live.

So much for the fabric of the church, what of its spiritual life? It would be interesting to contrast the religious life of today with a medieval year for which records exist, 1391. In that year, the church was probably already over 600 years old. King Richard II was on the throne and at his court most of the courtiers spoke French. The one notable exception was Geoffrey Chaucer, the first major English author to write in Middle English:

Whan that Aprill with his shoures soote
The droghte of March hath perced to the roote
Thanne longen folk to goon on pilgrimages,
And specially, from every shires ende
Of Engelond, to Caunturbury they wende,
The hooly blisful martir for to seke.

So Chaucer made the three-day pilgimage to Canterbury to pay homage at the shrine of Thomas à Becket whilst the poor villagers of Uplyme, who would in the course of their lives never travel further than Bridport or Honiton, faced up to a new and deadly menace. The Black Death had arrived in England; Uplyme itself would not be exempt. A total of 11 rectors were appointed in the space of 50 years! The incumbent in 1391 was Stephen le Eyre, the only man in the whole parish who could read and write. That is why he was called a 'clerk in holy orders'. He had three principal functions – to hear confessions, to say Mass, and to preach the Gospel. He was answerable

solely to the Bishop of Exeter, although he could have been checked by his synodsmen or sidesmen. He had a sexton to dig the graves and keep the churchyard neat and tidy; and a bell-man who would ring the bell at weddings and funerals and act as the town crier, disseminating village news and announcements as necessary. The population of Uplyme in the fourteenth century was less than 200 souls. Every single person attended church every single day of the week. At 6a.m. Stephen le Eyre celebrated what was called the Morrow Mass in Latin (it wasn't until the Reformation in the sixteenth century that services were conducted in English). This service was for travellers. High Mass was celebrated for all the village at 9a.m. every day. On Sundays, matins was at 6a.m. with consecration of the Holy Water. High Mass was said at 9a.m. and Vespers at 2p.m. There were no seats in the body of the church (the weakest went to the wall where there were a few seats for pregnant mothers and the elderly). The nave was literally the centre of the village. There was a wooden rood-screen separating the nave from the chancel and lots of vivid wall paintings, all in colour, depicting scenes from the Old and New Testaments. There were no lights in the church, merely a few candles, and plain glass in the windows. Babies were baptised a few hours after birth, and certainly on the day of their birth. The villagers lived in primitive houses with little or no land to grow vegetables. They worked long hours in the summer and winter for the lord of the manor, and paid tithes to the rector. Life was harsh, brutish and short.

So much for the fourteenth century, what of 2003? How does Jeremy White, rector of Uplyme and vicar of Axmouth, divide and fulfil his duties between his two parishes? Who is involved in helping Jeremy? Does anybody still come to church? What is the pattern of services? How much does it cost to run the church? Jeremy cannot possibly satisfy the demands of two parishes without the help of a lay team ministry who take services, read lessons, preach, clean the church, do the flowers, ring the bells, serve on the Parochial Church Council (PCC), edit the *Parish News* and help to distribute it to every house in

The grave in the cemetery of Sarah and Clare Baxter with their mother, Bridget, designed by Laurence Whistler.

the village, act as churchwardens, treasurer, sides-men, organist and choirmaster, members of the choir, youth worker and contribute in many other ways. But, bucking the national trend, many people in Uplyme and further afield regularly attend services in Uplyme church. On average about eight go to Holy Communion (the 1662 service) at 8a.m. on Sundays. The Sunday mid-morning service starts at 10a.m. and varies. On the first Sunday of the month it is Morning Prayer, the old-fashioned traditional matins. On the second Sunday it is Family Communion. The third Sunday sees a Family Service. On the fourth there is Parish Communion and, finally, when there is a fifth Sunday in the month there is a United service, alternating between Uplyme and Axmouth. The mid-morning service attracts a congrega-tion on average of about 60 people. In the evening, there may be 20 regulars, more for the praise services. On Sunday evenings at 6p.m. there is also variety. On the first Sunday there is a

The west door of the church.

so-called Village Praise service which attracts plenty of young people. On the second and fourth Sundays, there is evensong in Axmouth, with no service in Uplyme. On the third Sunday there is traditional evensong from the Book of Common Prayer with a choir. Finally, on the occasional fifth Sunday, there is Agape (the Greek word for love), which is either an informal evening Communion or Bible study. But of course on special occasions such as Harvest Festival, Christmas Eve Midnight Mass or the carol services, the church is absolutely packed.

So what does it all cost? In 2002 the Common Fund, as it is called, which went to pay for clergy pensions, was £32,663, a sum which the parish had to find and pay, bearing in mind that there are only 175 people on the electoral roll of the church. In addition to other expenses (lay staff, music, incumbent's expenses, property upkeep, etc.) the total budget for the year was £48,178, a staggering amount to have to raise but which was triumphantly achieved with the help of much hard work, effort and prayer. Uplyme church costs nearly £1,000 a week to run.

So there you have it; a vibrant church is alive and kicking in East Devon. St Peter and St Paul who have looked down benevolently on their church for the past 12 centuries need not be dissatisfied with the current trend. Uplyme church continues to proclaim the Gospel of Christ to those who have ears to hear.

But in past centuries there have been other reli-gions practised in Uplyme besides the Church of England. Just as the Dissenters in Lyme were perse-cuted, so it is entirely probable that those professing to dissent in Uplyme 'went underground' and held their services in secret or secluded places. One such place which may have been used is Pulpit Close

above Whalley Lane. The names hereabouts are evocative of a strong Nonconformist element in the village – Jericho, Heaven's Gate, Hell Lane, Mount Pleasant and Happy Valley. But in 1821 it was recorded that there were few Dissenters in Uplyme, most Nonconformists being Anabaptists.

The first chapel to be built in Uplyme would have been the Baptist chapel, opposite Harcombe House (then called Beulah Villa), where the local inhabitants regularly attended services. On adjoining land there are two graves. The Methodist chapel at Rocombe and the Gospel Hall in Uplyme were built later. From the 1850s onwards Job Fowler, who ran the village Post Office, assisted by lay readers and others, regularly led the Methodists in a Sunday afternoon service up at Rocombe Chapel.

Down in the centre of the village, a house called Avalon used to be the meeting-house for members of the Plymouth Brethren. Opposite Shapwick House (then called Loom House) there is an old chapel burial-ground. And, of course, the Quakers hold regular meetings in the Village Hall.

'WORCK DON' ABOUT THE CHURCH
By Molly Matthews

The churchwardens' accounts of Uplyme church date from the middle of the seventeenth century. Originally kept in an oak chest in the vestry, at the time of writing they reside and may be seen, together with the parish registers, in the County Record Office in Exeter. These accounts are full of minute detail. In them we seem to hear the natural voices of simple Uplyme folk going about the church's business. Traditionally there were always two churchwardens in a parish, one chosen by the rector and the other by the congregation. Their chief function was to oversee the finances of the parish and to maintain the fabric of the church. But other duties crept in and they were helped in their tasks by a few more parishioners who formed what was known as the Vestry, since that was where they originally met. This group became in time the Parochial Church Council or PCC.

In rural parishes such as Uplyme, churchwardens would nearly always have been farmers – honest, reliable men whom everyone trusted, but no schol-ars. Their spelling was decidedly unsophisticated and idiosyncratic. The following list is a reproduc-tion of part of the first page of the churchwardens' accounts for 1649/50. The handwriting, although fluent and graceful, is somewhat old-fashioned for that date. It is not easily read unless one has made a study of Tudor and Jacobean hands. By 1650 many people were writing in quite a modern style, but in rural Devon the latest fashions were slow to arrive.

The writer of these accounts belonged to the old school. The spelling is his very own and gives a personal charm to the document, for it echoes his pronunciation. It is as if over the centuries we can still hear his voice. For 'old timber' he writes 'wold tember'; 'windows' are rendered as 'wendoes'; the verb to 'fetch' becomes 'fach'. But there is not much consistency; the same word may appear in three different spellings within the space of three lines:

For the past eight years England has been riven by Civil War, a war which has finally ended in 1649 when on 30th January Charles I has been executed in Whitehall on a bitterly cold day.

> *He nothing common did, or mean*
> *Upon the memorable Scene:*
> *But with his keener Eye*
> *The Axe's edge did try:*
> *Nor call'd the Gods with vulgar spight*
> *To vindicate his helpless Right,*
> *But bow'd his comely head*
> *Down, as upon a bed.*

The King is dead and Cromwell, the Protector, is master of the Commonwealth.

Uplyme has been in the firing line too. Lyme Regis has successfully endured and repelled an eight week siege in 1644 by Royalist forces led by Prince Maurice. Many of the Royalist army have been camped in the hills about Lyme and of course they were billeted right here in Uplyme, making use of every large building and eating up the local supplies.

It is almost certain that troops were billeted in Uplyme church, judging by the major repairs that were needed afterwards. Here are just some of the items recorded:

An Accompt of such Monayes as have been Disbursed for repayring of the Parrish Church of Uplyme, in the year of our Lord 1649. £ s d

pd Thomas Whitte for seting up the Roofe of the Church and the wold tember 56 0 0

pd Thomas Whitt for seting up new settes [seats] in the Bodey of the Church at 11 £ beside the tembers Henerey Rosewell gave towordes the Church 11 0 0

pd Tho: Whit for Worck Don About the Tower Windoes Belles seates Dores and threshelds 1 10 0

pd Henery Tucking for the glas of the wendoe by the pulperd [pulpit] 13 0

pd John Levermore for the New glase in the bodey of the Church and in the Ille [aisle] 1 12 0

pd George Lues [Lewis?] for tiling the church 15

pd Gorg Paddon for the pineckell of the Tower 6 8

pd for a barson [basin, i.e. font] 2 6

pd Thomas Banks & Thos Lathey for paving the church 10 0

Richard Gammage for 2 bell ropes 5 0

Abraham Carter & William Arnold and their wifes for cleansing Church and Churchyard 4 3

pd for 3000 of lathes and the careag [carriage] of them hom 1 18 0

pd Edward Flood and his Company for 3 dayes Worck About the walles and for 2 bushelles of Lime 17 10

pd Simmon Woods for himself and his hourse to fach Lime 1 6

pd for lathes and for the old Blackamore for Clensing the Churchyearde 1 2

pd for the Communion Tabell 10 0

pd John Fowler for mending ther Great bell Whell [wheel] and nailes 3 6

These items constitute less than half the list of repairs needed after the ravages of the Civil War. There is hardly one feature of the church that is not mentioned. The roof, floor, pews, altar, pulpit, furnishings, stained glass, bells, tower and churchyard all required substantial repairs which amounted to £118, the equivalent of at least £20,000 in today's money.

But the churchwardens had other expenses to deal with besides the church. They were obliged, for instance, to contribute to the 'gaill and ospitaill' (gaol and hospital), even though these institutions might have been as far away as Exeter. They also had a duty of charity to the poor.

Casual vagrants who wandered into Uplyme were entitled to some small help, mainly given to encourage them on their way. So we find in the accounts small sums of money given to 'maimed soulders', of whom there must have been many in those sad times, 'Egyptions' (gypsies), 'Ireshe' and others. Then we find this entry:

pd Unto 5 maimed soulders and tow Jewish gentelmen and one gentelwoman. Midelton and Whitte wich ware tacken by the tourkes, pd to 8 Iresh peopell, mor pd to travelers at several times, all is 13s.

In the seventeenth century, Jews who were being persecuted in Spain fled to England. The mention of Turks refers to the Barbary pirates of North Africa who infested the Mediterranean and the coasts of Spain. They were really Moors who made a regular business of capturing English and other sailors and then demanding ransoms for them. Midelton and Whitte must have been local men or their names would not have been written as if they were well known.

There is one more item which concerned the Vestry. Consider these entries: 'pd Anthony Hart for 2 fox heads 2. pd Cyprus Osborn for a grays head 1.' Anthony Hart was paid two shillings for bringing in two foxes' heads and Cyprus Osborn earned one shilling for his badger's head. For lesser 'varmint' the Vestry paid fourpence each for hedgehogs' and polecats' heads (is Cathole Lane in Uplyme named after polecats?). Jays' heads fetched twopence each while bullfinches (also known as upps, oups, opes or hoops) were worth a mere penny. Omitted from the list are crows, magpies, ravens and buzzards. Hedgehogs are included, presumably because of the old belief that they sucked milk from cows.

By far the largest item that the Vestry had to pay out for in that momentous year of 1649 was £56 for the repair of the church roof. The smallest sum was tenpence paid to Abraham Carter 'for Drawing of Stones'. That is not much for what sounds like hard work. On another occasion he was paid 7s.6d. for working with 'the old Blackamore Clenesing the Church and Churchyard att severall times.' The 'Blackamore' mentioned here almost certainly refers to a negro. Perhaps the old man ended up in Uplyme from one of the Lyme slavers. But in those days the word was used to describe anyone with a dark skin, not necessarily a negro. However, the picture emerges of Abraham and the old black man labouring in the churchyard while people traipsed up the church path carrying the bloody heads of vermin. The money for all this came from the village. The squire paid the most, the very poor nothing. The lord of the manor might well have paid the princely sum of £20 while Abraham and the old blackamore would have coughed up nothing, provided, that is, that they did not earn a lot of money by catching foxes and badgers.

THE RECTORS OF UPLYME

There have been 50 rectors of Uplyme since Robert Everard in 1259, an average of nearly 15 years for each incumbent. But a closer look tells a different story. By far the most stable period in Uplyme's history was the eighteenth century, when only five rectors served Uplyme. There is one exceptional period – whereas in most centuries there were between six and nine rectors, in the fourteenth century there were no fewer than 13, four of whom succeeded each other in four successive years. We may know that the Black Death wreaked its deadly toll on Uplyme rectors during the second half of the fourteenth century.

According to *The Register of the Black Prince*, Nicholas Pinnocke (also spelt Pynnoke) ceased to be the rector of Uplyme in 1346. This was the year in which the Battles of Crecy and Neville's Cross were fought, with spectacular victories over the French and the Scots respectively. Pinnocke became a member of the Black Prince's Council. At the same time he was made the rector of a parish in Cornwall. The Black Prince employed him as a clerk, in which capacity he audited the Prince's accounts and acted as his commissioner for leasing lands in Cornwall. But Nicholas Pinnocke still owned considerable property in Uplyme when he gave the land to Glastonbury.

Forty years later another rector was being both contentious and litigious. In 1385:

Licence of non-residence was granted to John Vax, Rector of Uplyme, to enable him to prosecute his suit, respecting his right to the church, against John Couley, who claimed the same, subject to the proviso that the church was meanwhile properly served, that a proctor was appointed, and that he occasionally, more especially in Lent, visited the church, to look after the souls of his parishioners.

The smoke of embittered and angry parishioners still drifts across the Uplyme landscape.

Five rectors deserve especial mention for the length of their ministries. Richard Sant in the fifteenth century served 47 years; Simon Norrington and his son (?) did 79 years between 1560 and 1639; and Nicholas Vere was rector for 40 years in the peaceful eighteenth century. But it is Charles Wickstead Ethelston who holds the record for longevity of service. First he was curate for 17 years to a non-resident incumbent, and then he was rector for 31 years. Mr Ethelston, therefore, served the parish of Uplyme for half a century, as well as being a major benefactor of the church. His grandson, Alfred Watlington Parke, carried on the family tradition as rector for another 37 years.

Uplyme has produced one bishop, three prebendaries, an 'intrusive' rector and three 'warming pan' rectors. The bishop was Henry Morgan, LLD, rector during King Henry VIII's reign. He was also a prebendary of Exeter cathedral, much employed by Bishop Veysey as his Vicar-General. When Morgan resigned the living of Uplyme after 40 years of ministry, he seems to have been determined to make his retirement reasonably comfortable:

He secured for himself a yearly pension of £6.13s.4d; the use of two fields belonging to the church, called Brod Walley and Showytt Close; the hall of the Rectory; a small house near the barn; a kitchen and a woodhouse, with free ingress and egress during his life.

But, despite feathering his nest so snugly, duty called. Queen Mary appointed him to the see of St David's in distant Pembrokeshire. There he stayed until Queen Elizabeth, Mary's sister, deprived him of his seat in midsummer, 1559.

Nicholas Vere was not only rector of Uplyme in the eighteenth century, but also a prebendary of both Wells and Winchester cathedrals. He died on 16 January 1809 and is buried in the chancel of Uplyme church, to be followed soon after by his venerable clerk and sexton, John Marshall, who was buried on 31 March 1810, aged 85. And the third prebendary was Stuart Worth, a much-loved and respected rector of the parish for 21 years, who was made a prebendary of Exeter cathedral in 1986.

During the Commonwealth John Godwin 'intruded' himself as rector in 1650, being deprived of his living in 1663 after the Restoration of Charles II. The so-called 'warming pan' rectors were three parsons who succeeded Mr Ethelston until his grandson, Alfred Watlington Parke, was old enough to succeed to the living that had been kept warm for him.

When Francis Drake (not the famous sailor and bowls player) was rector of Uplyme in 1759–69, he was also vicar of Seaton and Beer. He employed a curate to look after Uplyme while he lived in Seaton Vicarage – talk about absentee landlords! During Drake's time, a parlour and 'two commodious rooms' were added to the Rectory in Uplyme. As a Justice of the Peace, Drake was very active against the numerous smugglers who plied their illicit trade along the coastline. Tradition says that he was eventually murdered by the smugglers on Rossell (Boss) Hill.

The rectors of Uplyme have lived for centuries in the handsome Rectory, later the Devon Hotel. Records show that a 'parsonage house' existed in Henry VIII's reign. A survey in 1680 mentions a 'kitching, a milkhouse, an apple chamber, a turfhouse, a schoolhouse, a barn, a stawl [sic], a mow-barton and two nurseries.'

Revd Ethelston enlarged and much improved the building in 1838, when tithes were commuted for £461. He was a wealthy man who employed seven servants in his house. But because he disliked seeing them about, he had many passages made, one of them leading from the road and emerging inside the house near the kitchen. A later rector had this passge blocked up as it was far too tempting as a meeting-place for courting couples! For many years the villagers held their meetings in the largest underground room in the Rectory, which was so large that it could accommodate 80 people.

When the church was extensively restored by Revd Ethelston in 1876, much of the fine carved panelling on the rood-screen and in the choir was removed by him and placed in the Rectory, where it remains at the time of writing. In 1934 the Diocese of Exeter built a new rectory in Rhode Lane and the old Rectory became the Devon Hotel. Revd Bestic was the first rector to live in Rhode Lane.

The incumbent at the time of writing, Revd Jeremy White, is Uplyme's 50th rector. He arrived more than 700 years after Revd Robert Everard, who first set foot in Uplyme in 1259.

RECTORS OF UPLYME
(WITH THE YEAR OF THEIR INDUCTION)

1259–60	Robert Everard	1639	Edmund Hunt
1284	John Lovel	1650?	John Godwin
1309?	William Tyffant	1663	Thomas Ayshford
1330	Nicholas Pynmoke	1676	Charles Hutton
1349	John Jenkyn	1690	Gilbert Budgell
1350?	Thomas de Avebury	1710	John Ayshford
1360	Walter de Marlbergh	1744	Thomas Tothill
1362–63	Alexander de Somertone	1759	Francis Drake
1384	John Vax	1769	Nicholas Vere
1387?	John Colyn	1809	George Tucker
1390	Stephen le Eyre	1816	Richard Lewis
1397	John Parys	1823	Henry Tippetts Tucker
1398	Richard de Skelton	1842	Charles Wickstead Ethelston
1399	Nicholas Wilton	1873	Brooke de Malpes Egerton
1400	William Musket	1879	Frank Salmon
1430	Philip Lewys	1881	Henry Edwards
1438	William Fuleford	1883	Alfred Watlington Parke
1443	William Dygon	1919	Ernest Bramwell
1466	Richard Sant	1927	James Henry Scott
1512	John Vaughne	1934	Alex James Bestic
1528	Henry Morgan	1946	Philip Marling Roberts
1550	Christopher Pytt	1950	Robert Lionel Seale
1554	Richard Hart	1972	William Charles Wordsell
1560	Simon Norrington	1978	Frederick Stuart Worth
1609	Samuel Norrington	1996	Jeremy Spencer White

In 1986, Uplyme was united with the parish of Axmouth to become the United Benefice of Uplyme with Axmouth.

Above: *Uplyme bell-ringers, 1955. Left to right: Revd Seale, Jack Guest (the local policeman), Bob Peach, Gilly Peach, Margaret Harniman, Bill Cross, Jack Stamp, Arthur Start, June Cawley, Charlie Stocker, George Tucker and Fred Peach*

Left: *Revd Jeremy White, rector of Uplyme and vicar of Axmouth. Jeremy is the 50th rector of Uplyme since Robert Everard was inducted in 1259.*

Right: *The earliest known picture of Uplyme church with its fourteenth-century tower and venerable yew tree* (COURTESY OF THE LYME REGIS MUSEUM).

VALEDICTION

Written with affection by Jack Thomas upon the occasion
of Stuart Worth's retirement as Rural Dean.

Just now forsythia's in its prime
In all the lanes about Uplyme
And primroses can blow their fill
In Venlake and on Woodhouse Hill.
In Cathole there is celandine
And daffodils are doing fine
On Whitty Down in this springtime.
And when we hear the church clock chime
It is not far we have to search
Along Pound Lane to find our church.
In every season, rain or fine,
We worship God, Our Lord Divine.
Each Sunday morn we hear the call
From St Peter and St Paul,
Summoned by the bells which sing
The praises of Our Lord and King.
Our shepherd is a man of mirth
And friendly too, one Stuart Worth.
In all we do he is our Pastor
Who teaches us about the Master.
Between his parishes he drives
And leads his flocks through all their lives.
He is our friend and our protector,
Of Axmouth and Uplyme the Rector.
For eight years past as well he's been
Of Honiton the Rural Dean,
A title both obscure and grand,
Suggesting property and land.
But Dean of whom we humbly ask
And what precisely was his task?
It matters not. The job is done.
The Rural Dean has had his fun.
The Rural Deanery shuts its door
And Rural Dean he is no more.
When monarchs die, 'tis time to sing,
'The King is dead! Long live the King!'
And so we say, 'Farewell, dear Dean,
But welcome to our Rector keen.'
Of course he's never been away
But all the same it's nice to say,
'Good morning, Rector, how's it been?'
Instead of 'Greetings to you, Rural Dean.'
The chestnuts blossom, tulips flower,
Bluebells burgeon hour by hour.
As spring comes back to Whalley Lane,
We greet our Rector, title plain.

Uplyme School group in 1912 with Miss Irish, the headmistress. Note the fine collar of the boy behind the board in the front row.

Mrs Ethelston's School, Uplyme, 1926. Left to right, back row: *Miss Newton, Fred Hoare, Vic Selway, ?, Jim Finnemore, Dick Keeley, Dick Austin, Cecil Quick, Nelson Finnemore, Mr Freeman (headmaster),* third row: *Tommy Crichard, Freddie Seward, ?, Austen Bishop, Arthur Rendell, Tom Matthews, Frank Stretch, Tom Stamp,* second row: *Win Stocker, Mary Sullivan, Hilda Hutchings, Sylvia Matthews, Joan Crabbe, Edie Rowswell, Agnes Harris, ?, ?, Hilda Norman;* front row: *Cecil Fisher, Frank Stocker, Joan Curtis, Wilf Tapper, ?.*

Chapter 9

EDUCATION

MRS ETHELSTON'S AND OTHER SCHOOLS
By Imogen Thomas

For as long as anyone can remember there has been at least one school in Uplyme. In 1746 an anonymous schoolmaster reported that in Uplyme there was:

... only a private school of about 8 or 9 children, 3 being of our parish, that I teach myself to read, write and cypher [i.e. to do arithmetic], as I have taught these seven years. These are very small.

By 1833 the Parliamentary Returns reported that in the whole of Devon there were 29 villages with no school at all. Happily, Uplyme was not one of them. It had a day-school with 13 boys and 13 girls attending, supported by the minister (Revd H.T. Tucker) and the squire. There was also a Sunday school (supported by subscriptions) which was attended by 32 boys and 48 girls. There have also been schools in Myrtle Cottage at the top of Church Street and in Mona House.

There was certainly a school in Uplyme before 1838, the date of the Tithe Apportionment. It stood on the roadside on a piece of waste ground approximately west of the church and almost adjoining the graveyard. The land was owned by the rector, churchwardens and overseers. On 6 January 1854, Anne Ethelston, wife of the rector, died. In her memory Charles Ethelston, her husband, put in a stained-glass window at the east end of Uplyme church. He also had a new school built which he conveyed to the trustees, endowing it with £80 a year, stipulating that it should be known as Mrs Ethelston's School, a school that still flourishes to the time of writing. Indeed, head teacher Roger Grose still gets letters addressed to Mrs Ethelston, in the mistaken belief that she is alive, even though she has now been dead for nearly 150 years!

The main building of Mrs Ethelston's Church of England Primary School was finished in 1873, unfortunately a year after its benefactor and founder had died. In Mrs Ethelston's School there are four logbooks which detail the daily running of the school from 1873 to 1947. The first one starts:

Sept. 1. (1873) This school opened as a public elementary school. Master. R.G.D. White. provisionally certified

Paid Monitor.   T. H. Burrell
Sewing Mistress. Mrs Adams
Number present: 21 Boys. 11 Girls.
Total 32

From then on equally terse entries were made by the master, usually about once a week. That for 15 September reads: 'Attendance increasing (but children extremely backward in their work, especially Arithmetic and Writing).' On the 19th Mr White noted: 'Many children Harvesting, others gleaning. Rather irregular in consequence.' By the 26th he reported: 'Harvest nearly over. Children more regular. Cautioned about coming late, irregularly and dirty.'

The school grew rapidly. By 1881 there were 153 on the register, and by 1904 there were 170, but absenteeism was a great problem. There were three main causes for this. The children were kept home to work on the land. As well as harvesting, there was potato planting, and later potato digging, bush beating (presumably for shoots) and haymaking, all of which would have employed every member of the family. There were local events which many children attended. Mr White soon learned to give a holiday for the Lyme Regatta, the Uplyme Fête or the circus when it was in town. These extra holidays also occurred for such distant attractions as a Choral Festival at Honiton or Colyton, or the Regatta at Seaton, or the Lamberts Castle Races. And the weather also played a part. Mr White noted frequently 'windy and wet, very few children' or 'Boisterous, weather, poor attendance', and occasional floods prevented even the teachers from getting to the school. He commented with typical schoolmaster's irony that he had 'Told the children not to be afraid of being dissolved by the rain.' But their reluctance was understandable. These pupils would not have had the waterproof anoraks of today's children. There is a reference to cloaks and shawls as being their outerwear. They would have arrived at school wet through and sat in a cold classroom developing coughs and colds, which, before the days of antibiotics, soon became something more serious. On 29 December 1873 he wrote: 'Very small attendance. Sickness increasing, some deaths, others at the point of death.' Epidemics of measles and whooping cough swept through the village,

Mrs Ethelston's School, Uplyme, 1921. The picture includes: *Frank Hutchings, Daddles Mence (back row); Winnie Cawley, May Irish, ? Wallman (second row); Joe Turner (front row).*

Mrs Ethelston's School, Uplyme, 1931. Left to right, back row: *Dorothy Meyer, Fred Meyer, Stan Marchant, Arthur Hutchings, Joe Crabbe, Stan Gudge, Walter Jelly, Ernie Marchant, ?;* third row: *Fred Quick, Roy Stapleforth, Doris Fisher, Hilda Hutchings, Lucy Hutchings, Joan Crabbe, Edie Bevis, Cecil Fisher, Cecil Quick;* second row: *Maurice Tucker, Horace Holman, ? Welch, Mary Holman, Olive Welch, Rosie Welch, Eileen Jelly, Ida Quick, Jack Bevis, Bill Stapleforth;* front row: *Fred Bevis, Ron Tucker, Cecil Bevis, Charlie Hutchings.*

Mrs Ethelston's Primary School's recorder band in around 1960.

sometimes closing the school. There were also more serious illnesses. In 1903 it was shut for a week for scarlet fever and in 1905 for diphtheria, from which L. Larcombe died. Other children died from rapid consumption and peritonitis.

Those pupils who did attend were divided into standards, numbered from I to VI. This was both the name of the class and the level of attainment. Regular tests were carried out and those who passed moved up to the next standard. The rector inspected the school once a week and Government inspectors came once a year. They commented on school work, including singing and sewing, and on the general state of the school. In 1882, for instance, they reported that 'The lighting and warming of the school room is defective. More slates are needed...' (the children worked on slates). In 1886 they commented that 'The children in Standards have not done well on the whole. A bad habit of working arithmetic aloud prevails throughout the school.' Religious instruction was taken very seriously and was also examined annually by a Diocesan inspector. As well as writing, arithmetic, history and geography, the children in the standards learnt poetry, drew maps and studied objects, from a list of 100 sent out each year in a Government circular – a sort of general knowledge lesson. One day in 1901, for example, the subject was 'lamps and their dangers', and the children had to copy out the information to take home, as house fires were all too frequent. In 1903 Sgt Major Britton started to take a drill class once a week.

The infants were taken by the sewing mistress. At the start they were a very mixed bag. Many were not yet three years old, but there were 'several children in the Infants Class who are above seven years of age but cannot be put in Standard I, not having been to school before.' In 1885 Mrs Adams, the first infants' teacher, was replaced by 15-year-old Florence Irish. She was to become an excellent and dedicated teacher, instructing up to 50 infants and taking needlework throughout the school. The inspectors were soon reporting that the infants, in particular, were alert and intelligent and 'sensibly and kindly

managed and thoroughly well taught.' As they moved up, the reports on the whole school began to improve. Miss Irish deserves much credit in the history of Mrs Ethelston's School. Her end was sad. In January 1913 Edwin Irish died of convulsions in the classroom. Miss Irish was clearly deeply upset. She suffered a nervous breakdown and a year later committed suicide.

The older six standards were taught by one master and a monitor, or pupil-teacher, who was completing his own education and would leave as soon as he had his certificate. The first pupil-teacher, Mr Burrell, was replaced by William Hodder, who was given a silver pencil-case when he left in 1880 as part of a continuing chain of student teachers. Mr White, the master, gained his certificate in 1880 and was replaced by Mr Bealby, who then left under a cloud in 1888. His place was taken by Hubert R. Morgan, 'Bumper' Morgan, who was to remain as master until 1924. By that time a second monitor was assisting with the teaching and keeping control of the children, who could be a rowdy lot. In 1885 Mr Bealby reported giving Tom Stocker a severe caning for 'swearing at him and kicking'. The usual punishment was a stroke of the cane, either on the hand or back. In 1907 Dora Finnemore received 'a cut on back and box on head' (tut tut) for disobedience and obstinacy. Much less seriously, Charles Cross endured one stroke for 'inking girls' faces'. But children grew up quickly in those days. On completing their elementary education at 12 or 13, the pupils left to work, to take up apprenticeships and, in the case of the girls, to go into service.

The ladies of the village took an interest in the school. Miss Pittis started a botany class once a week in 1901. Lady Peek from Rousdon called in and the Prescotts gave a series of prizes in 1901 for the greatest number of wild flowers found in the vicinity, which Frank Leeson won with a total of 90.

Uplyme School Sports in around 1968. Left to right, back row: *Yvonne Rowsell, Richard Spiller, Karen Walker;* front: *Sarah Gosling, Kevin Stokes, Teresa Powell, Julie Paull.*

Mrs Ethelston's Primary School Sports Day in the King George V Memorial Playing Field in around 1950.

Mrs Ethelston's Primary School choir seem to be in good voice around 1962. Those present include: Michael Batten, Angela Cross, Susan Cross, John Denham, Frank and Monica Finnimore, Roger Fisher, Robert Fowler, David and Jenny Silverlock and Jenny Wood.

The first-year pupils at Mrs Ethelston's Primary School around 1970.

HEAD TEACHERS OF MRS ETHELSTON'S SCHOOL

1873	R.G.D. White
1880	G.H. Bealby
1888	H.R. Morgan
1924	C.H. Freeman
1947	E. Bessell
1950	F.J. Lake
1955	A.E. Denham
1977	P.J. Newnham
1988	Susan Barton
1996	Lynne Moore (acting head)
1997	R. Grose

The school year appears to have been longer than it is in the early-twenty-first century. It started on 1 September and broke up for a week in October for Harvest Thanksgiving. There was a week's holiday at Christmas, a week at Easter, a week at Whitsun and at first three weeks for the Harvest holiday in August, later increased to five weeks.

From these rough beginnings the school has grown to be a flourishing, happy and very successful establishment. Mrs Ethelston's is a Voluntary Aided Primary School in 2004, organised within the principles and doctrines of the Church of England. In the summer term of 2003 there were 150 pupils in the school, taught in five classes. The classes are named after planets – at the bottom is Earth where the five- and six-year-olds flourish; Mars caters for six- and seven-year-olds; Jupiter has the eight- and nine-year-olds; Saturn is where the nine- and ten-year-olds are taught; and finally Neptune is the home of the senior class for ten- and eleven-year-olds. These senior pupils leave Mrs Ethelston's in July to go on mostly to the Woodroffe School, Colyton Grammar School or the Axe Valley School.

Roger Grose is the head teacher at the time of writing, supported by seven assistant teachers. There are also five teaching assistants on the staff, five mealtime supervisors and two people working in administration. For some 130 years this school has faithfully served generations of Uplyme children. The original building has been constantly expanded and adapted and is now bursting at the seams. Indeed, there was a time in the late 1970s when growing numbers led to classes being held at the Scout hut in Rhode Lane and at Hook Farm up Gore Lane! Because of the increasing demands of the school curriculum in the twenty-first century, the building has been euphemistically declared 'time-expired'. Its replacement is now overdue. Where the new building will be erected is a subject for debate in the Parish Council and elsewhere.

What is certain is that the history of Mrs Ethelston's School has been a success story. There are countless 'Old Ethelstonians' who will remember the school and its personnel with lasting affection.

FLOREAT ETHELSTONIA!

A 1960s view of Mrs Ethelston's School, Uplyme, before the birth-rate explosion led to the development of the 'new' buildings. Ted Denham, the headmaster, is checking on latecomers!

HIGH WYCH SCHOOL

After the Second World War there was a school in Mona House, run by Mrs North and Miss Williams. In due course they moved up to St Mary's which is still (just) in Uplyme. There they were taken over by Raymond Birkett, MVO, DFC, BA, who started a very successful prep. school which flourished for more than 20 years, helped by his wife who was a housemistress. The school was called High Wych School and occupied a large stone-built country house at the end of a mile-long avenue, standing in 250 acres of woodland and moorland. Raymond Birkett was a talented musician who gave the school a reputation for excellent music teaching. High Wych closed in the 1980s.

High Wych School was a large stone-built country house standing in 250 acres of woodland and moorland at the very top of Uplyme.

High Wych School up at St Mary's.

The gardens of High Wych School.

Right: *Raymond Birkett MVO, DFC, BA, principal and headmaster of High Wych School with Mrs Birkett, MA, housemistress.*

Left: *A dormitory at High Wych School.*

Uplyme Rectory (later the Devon Hotel) in 1930. A handsome seventeenth-century building, it was completely redesigned and rebuilt by Revd Ethelston in 1838. Charles Wickstead Ethelston was curate of Uplyme during the rectorship of an absent incumbent and rector between 1842–73. In all he served Uplyme for 49 years. A man of substance, besides rebuilding the Rectory, he also built the village school and restored the Parish Church.

The Uplyme Men's Club on the cricket field on Whit Tuesday, 1912. After this formal photograph the members repaired to the Talbot Arms where the Court Leet was held annually to pay village tithes to the lord of the manor, Mr Alban Woodroffe JP. Note the tiny cricket pavilion behind the group and the sashes worn by the officers of the club.

Chapter 10

RECOLLECTIONS

Hubert R. Morgan wrote these memories in 1938. Born in 1867, he was a former headmaster of Mrs Ethelston's Primary School (1888–1924) and organist of St Peter and St Paul's Church (1887–1924) when he retired. He helped to start cricket in Uplyme and was secretary and treasurer of the club (1893–1923). A bachelor, he lived with the Plum family at Coombe House, Coombe Street, opposite the Conservative Club in Lyme Regis. He walked to Uplyme and back every weekday and twice on Sundays to play the organ. He was a strict disciplinarian who never spared the rod. He was quite prepared to give a second chastisement to victims who scuffed or stamped their feet on returning to their desks. Known affectionately to his pupils as 'Bumper' Morgan, he records many names and aspects of Uplyme long since gone. He died in 1952 and is commemorated with a plaque on a seat outside the church. He wrote:

On Whit Sunday, June 1890, at about 5.30 pm, a cloud burst over Uplyme. The little river Lym became a raging torrent and broke its banks. The cricket field, the football field, Venlake, Pound Lane and all the lower parts of the village were submerged. The hedges were covered and water poured through the backs of the houses and school and out at their fronts! Carts, putts [a 'putt' is a small farm cart], wheelbarrows, pigs, poultry, as well as every bridge between Uplyme and Lyme, were carried out to sea. Fortunately, the tide was out! At Lyme, people were taken out of their bedroom windows in boats. The damage to Lyme roads and the renewal of bridges exceeded £1,000.

The Revd Charles Ethelston, who married a Miss Peel, added a wing to the older part of Uplyme church, which dates from the twelfth century. His wife had the school built that bears her name. It has since been greatly enlarged and improved. The school was endowed with the rent from Court Hall Farm that belonged to Miss Peel and was subsequently bought by the Manfield family. The poor children of the village were taught free of charge and wore uniforms. On Sundays they were seated in the gallery of the church.

The old Rectory where Mr Ethelston resided had very extensive grounds, now much reduced. Broadway House, Park House, the butcher's shop, the garage rented by Saunders, a piece of ground just above the two

lock-up shops, the two shops themselves, and the three new bungalows in Church Street all occupy portions of the former Rectory garden. The field extending from the schoolmaster's house to that of Mr Budgett at Lane End was planted with trees (on which the squirrels used to play) by Mrs Ethelston to prevent people overlooking the Rectory grounds!

St Mary's used to be the property of the Holland family but is now owned by a Mr Williams. Woodhouse (now occupied by the Misses Prescotts and Mrs Sinclair, their sister) was built by Sir George Baker. Waterside, where Sir Thomas Jackson resides, was originally quite a small place but has been considerably added to by successive owners. A Mr Boon of Axminster formerly owned it. Where the present stables and garage are used to be stalls where he kept his pedigree bulls!

There used to be a tree on the top of Knoll Hill which, taken in a line with the vane on Lyme church tower, formed one side of a triangle, the apex of which used to be a spot to drop a kellick or anchor for the most successful blinning. A blin is a kind of rock whiting.

Pitt White in Mill Lane occupies the site of an old flax factory. The garden, now full of bamboo, used to be full of water to work the wheel. The course of the water can be seen under the wall of Waterside leading to Pitt White House. The cottages in Church Street, formerly occupied by the Spillers (blacksmiths) were also used in the flax trade. Besides providing the power for the flax mill, the little river Lym worked a grist mill at the end of Mill Lane and another grist mill just after leaving the fields in the direction of Lyme, a silk factory (now the Steam laundry), a woollen factory (opposite the Dolphin Inn), and a flour mill in Mill Lane, now White Rose used by the Corporation for various purposes.

Pitt White with its bamboo garden.

At Knoll Side there used to live a Mr Pearce, the author of the well-known Pearce gambit in chess. At Rhode Hill resided the Talbot family, descended from Talbot de Malehide of Dublin. A Mr Hargreaves, a Yorkshire gentleman and proprietor of the Lyme Regis Cement Works, formerly owned Harcombe House, now in the possession of Mrs Francillon. The residence known as Clevelands at Pinhay [called Whitlands in 2003] used to be inhabited by a Mr Ames, or 'Squire' Ames as he was usually designated. Captain Fullerton's house, Ware House, was occupied by Mrs Platt, three Miss Platts and two sons, both of whom became Majors in the Dorsetshire Regiment.

Whit Tuesday used to be a Red Letter Day in Uplyme when the annual Club Festival was held. Preceded by the Lyme Volunteer Brass Band, the members perambulated around the village, went to a service in the church and adjourned for dinner in a marquee set up either in the field opposite the Devon Hotel or in the field at the back of the Talbot Arms (Hacker's Mead). After dinner the remainder of the day was given to jollity and sports!

The lane leading from The Black Dog (Haye Lane) via Waterside, past Dr Cook's to Marven through Rocombe to Hunters Lodge and then under Lamberts Castle, is the one passed through by Monmouth's army on its way to the Battle of Sedgemoor where it met its Sedan!

MEMORIES OF OLD UPLYME
1895–1951
By Alice Cartwright, née Prescott

We came to Woodhouse 56 years ago in 1895. There was no railway in those days; that was built some eight or ten years later. The only way of getting to Axminster was by walking or taking the Lyme Coach which ran twice a day. On one occasion the coach raced a bicycle from Hunters Lodge to the Talbot Arms. The coach took six minutes, the bicycle did it in three!

In the village were three pubs, the New Inn, the Talbot Arms and the charming old Black Dog where one could hire a carriage and pair. The Black Dog was a very picturesque long, low thatched building. On moonlight nights a black dog was supposed to haunt Haye Lane just behind the pub.

Skirts were worn ground-length in those days and the roads, which have greatly improved with the passing years, were thick with mud. In wet weather, especially by the old Rectory [now the Devon Hotel], a thick row of chestnut trees in the field opposite [now Barnes Meadow] used to shed their leaves on the road and make us all covered in mud.

Our old Rector, Mr Parke, was the typical old-fashioned 'Father' of the parish. His word was law. When in the saddle, he was part and parcel of his horse. He was a good shot and a keen fisherman. During the week he would wear knickerbockers and an old green coat. But on Sundays he always appeared at church in a top hat, frock coat and immaculate white tie. No dog collar for him. On one occasion when he was preaching a rather censorious sermon, an ancient member of the congregation stood up and interjected 'Mind what you are saying, Parke!' He obviously felt the cap fitted.

There was no such thing as a committee in the village in those days. Mrs Parke managed our Nursing Association, which consisted of Nurse French and Mrs Parke! Our predecessor at Woodhouse, Lady Baker, when she died, had left an invested sum of money, the interest of which was to pay for a Village Nurse. The Parkes supplemented this from their own pockets which brought the grand total up to a princely £60 per annum!

In those days before the First Great War everyone seemed happy and contented with the few simple pleasures of country life. There was the annual Fête on the cricket field with tea on trestles tables but no Village Hall to run to for shelter when it rained.

The Harvest Home was always on a Friday with tea for the whole parish in the school. Such a nice, friendly affair. Fruit and vegetables were brought to the school instead of to the church and prizes were given for the best products. The following day they were taken to Lyme Hospital. At 6.30p.m. we all went on from the school to the church for the Harvest Thanksgiving service.

For many years after we came to Uplyme there were only two, or possibly three, early morning celebrations of Holy Communion in the whole year. These services took place on Easter Sunday, Ascension Day and Christmas Day. There was a mid-day celebration on the first and third Sundays in the month.

Alas, one old custom has faded out. The 'Pudding Bell' no longer warns the housewife that the morning service is over and that the family will soon be home for Sunday dinner. This bell was always rung as soon as matins ended. I think the custom ceased during the 1914–18 War.

In 1919 Mr Parke retired after a ministry of 37 years. 'The old order changeth, yielding place to new.' Many changes were made. The Village Hall was built in 1923 for the use of various organisations, all run by committees. Benevolent dictatorship ceased to be the order of the day, oligarchy ruled in its stead. With the advent of the railway and motor buses, many more people became mobile. The population increased, bungalows and Council houses sprang up everywhere. Uplyme was becoming up-to-date and modern! Though much that was valuable has been lost, the new order has exchanged many bad conditions for better ones – better houses, better education and better wages.

Many years ago we used to visit an old woman on Sunday afternoons. She had been bed-ridden for nine years with arthritis but never made a complaint. She had been one of twelve children and her father, a farm labourer, earned ten shillings a week! They could not afford tea to drink but instead toasted bread till it was nearly black which they then soaked in boiling water to take the place of tea!

My mother used to read to one old woman who smoked a clay pipe and was reputed to have the 'Evil Eye'. As soon as she heard my mother coming, she slipped the pipe into her pocket, quite forgetting that the room was full of smoke! One evening her husband, rather the worse for drink, smashed all the china in the cottage. Next night she put all the bits into a saucepan on the stove. When the man asked for his evening meal, she pointed to the saucepan and said, 'There's your supper!'

A POLICEMAN'S LOT
By Frank Nunn

I was the local policeman stationed at Uplyme between 1932 and 1936. The police house was one of two semi-detached cottages on the right going up Wadley Hill from Venlake. The adjoining cottage was occupied by a family called Arnold. Frank Arnold, the father, drove two horses and a wagon, delivering for Mr Bate of the Yawl Mineral Water Works. When I first occupied this house, there was no mains water, electricity or telephone. We had to collect the water from a pipe jutting out of the hedge further up the road. Mr Thomas, the coal merchant, received any messages from Axminster police station and delivered them to my house. I think it was about two years later before all three services were installed.

Our milk was delivered by Cecil Turner of Combehayes Farm, our bread and groceries by Mr Perham who continued the practice for many years.

When I was in the vicinity of Hunters Lodge at night, it was routine for me to wait until closing time before walking back through Harcombe with a young man called Oliver Furzey. Two of the young girls were called Winnie Start and Hilda Stamp. Winnie Start's father was one of the postmen; the Post Office was the little corner cottage opposite the Talbot Arms. The post-mistress was Mrs Saunders and Wilf Saunders's mother, Grace Brewer, kept the shop further up the main road.

On one occasion I was on duty in the village after midnight on New Year's Eve. I met two men dressed in dinner jackets walking back from Lyme Regis. They were Tom Sloman of the Talbot Arms and Andrew Rutherford, the local vet. Andrew, who was Scottish, said, 'Do ye no ken, Tam, that it's Hogmanay tonight?' 'No, I didn't know what it was, Andrew, but it was a lovely tasty meal.' You may guess what followed!

The three licensees of Uplyme pubs were Mrs Stapleforth of The Black Dog, Mr Leedham of the New Inn and Tom Sloman of the Talbot Arms. Mr Leedham was a retired butler whom nobody ever dared to address in any ways other than as Mr Leedham!

Rousdon Manor was occupied by Sir Francis Peek, the director of the Peek Frean biscuit business. He kept a full staff of servants including gardeners and game-keepers. Occasionally, a certain Mr Selfridge from London would stay at the mansion, bringing with him his own staff of servants. Sir Francis would sometimes hold a ball, with ladies wearing elaborate dresses and all the men in tails. My job then was to deal with all the uninvited guests – gatecrashers as we would call them now – and a surprising number of them would turn up. All the guests would be identified by the head butler.

After the ball was over, I was invited into the kitchen with all the staff and helpers. Our job was to finish off all the food and luxuries!

A certain Bert Quick, a farmer's son, was always boasting to me and others how he had dodged me and all the previous policemen. One night he attended a concert in the Village Hall. I spotted his bicycle at the back of the building with a slow puncture in the back wheel. There was no pump or lamp. Just before the concert ended, I used my pump to blow up his tyre. Then I went up the road and stood in a gateway. Not long after, along came Bert Quick pedalling away without any lights. As I stepped out in front of him, he stopped and said, 'Well done, Mr Nunn, you've caught me!' He was fined five shillings by the magistrates. After the court case, I couldn't resist telling George Tucker, Stan Cross, Alf Gale and all the others. I'm afraid poor Bert never lived it down but he took it in good spirits with no ill feelings.

My duties in those days involved very difficult hours. The early duty was 10p.m. to 2a.m., followed by 6p.m. to 10p.m. Other duties ranged from 11p.m. to 3a.m. and sometimes 3a.m. to 7a.m. I had one day off a week, provided nothing happened. There was no such thing as overtime.

My wife and I are now 85 years old [this article was written in 1991]. We always insist that Uplyme was the best station during my service. We have kept in

Frank Nunn the village constable outside the Police House in Wadley Hill in 1932, where John Fowler lives in 2003.

Above: *Venlake in 1933 with PC Frank Nunn, the village policeman, on the lookout for miscreants. Standing beside him is Harold Pope, a Seatonian with a fine baritone voice, who was a fireman on the railway. The thatched building on the right burnt down in 1936 and was once a dairy owned by Mr Adams. Later Mr and Mrs Lawes did shoe repairs there and sold sweets and cigarettes until the 1960s.*

Right: *The hall of Woolcombe Manor with its fine Georgian staircase and Jacobean panelling.*

Woolcombe House being built in 1923.

touch ever since with various people from Uplyme. We still pay the occasional visit to the village, if only to have a cup of tea with Kate Cross in Cook's Mead.

When I left Uplyme in 1936, I was presented by Jim Tasker on behalf of all the people in the village with a clock. That clock still takes pride of place on my mantelshelf.

Has anything really changed?

PAM MORRISH REMEMBERS

A bomb fell in 1941 up at the top of St Mary's Lane between the main road and Woolcombe cottage. The only casualties were eight hens belonging to Mrs Hutchings. What's more, Frank Hutchings slept right through the incident! Fortunately it was at the very beginning of the war and it was only a light bomb. This was the second bomb, the first one fell at the bottom of what we call Steep Field. The German plane which was being chased got rid of his bombs.

When the first bomb fell, it blew out the windows in Woolcombe. Our maid was bending down at the time to pick something off the floor; it saved her, otherwise she would have been killed.

I was born at Woolcombe (now called Amherst) and my father, James Kenneth, always known as Ken, was a farmer. My brother was James or Jimmy. Woolcombe in those days was a modest but very old cottage, two up, two down, since considerably enlarged, as the photograph shows.

The river Lym which ran through our garden used to get flooded. When the great flood came, it started to rain in the night and my father put on his mackintosh

and Wellington boots to go out and rescue the pheasant chicks, but he couldn't find the bridge. It was underwater! And the following morning he found all the chicks drowned. What a disaster!

I remember on one occasion during the war the butter which we made at the farm tasted funny. We got a man down from the Ministry of Agriculture and he went all round the pasture smelling all the wild flowers until he found the culprit. It was the cowslips! Apparently when cowslips are very young and just appearing in the meadows, they have a pungent taste which the cows pick up. So from then on, we had to be careful where we put the herd in the early spring.

Of the rectors I have known, Mr Bestic, who was a bachelor, comes to mind. He was a man of means and the first occupant of the new Rectory in Rhode Lane. Mr Bestic was at one time the rector of Sark and he used to come down quite often to see my mother who was born in Jersey. So I regard myself as half a Channel Islander. I've still got a lot of relations over in Jersey.

STAN AND STEPH REMEMBER

Stanley Gudge has lived in Uplyme all his life. Here are his memories of an Uplyme long since gone:

I was born in 1917 in the lower buildings at the bottom of Cuckoo Lane. My father was a farm labourer who worked for Mr Harris up at Ware Farm where his wages were 32s.6d. a week on which he had to keep five of us. We had meat once a week.

Pam Morrish in 1928 standing in front of Woolcombe House (now Amherst) with her brother, Jimmy, behind her. A year later the River Lym burst its banks at Woolcombe, drowning 1,500 pheasant chicks. Will Crabbe had to walk a Jersey bull from Pinhay to Woolcombe for the two Jersey cows kept there for their milk and backdoor sales. The house subsequently burnt down in April 1974.

65

I remember there was a Mr Hockey who lived in Uplyme and maintained the roads. He used to quarry gravel from the fields. Stones were stacked up by the side of the road for men like Steph's father to spend days and days beating them into small pieces. I went to Mrs Ethelston's school when I was four. The headmaster was Mr Freeman, a very nice schoolmaster. In classes of about 30 we learnt the three R's. I can't honestly remember not wanting to go to school; in those days, school was fun.

Of course we also had religious education. The first rector that I can remember was Mr Bramwell who lived in the Rectory, now the Devon Hotel. On one occasion he was very ill and went away to convalesce. When he came back, the men of Uplyme stopped his car at the Village Hall and insisted on putting a rope on the car and pulling him back to the Rectory! In the 1920s there were only three cars in Uplyme – Mr Alban Woodroffe's up at Rhode Hill, the Prescotts' at Woodhouse and Revd Ernest Bramwell's at the Rectory.

I had a school friend called Charlie Hoare who died of TB, prevalent in those days. I helped to carry his coffin to the graveyard. I suppose I was about ten at the time.

I left school when I was 13 and went to work in the village shop. We worked long hours. We started at eight o'clock and didn't knock off until half past five. On Saturdays it was from eight in the morning until eight at night, with a half day on Wednesdays.

Stephanie Gudge with her mother in the Glen, 1926. In 2003 the Glen, which is part of the East Devon Way, runs alongside the Lym between Church Street and Springhead Road. This bridge crossed the leat which supplied water power to the old mill at Waterside.

Everything in the shop was loose and had to be weighed. Even the sugar and barley meal came in hessian bags. I put my hand into a bag once and there was a rat!

I can remember the Village Hall being built in 1923 when I was six. My great-grandfather, Mr Doble, was in his 90s. He and his wife were the oldest persons in Uplyme. He laid the foundation-stone with a glass bottle under it containing coins and documents sealed with wax.

Before the council-houses were built in 1922, there were only three houses in Whalley Lane. There was Higher Fold, Hill Top and our slaughterhouse below the railway bridge. The butcher's shop was where Pound Cottage now is [in 2003]. At the New Inn, the main road was so narrow that two vehicles couldn't pass.

Stan's wife, Stephanie Gudge, also a lifelong Uplyme inhabitant, recalls the past:

I was born at Harcombe in 1918. After the war we lived in Church Street. My father was a roadman.

Before the second war many people in Uplyme were in service at the big houses – Rhode Hill House, Ware House, Woodhouse, Lady Jackson at Waterside and the Rectory where my cousin was a maid. But I didn't go into service.

I didn't go to school until I was five and a half because I had diphtheria. Dr Cook of Marven called and put me to bed – in those days there was no isolation hospital so my father and sister had to stay at home for six weeks in isolation with a sheet hung up at the front door.

My mother wanted me to become a dressmaker but I stayed on at school and became a pupil-teacher from 15 and a half until I was 18. Then I worked as a cashier at the International in Lyme for 25s. a week until the war when I became a WAAF.

Stan and I were married in 1943. I've lived in only three houses all my life – Harcombe, Church Street and this house, 12 Whalley Lane, which was built in 1930 and where we have spent all 47 years of our married life.

These council-houses were built in groups of six. When we moved in the rent was five shillings a week. There was no running water, just a well between six houses, gas lighting and an outside toilet (an earth closet). We didn't get a flush toilet until 1956. The house next door was built and sold in 1927 for £300.

I used to travel by train. We relied on those trains as an alarm clock. The first train, a goods train, left Lyme at 6.20. The first passenger train was at 8.04. I paid £2.12s.0d. for a two-month ticket, roughly sixpence halfpenny per journey, which took 20 minutes. The last train used to get into Lyme at nine o'clock. On occasions we walked to Axminster.

Our next-door neighbour was killed on the line. Mr Marchant worked all his life as a linesman on the railway. On New Year's Day, 1949, there was a lot of wind and rain. He didn't hear the train coming and they didn't see him.

I can always remember my sister saying that I was sent up one day to Manfield's for cream out of the separator. *They teased me which made me mad and I came back and said, 'That's the last time I shall go up for you or mother either.'*

WILL CRABBE REMEMBERS
Will Crabbe reminisces about Uplyme in the old days.

My workmates call me Bill, some say John, and the very old address me as Wilf. Actually I was christened Wilfred John Charles in Yeovil where I was born in 1908. Soon after that we went to live at a farm near Forde Abbey. Then when I was nine years old, I came to live in Uplyme in 1917 when my father joined the army.

Because my mother could no longer live in a tied cottage at Forde Abbey Farm, she came back to Uplyme with six children to be near her mother who was granny to the whole village. Granny used to wear one of those starched bonnets with a tail.

If I could go back to those far-off days in 1917 and stand on top of one of the hills, I would look down on Uplyme and see just a few isolated farmhouses with their cottages and some big houses like Rhode House, the Rectory [later the Devon Hotel], Ware House, Rousdon Mansion [later Allhallows School], Pinhay where I worked for 25 years, Whitlands, the dower-house to Pinhay House, and Woodhouse which was fairly new then. [Three of the houses that Will mentions – Pinhay, Whitlands and Rousdon – are actually not quite in Uplyme parish.]

When I went to Pinhay, which was owned by Major Allhusen, it was still Victorian. There were seven servants indoors to look after four people and out of doors five gardeners and a groom for the horses.

On the day I was 14 I started work, that is five full days and a half day on Saturdays, for which I was paid seven shillings a week. Maids were paid about £75 a year with their keep and uniform. An agricultural labourer, like my father, was paid 17 shillings a week (that is just over £44 for the year). The rate per hour for a jobbing gardener was 5d (2½p) an hour. Eventually my father was paid 28 shillings a week (£72 annually), I used to give all my wages to my mother. Then when I wanted to go to the pictures, she would give me sixpence.

When I first came to Uplyme, the Undercliff which had slipped away in 1839 wasn't fully grown over. I can just remember as a boy paying sixpence to a farmer to walk across his land to view it.

If we wanted to go to Axminster or Lyme, to save the train fare we would walk. But the roads were terrible – dusty and full of potholes because they were all built on flint. I remember riding a bicycle down from Hunters Lodge and when I got off, I was shivering from the continuous shaking I had received.

My mother and father rode the train from Lyme to Axminster on its first journey in 1903. The train was often crowded. It was a beautiful ride – the engine puffing its way up to Combpyne, the highest point, then downhill all the way to Axminster past beautiful blue-bells. There was no need to carry a watch (we couldn't afford one, anyhow); you knew the time by the trains. There was one train every hour and a goods train at 20 minutes past six in the morning. By the way, my return fare was tuppence (1p).

I went to school at Mrs Ethelston's. There were about 90 pupils, 40 to 45 in two classes, all writing on slates. The headmaster was Mr Morgan – he was very strict. He was fond of his drink and used to come to school the worse for wear. He used to hit us with a stick or with his hand. He wore a ring and sometimes he split your ear. I look back now with resentment and think he should never have done that. I didn't learn anything at my school, either. I'm a dunce! I wish I'd had a good education.

There was an old charabanc called 'The Pride of Lyme'. My mother went to Torquay for the day in it, with her two sisters. She brought me back from that trip a razor which I've still got! That's a safety razor which I've used all my life.

In those days we made our own entertainment – kicking an old can around, skipping, playing with hoops, or birds-nesting. You used to see flocks of yellowhammers. And sparrows, there used to be thousands, whereas there's not so many around now. The same is true of rooks. We used to catch foxes and skin them. We were paid half a crown for the skin (2s.6d. = 12½p). Same with badgers. I've done badgers, got maybe £5 for them. But I wouldn't do it now.

In those days the inns of Uplyme had either a beer or a spirit licence. A pint of beer was 2½d. The New Inn was a beerhouse. Hunters Lodge, which was the only house up at the top of Uplyme and very isolated, was a farm. The pub was a sideline.

They used to have a Slate Club in the Club Field where you paid in a subscription to get a little when you were ill. We paid 2s. a month and then, if we were ill, we got 10s. a week for five weeks, if we needed it.

When the Village Hall opened in 1923, I was there as a Scout. Mrs Doble, the oldest parishioner, was supposed to lay the foundation-stone but she was ill so John Doble, her husband, performed the ceremony. Under the stone they put a 6d., a cutting from Pulman's newspaper and other objects.

Mr and Mrs Crabbe with their family in 1910. The Crabbes eventually had five girls and four boys, the second of whom is Will on his mother's knee.

The Post Office is where Wendy's Stores was in the 1980s. Miss Brewer had a little shop beside what is now the Post Office. She used to cut the slices of bacon with a knife. Her brother had the bakehouse at the time. The baker was called Salter.

Then there was a forge at the end of Venlake which was a square thatched building with a chimney going right up the centre, coming out of the middle like an umbrella. It should never have been altered. People used to queue up there to get their horses shoed. Only one old chap called Simmonds shoed the horses and you used to try and get down there by six o'clock in the morning, or even half past five. Otherwise, you would be wasting the whole day.

My father who was a lengthman used to have the length of road for the County Council. His length was from the county boundary at The Black Dog up to Hunters Lodge. He had to clean the ditches and cut the hedges alongside the road. The gangers repaired the roads.

I became a roadman because it paid so well. During my working life I've been a gardener, a farmworker and a roadman. I retired in 1977.

I was working at Pinhay in 1939 when the war broke out. Major Allhusen got all of us workers into the Bailiff's house where he made us sign up with the Local Defence Volunteers, later called the Home Guard or Dad's Army. I was in the Home Guard for four years. We had no uniform or weapons at first – just a cudgel! We used to go up the tower at Allhallows School and watch for the German invasion.

I have never had a wish to live anywhere else but in Uplyme. I just love this spot and this valley where I hope to end my days.

EDNA WOODMAN REMEMBERS

My father, William Larcombe, was the local builder here in Uplyme. He bought this piece of land [at the end of the Glen by Church Street] from Court Hall Farm in 1927. Before that, this was a pound where the farmers kept their animals. My father was also a diviner who found water with hazel sticks. He paid £300 for the rights to the water up on Springhead near Marven where there was a well. He brought the water down in pipes and built four bungalows in the Glen as well as this house, Cranbrook, in 1928. These were the first working-class houses in Uplyme to have running water – flush toilets and baths.

I've lived in Uplyme all my life from the age of four. My father brought me from the centre bungalow in Church Street to this house, Cranbrook, when I was four. So I've lived here and within a few hundred yards of here for 82 years. Terrible! [big laugh].

The Devon Hotel which had been the Rectory was bought by Clifford Stapleforth in 1934. He built the three bungalows in Church Street. But before that it was the back entrance to the Rectory. It was all laurels and rhododendrons. The rector used to come down through that area and go to church that way. In the Rectory there were subterranean tunnels put in by Mr Ethelston for the servants to use. My father blocked them up. I can remember Revd Scott who used to ride around on his horse. He is the first rector I can remember and he was the last rector to live in the Rectory before it became the Devon Hotel.

Mr Freeman, a very nice man, was the headmaster when I was a child. He lived in Knapp House, the school house. Mrs Freeman taught Sunday school. She was a great friend of Mrs England who lived in the Havard and bred smooth-haired fox terriers. Mrs England and Mrs Freeman were great WI people, like most of the village. They belonged to the WI choir. Mrs Freeman used to be the pianist and conduct the choir at the shows in the village which Mrs England organised.

Dr and Mrs M. Mutch lived at Pitt White which was their country residence. He was an ENT specialist in London who created the bamboo garden at Pitt White. He had travelled to many countries collecting different specimens of bamboo and other trees. His garden became famous for its collection of hardy bamboos, probably the most comprehensive in Europe. Mrs Mutch smoked a pipe – you used to meet her coming along smoking a pipe. They had four children and they kept their nanny well into her 90s. Then there was Mr and Mrs Gear, parents of David, who lived in the cottage and was the first head gardener. Mr A.H. Lawson was their next head gardener. He wrote an authoritative book on bamboos.

Admiral and Lady Jackson were lovely people who lived in the big house in Mill Lane, Waterside. They had two daughters, Prudence and Nancy, who hunted riding side-saddle, wearing white jabots round their necks. They housed a pack of hounds all the winter in the garden which was surrounded by iron railings to keep the hounds in. The Jacksons used to give lovely Balls in the ballroom of Waterside.

Years ago Church Cottage was two houses. In the higher cottage lived Mr and Mrs Holdway and their two daughters. Now one daughter was Topsy who ran the Dorset Hotel in Lyme and the other, now sadly in a nursing home, was Steffi Gudge. In the bottom cottage lived Newy Newbery with his aged mother. When we were girls Steffi and I sat for hours on a newly-felled tree in the Glen blowing soapy bubbles. Lovely memories.

My father used to keep three full-time plumbers and three full-time carpenters. Sid Marchant was one of the carpenters. He built the cupboards in this house. Sid worked on the railway where he was killed on New Year's Day, 1949. It was his last day on the railway, just as he was due to retire. It was a very windy day and he never heard the train coming round the cutting at Hook's Farm. So, so sad.

My husband and I married in 1938 on £3 a week but we could still afford a bunch of bananas! I've lived in this house all my married life with the exception of two years in Exeter during the war when we were blitzed out.

My husband Tom was one of the youngest engine drivers when he started at Exeter. He became a driver on the Uplyme line in 1950. He did two shifts. He took the first train to Axminster and shuttled to and fro. His first shift was from six to two; the second shift was from two o'clock to ten. We had a railway strike and Tom would not strike. He didn't approve of their principles for striking. He maintained that if they'd struck for sick pay that would have been a much better thing to strike for. So he did all their shifts. To keep the line open he did the work of two men. There were just two drivers, Tom and a chappie from Axmouth, George Johns, plus two firemen. Tom missed his father's funeral because of the strike. He felt that it was more important to keep the line open than attend his dad's funeral. Tom fought very hard to keep the line open when Dr Beeching threatened to close it. He said that the goods coming into Lyme maintained the railway and covered their costs. In summertime there would be six coaches packed with holiday-makers pulled by two engines with bogey wheels. And the taxis and buses would be full up at Lyme. It was such a hectic place in those days. We could hear the train from this house; you never bothered about a clock. If you were in the garden, you would say 'Oh, that's the one fifteen coming in.' Tom said that he knew almost every stick in the hedges. The bluebell line – it was a great loss.

There was so much happening in our village. Isn't it sad that we are losing so many of our large houses and estates?

MURIEL ARBER REMEMBERS

Muriel Arber, in her 90th year in 2003, has been coming to Lyme Regis and Uplyme regularly since 1922. A graduate of Newnham College, Cambridge, she is a distinguished geologist with a wealth of knowledge on many scientific and cultural aspects of life and with an astonishing memory. Here she recalls some aspects of life in an Uplyme of a bygone era:

I got to know Uplyme in the 1920s when the Listers, who lived at High Cliff in Lyme, took us for walks, not very lengthy walks, but then I used to have riding lessons with Gladys Stapleforth whose father was the landlord of the newly rebuilt Black Dog. That was when I really got to know parts of Uplyme – Cathole Lane, up at St Mary's, that sort of thing. Gladys Stapleforth's brother Henry was a taxi driver. It was Henry who rescued old Mrs Jones from Mona House in the first fire it had. I think it must have been in 1924 or 1925, in April, I wouldn't like to put an exact date on it, but I was about 11 years old. What I do remember is that it made an enormous impression on me because I had a nanny when I was a child and nanny had a horror of thatches. She brought me up to believe that anything thatch always burnt. One year, which I think must have been 1925, a friend of my mother's brought her little girl Anita to stay in Lyme and we used to go for walks together. One day we were playing a game – animal, vegetable, mineral – one person thought of something and the other had to guess what it was. We saw Mona House with its thatched roof on the extension facing towards Uplyme. I noticed this thatch and chose the subject 'fire-engine'. That night Mona House burnt down. It did give me the most awful shock. I have had several examples of second sight since then but that was my first experience.

We were told afterwards that old Mrs Jones, a semi-invalid in Mona House, was in bed at the time when the fire broke out. She was in a room on the first floor with a bay window which looked out towards The Black Dog. She was asleep at the time and Henry Stapleforth found a ladder and got her out. Whether he saved her life or not I don't know but it was regarded as a very heroic thing to do.

I do remember Alban Woodroffe standing for some local election and all the children chanting:

Vote, vote, vote for Mr Woodroffe
Vote, vote, vote for Mr Woodroffe
He is our man
We'll have him if we can
And drive the others out of town

As for the geology of Uplyme, the valleys are carved in the lias but with this capping of greensand. Just about on the old railway line there was a top of the lias but overlaid with greensand. I regard the land opposite the Devon Hotel as very unstable because not only do you have the greensand washing down over the lias, but also the lias itself turning to slumpin. Years ago I noticed that if you go along Mill Lane to the Middle Mill and look up towards Haye Farm, which Ken Gollop calls Bumpety Field, the lias is slumping down that field.

I remember the railway vividly. It was heaven coming to Lyme, I loved it. Cannington Viaduct was a thrilling experience; you didn't know whether to look to the right or the left. I must have travelled that line about 20 times each way. It only had two coaches. In the late 1950s I got to know the chief engineer of the Southern Railway and he told me that he was very worried about the Lyme line and the fact that the coal sheds in Lyme station were filling up with water. Would I like to write an informal report and they would pay for my photographs? I got a letter from him authorising me and I went to the station master at Lyme – I felt very grand – and I gradually worked out that the water was coming from Springhead and all the springs were joining up at the Roman road, and it was that which was causing the flooding in the railway station and washing away the foundations of the engine shed.

I remember going up St Mary's Lane where the road goes round a hairpin and there was a vast quantity of moss, masses of moss.

My grandmother was brought up in the Haymarket over a soap factory, where Burberry's is now. I suppose that Hyde Park was the nearest open ground for the children to play on. My uncle Ben, aged I suppose about five, rolled his hoop into the Duke of Wellington's legs and the Duke of Wellington swore at him roundly. That is really rather a long link with the past.

Above: *Glowing translucent jellies by Thursday Cottage Jams.*

Left: *In the 1990s the Yawl Spring Water Company re-introduced the distinctive shape of the original company's bottles.*

Chapter 11

COTTAGE INDUSTRIES

QUAINT ARTEFACTS AT QUAINTWAYS

Fancy a display case containing 13 insects ranging from a stag beetle to a ladybird? The case is made of copper beech from a tree that grew outside Sir Winston Churchill's study. All the insects have six legs, two antennae and an inscription. They come with a certificate of authenticity. They are of course millennium bugs 'which never came'. Oh, I forgot to mention that the case, which costs £100, measures 2 inches by $1^1/_2$ inches.

David Rubie has made them with a twinkle in his eye, infinite patience and a craftsman's skill out of... but no, that is a trade secret. 'I'm the only doll's house shop where the pieces are made on the premises and you can meet the maker,' says David proudly. His shop, Quaintways (www.quaintways.co.uk), stands next to the Post Office in the centre of Uplyme. Enter it and you are standing in a veritable Aladdin's cave of miniature marvels.

Dave started making doll's houses in 1987, with the help of Denise, his partner. He set up shop in Uplyme in 1992. He explains that:

At that time there were an awful lot of grandfathers making doll's houses. It was a very competitive market. I began by making one-off speciality houses, like the one I made of Colin Chapman's house which has gone to Singapore. I built a number of copies of Miss Reed's Schoolhouse, all bought by teachers. I made a $^1/_{12}$ size copy of Holcombe Manor at Ottery St Mary with all of its 22 rooms and oak-carved stairwells. That is now in Australia. And I've made a copy of Queen Victoria's 1898 Royal Train carriage.

David Rubie, master craftsman in Lilliputian design and workmanship, studied fine-hand bookbinding at the British Museum. In 1987 he turned his skilled hand to miniaturism, since when he has gained international recognition. His work is on permanent display at the Doll's House Museum in Petworth, the Miniature World at Bourton-on-the-Water, the Bokuskin Gallery in Tokyo and Puppenhausenmuseums in Basel, Switzerland, and Heesch, Holland.

David's highly original craftmanship has made his products internationally collectable. 'Virtually everything I do is based on an original idea,' he says.

David welcomes callers to his shop where he works when he is not busy next door in the Post Office, which he owns. 'You'd be surprised how many hours I work.' He also exhibits at three miniature trade fairs, writes articles for specialist magazines and has been seen on TV.

The tools he uses are a swan scalpel, a miniature lathe and a miniature router. He works in all types of wood ('If you want a rosewood chair for your doll's house, it will be made of rosewood.'). He also makes use of thatch, brass, aluminium, silver, copper and glass (0.5mm thick). He creates his mirrors out of surgical steel. His adhesives are white wood glue and contact adhesives.

So what does he make to furnish a doll's house? The answer is almost everything that you might find in any house, however small or big, however bizarre. Thus he will dress my lady's boudoir with a half-tester bed and screen, a marble-top washstand, a dressing-table, a chest of drawers, mirrors and a wardrobe. In the 1930s kitchen he can supply a kitchen cabinet, a dresser, a kitchen table with an enamel top and central drawer full of cutlery, a sink complete with taps and pipes, a pine wood plate rack and a 'mains' hot-water geyser. Elsewhere in this house you might come across a mahogany hat stand, a Tudor fireplace (made out of fibreboard with a stone finish), a pine rocking-horse, a Burmese elephant gong, a Bavarian hall seat, a Black Forest chair supported by a bear, a pedestal desk in mahogany, a Spanish Galleon mounted in a walnut display case, a Japanese sideboard, an eighteenth-century Dutch display cabinet, an umbrella stand in white elm with a model of a heron holding a snake and a fossilised Ichthyosaur hanging on the walls. Talking of walls, you will undoubtedly want some ducks flying across them. They're there too.

Would you like a bar in a pub? No problem. There it is in David's shop under a pub sign complete with beer pumps, ice buckets, a veal and ham pie, pork pies and ashtrays full of disgusting fag-ends. His attention to detail is astonishing.

You would like an exact copy of the house you live in, fully furnished? No problem for David. The cost? It might set you back £12,000 to £17,000. Oh, by the way, don't get the mistaken idea that these houses are children's toys. They're not. Little fingers, grubby or otherwise, should be kept well away. David's products are strictly for adults to place on shelves or tables and to gaze at and admire.

David has recently made seven butterfly bureaux for a dealer in New York. They have been constructed in a variety of woods – ebony, burr elm, copper beech, rosewood, walnut and oak. Some of these woods come from Windsor Great Park. The three-drawer bureau with a top display area contains under glass a set of butterflies which have been named. The drawers have burr inlay, ebony string-ing and brass furniture. Each butterfly wing has been hand painted on tissue and then attached to the body, along with its antennae. The complete butterfly was then mounted, slightly raised in a drawer. Because David is working on a scale of one to 12, the standard of his workmanship has to be that more precise and accurate. Two months' painstaking work completed the project and the finished articles were shipped off to Westchester Avenue, Pound Ridge, New York.

What shall we buy in Quaintways? Shall we treat ourselves to a bear umbrella stand as exhibited in Fawlty Towers? It's a snip at £750.

In one corner stands a rather intriguing adult toy – for the seriously rich man who has everything. It is a model of the attic of a brewery which brews Badger Ale. What's more, it is haunted (Harry Potter would love it here). In the middle of the attic stands a badger with a yard of ale in his paws. Press a butterfly on the outside of the cabinet and the badger proceeds to drink the yard of ale with evident enjoyment (don't ask me why). Out of one of the many barrels emerges a rabbit. A hand comes out of a crate to pinch an apple, a still in the corner vibrates with heat and all the candles flicker realistically. This automaton with its own transformer comes complete and is yours for a mere £1,200.

Or you might prefer a magician's chair which he made last year, inspired by the Harry Potter books and films. The chair is a swan with outstretched wings to form the arms. Harry can loll safely on his wizard's chair, admired by the American owner who purchased the seat.

But if you think that is a bit steep, why not indulge yourself by parting with just £395? For that you get a station lavatory (the station is called Bucket Under Loo), complete with a gentleman who rotates while on a bucket with dog-eared copies of the *War Cry* hanging on the back of the door ready for his every sanitary wish once he has finished. It is a sure-fire party ice-breaker. I forgot to mention that there are even the obligatory dog-ends in the fire bucket hanging from the rickety wooden fence. But then David thinks of everything.

THURSDAY COTTAGE JAMS

In the rolling green hillsides and beautiful valleys of Uplyme, you would not expect to find many industries. But if you had taken a walk between 1990 and 2002 up Rocombe Bottom to Carswell Farm and looked in the pig unit, you would have found, no, not 500 pigs fattening themselves, but large preserving pans bubbling over gas rings. The wholesome smell of marmalade or strawberry jam pervaded the atmosphere.

It all began in Somerset. A Swiss gentleman called Kurt Kunzli, who married a Somerset girl, was living in Spaxton, a village near Bridgwater. There in 1964 he started making and selling home-made jams of the highest quality. For reasons that are too arcane to explain, he called his jams after the name of the cottage in which he lived. Thus Thursday Cottage was born.

On 5 May 1989, Hugh and Pam Corbin bought the business from Kunzli and looked for suitable premises in Uplyme. They found Carswell Farm and started their project on 30 March 1990, to make quality jam. The business, which employed a dozen people, thrived and the name of Thursday Cottage is synony-mous with jams of the highest quality. The name, which derives obscurely from G.K. Chesterton, has a nice aroma about it, redolent of grey-haired grannies in thatched cottages producing divine jams to secret recipes handed down from generation to generation. But there was nothing old-fashioned within the 4,000 square feet of floor space where the jams were produced. All was modern, gleaming, sterile and hygienic. Every working day at least a ton of home-made jam rolled off the production line; sometimes even a ton and a half. That represented 350 dozen pots of jam, or 4,200 one-pound jars in one day. That's an awful lot of jam. Someone, somewhere must be spreading it a bit thick!

So how was it made? (Members of the Women's Institute, please take notes.) Basically it is the same process as all the best jam-makers in the world (your mum) use to make their products. As Mrs Beeton

Making jam.

would say, first catch your fruit. Be they citrus or soft fruit, only the best are used and are sourced from all around the world, depending on the season. There are eight stages from the raw fruit to the finished product. First the fruit is fed into a slicing machine which clinically and ruthlessly dissects each orange (pith, rind, pips and fruit) into very thin slices. These slices are then steamed. The sliced fruit is weighed. It is placed in 20lb preserving pans which boil on gas for about 25 minutes. There are 14 of these pans all boiling at the same time whilst being carefully stirred. To the fruit is added raw cane sugar. There are no other additives. Once it has cooked, the jam is placed in honey bins where it is drained. The jam is then poured into clean jars by hand. Each jar is sealed by hand with a cap which makes it airtight. Now comes automation. The pots of jam on a conveyor belt are labelled by a machine before proceeding through a heat tunnel which encases 12 jars at a time in plastic. The finished products are neatly stacked on pallets ready for distribution.

So where does all this jam go? Firstly, you will find it on sale in the Post Office in Uplyme. Further afield, it is in most health-food markets. Eight wholesalers distribute it nationwide. You can buy it in Selfridges or Fortnums. You can go right across the Continent and you will find Thursday Cottage in any and every prestigious store. People in the USA, even though they call jam 'jelly', sell it.

Hugh and Pam are rightly proud of their products which are, in their words, 'wholesome, good value and delicious'. They have become well known as 'The Jam Specialists' and the glowing and growing range includes a variety of marmalade, including the ubiquitous Seville orange in different styles – fine cut, chunky, vintage, with whisky, or with Somerset cider brandy. The marmalade range extends to include three fruit, grapefruit, ginger and grapefruit, tangerine, and lemon and lime. Strawberry is the heart of the jam range but others follow closely – raspberry, blackcurrant, tayberry (a cross between a blackberry and a raspberry), damson and dear old-fashioned gooseberry jam (a wonderful accompaniment to freshly caught and lightly cooked mackerel in the summer). The five fruity diabetic products provide a special treat for diabetics (and those who like a less-sweet preserve). In total, they have made 40 different products with their old-fashioned lemon curd being their best-seller, hugely popular in the home market and abroad.

You only have to read their *Jam Journal* with its succulent descriptions of their three new jellies –

The grave of William and Lydia Beer.

'jewel-like and bursting with flavour' – to get the old taste buds bursting. The descriptions continue:

Bramble Jelly, made from rich, ripe blackberries, is a poignant reminder of the olden days with tea and hot crumpets in front of the fire. Our Raspberry Jelly will ensure you never get the pip! This crisp, clear jelly is full of the sweet fragrance of an English summer and is perfectly served with freshly baked scones! Redcurrant Jelly is luscious.

Over the course of the years Thursday Cottage has won an impressive array of awards. It would be invidious and tedious to list the plethora of awards it has won. The icing on the cake was when, in 2001, they were named 'Best Speciality Food Producer' at the annual Great Taste Awards with their products winning four gold and five silver awards at the same prestigious event.

For commercial and private reasons Pam and Hugh have sold their business. Messrs Wilkin and Son Ltd, popularly known as Tiptree of Essex, have bought them out. Tiptrees have built a special unit to produce Thursday Cottage jam under its own label at a factory near Colchester. Hugh and Pam will be keeping a fastidious and benevolent eye on that factory to make sure that the impeccable standards which they established are maintained.

Uplyme may have lost its world-famous jam but the name lives on. Pam says graciously, 'My baby has become my teenager and moved home. The jam may actually get better.' We shall wait and see.

SNUFF AND CHEESE

William Beer was born on 8 March 1811. He used to live at Enmore Castle up at the end of Yawl Bottom, the last house up the valley, except for Burrowshot. He dealt in cheese and was known as Dr Beer or Dr Cheese for reasons which are now lost in the mists of history.

When his load wasn't very heavy, he would come up over the main road just below Hunters Lodge. But when he was heavily laden, he would go across the stream and along and up St Mary's Lane through Yawl.

His wife Lydia, who was born in 1793 (the year that the French guillotined King Louis XVI), used to take snuff. If men working for him went into the cottage when Lydia was preparing dinner, they would see her taking snuff and blowing it out all over the food. Often they would find an excuse not to eat

The bottling department of Yawl Spring Water Company at Yawl House in 1991.

*For a spell the Yawl Spring Water Company sponsored Gavin Wills
and his Formula One racing car.*

her meals when they were offered them after they had seen the snuff flying all over her kitchen.

There was a popular rhyme in Uplyme which went:

If you work for Doctor Beer,
You'll get plenty of cider but not much beer.
Twice a day you'll get some duff,
And tiddies and cabbage,
Well seasoned with snuff.

William Beer died on 4 June 1887, aged 76. His wife outlived him, dying on 10 October 1890 at the venerable age of 97. As we walk up the path to the church, we pass their grave on the left where they lie side by side.

YAWL MINERAL WATERS

The art of manufacturing carbonised water was discovered in 1772 by Joseph Priestley and popularised by Joseph Schweppe, who started his business in Bristol in 1794. But there was a severe problem with bottling the fizzy water. Either the liquid went flat in the bottles or, worse still, blew up.

A satisfactory solution was not found until 1875 when Hiram J. Codd, an American, designed a bottle known as a pop-alley. Codd designed a bottle in which closure was effected by a glass marble being forced onto a rubber ring in the neck by the gas generated by the carbonised drink. A wooden cap and plunger were supplied to each customer to force the marble down until it was trapped by two lugs built into the neck. The drink could then be poured and the marble released to return to the rubber ring. The Codd system survived until the 1930s, when it was replaced by a screw top with a rubber ring.

In the 1700s, nearby Lyme Regis became a popular holiday resort and, throughout the eighteenth and nineteenth centuries, people used to travel to Yawl to take the waters which had become renowned for the health-giving and rejuvenating qualities.

It was in 1896 that Yawl Mineral Works began bottling the local water in a factory owned by Mr Harold H. Bate. Among the many aerated products marketed were lemonade, cherryade, ginger beer and soda water. Local distribution was by horse and cart with the railway network being used to cover the entire South West. For the latter Axminster Station was used at first, and when the Lyme branch line was opened in 1903 that was used as well.

At first the various products were contained in glass Codd-style bottles sealed with an internal marble, stoneware jars and glass soda siphons; many of the original containers have been uncovered within the factory grounds and have come to light after having been buried in Uplyme gardens for many years.

That the factory owner, Mr Bate, took an active interest in village life is established by his inclusion in many postcards depicting the annual fête and sports in Edwardian times. In them he can be seen in what is obviously an official position.

At one time the mineral waters and lemonade were sent each week to Exeter, an old countryman called Frank Arnold (1861–1938) driving the horse and cart. Later, when a motor lorry was used, Frank Arnold still went to Exeter, accompanying the driver. When the lorry inevitably slowed down going up a hill, Frank would say anxiously, 'Come along now, Major, come along! You know you can do better than that!'

Around the end of the First World War, and certainly by 1923, the works had been purchased by Mr Horace Ashton Jewell who, along with experiments in jam- and coffee making, continued the production of mineral water until 1938 when the Water Authority took over the springs to supply the village with its water.

Reg Stephens, a retired naval officer, bought Yawl House and the closed factory, together with the springs, in 1969. In 1990 his son Richard formed the Yawl Spring Mineral Water Company and, with two former school friends, reopened the old boreholes and factory and began producing high-quality bottled spring water. Standard 25ml and one-litre glass bottles were used for both still and carbonated water, together with a five-litre PET container for bulk still water. An extensive search resulted in the discovery of a source that could supply the factory with the traditional half-pint Codd style bottle. Sadly there was considerable competition in what was already a lucrative business and, being unable to provide bottled water in such quantities as the 'bigger boys', the factory was closed after a few years.

The 1991 brochure of the Yawl Spring Water Company showing Mr Harold Bate, the proprietor of the original firm. The picture is taken from a postcard of an Uplyme Edwardian village fête.

A hunt meeting at Rhode Hill House in the 1900s.

Alban Woodroffe's Austin standing outside the front door of his home, Rhode Hill, in the 1930s.
The chauffeur is William Bastin with Mrs Laura Woodroffe in the back seat. Laura was the granddaughter of
Sir John Talbot and married Alban in 1904. She was the sister of General Sir David Mostyn's grandmother.

Chapter 12

HOUSES & INNS

RHODE HILL HOUSE
By David Mostyn

I regret that I do not know when Rhode Hill House was built, by whom, or who owned it until 1815. However, in that year it was bought by my great-great-grandfather, Admiral the Honourable Sir John Talbot, GCB. It was then a typical, although somewhat severe, stuccoed Georgian House, rather larger than it is in 2003.

Admiral Talbot was a most interesting man, the third son of the Talbots of Malahide in Ireland. (For a full account of his distinguished naval career see Chapter 21.) Admiral of the Fleet Lord Lewin once described to me Talbot's fascinating career as 'reading more excitingly than Hornblower's'. The estate comprised approximately 1,500 acres and ran from Horn Bridge up Colway Lane and Timber Hill, around the golf course and along the Charmouth Road to Penn Cross and on to Penn. Then it went along the Roman road, the A35, to the junction opposite Raymond's Hill Post Office where it turned left back down Springhead Road, including Rocombe Farm and Winters Farm, along Yawl Lane to its junction with Springhead Road again. From there it ran down the road to Lane End Crossroads (including Lane End Farm), down to and along Mill Lane and along the River Lym to Horn Bridge. The owner of Rhode Hill was the lord of the manor of Uplyme, a medieval title which persisted until the 1960s.

The Admiral lived in happy retirement until his death in 1851. His son, John Reginald Francis Talbot, inherited the estate. Over the next 50 years he reared a large and happy family of nine children, including my grandmother Cicely and a great-aunt Laura. John Talbot died aged 80 in 1906 and is buried just by the front door of the Roman Catholic church in Lyme. Unfortunately, his wife, Sarah Elizabeth, had died in 1878, some 28 years before he did. Subsequently, Rhode Hill and the estate were run by his eldest son, John Reginald Charles Talbot, a Justice of the Peace for both Devon and Dorset. He was helped by his wife, Josephine (née de Stacpoole). She was a great entrepreneur who had a hand in many ventures in Lyme, including the establishment of the Alexandra Hotel. It was she who started to transform Rhode Hill from a stuccoed Georgian House into the brick 'Edwardian' house that it is at the time of writing.

It was, incidentally, at this time too that our own house, White Ley, was put up as a wooden bungalow to house the overflow of guests to one of the many 21st-birthday parties at Rhode Hill!

Perhaps it is not surprising that Josephine and her husband ran into financial troubles. When he died in 1909, Rhode Hill was only half converted. Furthermore, because none of his male heirs felt able to take it and the estate on, in 1912 it was put up for sale.

However, in 1903 John Reginald Charles' youngest daughter, my great-aunt Laura, had married Mr Alban Woodroffe who owned the Ware estate. It was she who persuaded her husband to buy Rhode Hill estate 'to keep it in the family'. Between 1912 and 1915 Alban and Laura completed Rhode Hill's transformation, begun so many years before. In doing so, they demolished 18 rooms to the west of what is the front door in 2003.

They continued to live at Ware because between 1916 and 1919 Rhode Hill became a convalescent hospital for wounded soldiers. Alban Woodroffe was its commandant and it was staffed very largely by VADs. My paternal grandparents both died in 1916, leaving a large family of nine. My father and his two elder brothers were away fighting in France but my five aunts, all in their late teens, became VADs at Rhode Hill.

Alban and Laura Woodroffe also undertook the upbringing of my youngest uncle, John Mostyn, who was then only 13, the same age as their son, Rex. Although the Woodroffes and my uncle John finally moved back into Rhode Hill in 1920, it was still some years before they sold Ware. Although Laura was very happy in her old family home, Alban Woodroffe's first loves were Ware and his estanzia (ranch) in the Argentine.

In 1938 Laura became ill. That and the impending war persuaded Alban to sell Rhode Hill House but to keep the estate and build a rather smaller house on it. I have the architect's drawings for a really lovely house he planned on the coach road with what would have been one of the finest views in Europe. But getting water there in 1939 was a problem and he finally decided to build a house on the site of the old wooden bungalow, 'White Ley'.

Left: *During the First World War Rhode Hill House, the home of Alban and Laura Woodroffe, was turned into a convalescent home for soldiers. Arriving at Lyme Regis Station they were met by a small stretcher-carrying van belonging to The Black Dog. They were transported to Rhode Hill where they were kitted out with blue jackets and red ties, as worn by these men in 1918. Among the nurses were two of Alban Woodroffe's nieces, Maie and Teresa Mostyn.*

Below: *A humorous entry in Teresa Mostyn's autograph album.*

Tea !!

E.Wilkinson
R.F.A
'1918

Nurse Mostyn giving out "Tea" when the War is nearly finished.
A·D· 2006

Mrs Emma Moller, a German lady who worked at Rhode Hill, seen here in the 1930s. She died on 28 March 1938 and is buried in Uplyme churchyard where her grave carries the tribute: 'In memory of 57 years of devoted service with the Woodroffe family.'

Rex Woodroffe, son of Alban Woodroffe, in 1911. Born in 1905 he married Aileen Allen (a member of the lawn-mower-manufacturing family). Educated at Downside in Cheltenham, after service in the RAF he managed an estanzia in Argentina where he died in 1949. Aileen lived on until 1965.

So, in 1939, Rhode Hill House and park were sold to Mrs Francillon who, since 1911, had been running a most successful and well-known Domestic Science College for girls up at Harcombe House. In fact, almost as soon as she bought it, the house was taken over to house wartime evacuees. Later in the war it was used by American troops stationed in Lyme before the build-up for D-Day, 1944. So it was not until 1944 that Mrs Francillon was able to expand it into an extension of her Domestic Science College. It was run by Miss Monica Woods and her brother, Robin, both of whom lived in the Dairy House. Mrs Francillon retired in 1944; the Woods continued at Rhode Hill alone until 1968 when the college closed.

Once again Rhode Hill was sold, this time to Dorset County Council for use, most appropriately, as the girls' boarding-house for Woodroffe School. For 28 years it fulfilled this function until it closed in 1996. The Secretary of State for the Environment has declined to make Rhode Hill a listed building, although it is in an Area of Outstanding Natural Beauty where undesirable buildings are prohibited. Since then, with planning permission, it has been converted into three private apartments, each of

approximately eight bedrooms. There are further apartments in what used to be the stables and there is another self-contained house in the lodge.

Just to complete the story, I should perhaps explain that sadly Rex, Alban and Laura Woodroffe's only son, died in Argentina in 1949. Alban was going to leave the remains of the estate to my uncle John whom he had brought up. But John was a Catholic priest – a Canon in the Vatican – with of course no heir. It being historically a Talbot house, he wanted it to pass to a Talbot rather than a Woodroffe descendant. As the grandson of Cicely Talbot, I was the lucky one he chose! When he died in June 1964 I inherited it.

HARCOMBE HOUSE

Her full name was Mrs Winifred G.R. Francillon. Before her marriage in 1911 she founded a celebrated and remarkable School of Domestic Science. Harcombe House was originally a simple farmhouse which was considerably enlarged by a Mr Hargreaves, a Yorkshire gentleman who was the proprietor of the Lyme Regis Cement Works on Monmouth Beach.

The gardens of Harcombe House in the 1930s, which became a boarding-house for boys at Woodroffe School.

Many girls had their lives improved by the first-class training they received at Harcombe. The training consisted of a one-year course in cooking and housecraft. All the students boarded. Although discipline was very strict, there was a friendly, happy atmosphere. In their spare time, the girls enjoyed walking around the countryside or going to Axminster, Charmouth and the Undercliff. But it was not easy to gain admission to the school as Mrs Francillon was very particular whom she took.

Each week a group of students were nominated as 'drudges' whose duties were to get up very early and polish the passages with a weighted 'donkey', or skim the Devonshire cream from the surface of the milk which had been standing overnight in pans on the huge kitchen range. All their menial tasks had to be accomplished before the rest of the household awoke. Somehow the girls did not resent being treated as skivvies. Occasionally they visited a local woman who taught them how to pat butter into fancy shapes.

By 1934 Mrs Francillon found that she was so successful up at Harcombe that she needed more space. She therefore bought Rhode Hill from Alban Woodroffe and used both houses as domestic science schools. She put Miss Monica Wood and her brother Robin in charge of Rhode Hill. Mrs Francillon retired in 1944 and Harcombe House was let to Dorset County Council as a boarding-house for boys at Lyme Regis Grammar School, as it was then called. That was a long walk the boys had from their school to their boarding-house, uphill all the way after a day of lessons.

Rhode Hill continued for another 24 years as a domestic science college. When it closed in 1968 it was bought for the Woodroffe School, as Lyme Regis Grammar School was then known, and became a boarding-house for the girls. When boarding ceased at Woodroffe, both Harcombe House and Rhode Hill House were bought by developers and turned into apartments.

THE UPLYME MILL

In Tudor times, scarlet livery cloth was made in Uplyme. Tradition has it that the scarlet serge for Queen Elizabeth I's soldiers was made in Uplyme Mill. It was called Tudor or Elizabethan cloth. The link with Queen Elizabeth I was through Elizabeth Throckmorton, a maid of honour to Queen Elizabeth, who fell out of royal favour when she married Sir Walter Raleigh and was a daughter of the Mayor of Lyme. It is possible that one of her relatives owned the Uplyme Mill or that her father had shares in it.

There is no doubt that after farming Uplyme's most important industry was the wool industry, which was carried on at the Waterside Cloth Factory or Blanket Mill. Power for driving the looms was brought to the factory by means of a diversion of the River Lym, known as a leat. It was then led through the mill house which stood on the site where Pitt White stands in Mill Lane at the time of writing. On the far side there was a dam to provide water for a water-wheel which worked the looms in sheds at a lower level. The derivation of the name Pitt White goes back to the thirteenth century – in old Dorset, the house was called 'Pytt-Hwit', Pytt meaning a hollow or clearing, Hwit meaning near a stream.

The local wool was of a high quality and was not only spun at the mill but also dyed, woven and napped there. The livery for Queen Victoria's footmen was given its distinctive Turkey red in the dye pits of Pitt White. Teasles were grown in the field where Westhill stands in 2003, and were harvested and used for the napping process. The skins were stretched and cured nearby at what is now called Honeysuckle Cottage but was then known as Pitt White Cottage. The remnants of two skin-soaking pits on the banks of the river can still be seen at the time of writing. At Waterside Cottage, called The Roost in 2003, there was until 1990 a long attic where the lengths of cloth could be hung up to dry.

Hunters Lodge Inn, 1907. In the eighteenth century the Exeter Flying Coach came past here on its three-day journey from London to Exeter. The inn was rebuilt in about 1850 when it was owned by Captain Charles Cowper Bennett, a magistrate. Barney Hansford, who kept a fossil shop in Charmouth, is one of the boys in the trap. J. Hodder of Charmouth, the owner of the trap, is giving a scenic ride with graphic descriptions.

Unfortunately, Waterside Cloth Factory burnt down in 1868, shortly after a new boiler had been installed. Listed in Uplyme in the 1851 census is a John Edwards, whose profession was given as 'Miller'. Then, in 1871, a cloth manufacturer is listed, named James Boon. Elderly people in the 1950s could still remember Jimmy Boon, a wool-stapler and manufacturer of blankets in Uplyme. Hand-weaving was carried out in people's homes and located almost underneath the viaduct was Loom House (called Cannington House at the time of writing). When repairs were being carried out to the roof in the 1940s, a quantity of flax was found to have been laid out to dry in the attic and presumably forgotten.

THE VILLAGE'S INNS AND HOTELS

One of the more historic inns in the area is the Hunters Lodge Inn at the junction of the B3165 and A35 at Raymond's Hill. Despite its claims to the contrary, it was not a coaching inn. In the first place there would have been no need to change horses just over a mile away from the George, at Axminster, which was a coaching inn. Secondly, any casual coach passengers for Lyme Regis would have alighted at Red Lane or Harcombe Road, then the main roads to Lyme Regis. The Lyme Road at the time of writing, outside the inn, did not exist at the time, which, as mentioned earlier, does tend to disprove the old fable that a highwayman was hanged at the crossroads outside the inn. There were no crossroads there, the Crewkerne Road and the road to Lyme Regis not being cut until long after public executions had ceased to be carried out outside prisons; neither is there any proof that a highwayman was hanged there. But, if he had been, he would have met his grisly end at the crossroads that did exist – half a mile up the road at the junction of Green Lane and Red Lane with the main coaching road.

Hunters Lodge was a small sixteenth-century inn that had been considerably altered down the years to become long and two storeyed, made from stone and cobb and with a bow porch. Over the years it had served as a farm and a blacksmith's shop and,

The meet of the Cotley Hunt at Hunters Lodge in 1912. Imagine the consternation of today's motorist on the busy A35 if he were confronted with such a scene.

between the two world wars, sold petrol from two pumps that stood in the corner nearest the end of what is the car park in 2003. During the nineteenth century the inn had an estate of some 100 acres that included closes of orchards, meadows, pasture and arable land.

It was around that time that a man was killed in the bar. One landlord, well known for dragging troublemaking customers outside and throwing them in a pond that has long since vanished, came down to check everything was locked up for the night and, seeing a sack bag moving, picked up his shotgun and emptied both barrels into it. He cut the sack open to find a dead man inside. Apparently, two villains had been drinking there and only one had left. The other was inside the sack and would have cut his way out and let his accomplice in when the landlord had gone to bed. Robbery was their motive, of course.

The inn has never been short of personalities among its customers. Albert Manley's grandmother took him there in 1921 on the day the tenor, the Great Caruso, died for his first drink – lemonade. That was during the tenancy of Mr Willmington. In 1991 the then landlord, the Australian opera singer Craig Sullivan, threw a party to mark Albert's 70 years as a customer. The first drink was on the house – but it was not lemonade!

It was Craig Sullivan who discovered the inglenook fireplace in the lounge bar behind a rather mundane, and modern, open fireplace, and had it restored to all its former glory. It is now one of the outstanding features of the place, although it houses a table and not a fireplace.

The Black Dog and the New Inn both belonged to the Bridport-based brewers J.C. & R.H. Palmer Ltd, who closed them both towards the end of the twentieth century. The Black Dog, certainly there as early as 1840, went first in 1994. Originally thatched, it was rebuilt after its northern end was badly damaged by fire. In 1856 the landlord was Gabriel Hillian, and 20 years later a Mrs Hillian (his wife?) was in charge. By 1906 Mrs Sarah Ann Stapleforth was landlady. The first of that family to hold the licence, she was followed by George and Henry.

The inside of Fuller's Shop in 1960 when the special offer on Sqezy was 2s.5d. (just over 12p)!

Looking east towards the New Inn in the 1920s. Sadly, the New Inn closed in the 1990s and now sells insurance. Stafford Cottages on the left were demolished to widen the road. In 2004 a little park called Stafford Mount and a bus stop take their place. On the wall of the nearest cottage, which used to be a butcher's shop owned by Mr Irish, was an AA sign stating that London was 147½ miles distant.

The New Inn in 1987. Much to the surprise of most villagers, and after the above sign in varying shapes and sizes had greeted motorists as they passed through Uplyme on their way towards Axminster, a later and smaller sign for the Greenman Insurance firm that took over the premises when the New Inn closed, was turned down by the planning authorities.

Phil Webber, the last landlord, and his wife Val, the landlady, at the New Inn shortly before the pub closed around 1995.

A 1775 plan of the Hunters Lodge estate that then included Burough Shot Farm. The road on the left has previously been, in turn: a British trackway; part of the Roman Ickneld Way; and, as part of the Axminster Turnpike Trust, a section of the London–Salisbury–Dorchester–Bridport–Axminster–Honiton–Exeter coach road. Today it is the A35 and part of the Folkstone–Exeter Trunk Road. The Hunters Lodge Inn is adjacent to the field marked 14 on the map. Of interest is the absence of Crewkerne Road opposite the inn – it was not cut until around 1850. Also of interest is the track to Uplyme, which was replaced when the B3165 road was cut through Yawl around 1832. Before that traffic from Uplyme and Lyme Regis went to Axminster via Tapper's Knapp and Upper Rocombe to the main road above Hunters Lodge, as shown on the map. The track leading away from Hunters Lodge towards Uplyme became the B3165; in 1775 it does not appear to have the bend that the modern road has just below the inn. Burough Shot Farm no longer exists, it does not even warrant a mention on the Ordnance Survey map. But the name has been resurrected (and spelt incorrectly as Burrowshot) by the private placing of a village sign.

Two of the village's legends are based on the inn. Although one of them (reputedly) took place just over the Dorset border in Haye Lane, as it provides The Black Dog with its name it must be included here.

A local coastguard on duty in the quiet lane, which was ideal for smugglers taking their contraband inland, spotted a small black dog approaching him, but it grew larger and larger as it came towards him, finally changing into a towering black cloud as it sped past him. Even today it is claimed that only the bravest of dogs venture into the lane and those that do always cross to the other side at a certain spot.

The other story is that a farmer shared his half-ruined farmhouse, next to The Black Dog, with a huge, black canine ghost that was harmless and, as the farmer pointed out to all those that warned him of the possible dangers, 'It is the quietest thing in the house and it does not eat anything.' But, doubtless well into his cups one evening in the inn, the farmer grew tired of the taunts and rushed home. The dog soon gathered his intentions when the farmer picked up a poker and it vanished ghostlike through the ceiling. The farmer lashed out in fury at the spot where the dog had made its exit, his blows dislodging a small box that had been hidden in the roof. It contained several gold coins dating from the reign of Charles II.

The first reference to the New Inn is found in the 1923 edition of *Kelly's Directory*, which gives Henry Irish as the landlord. As it is not mentioned in the 1919 or any earlier editions, it seems safe to assume that the inn was opened around 1920. It was a cosy little place with the traditional jug and bottle, and it had not been spoilt by the subsequent interior enlargement and modernisation of its bar. Sharp increases in the rent asked by Palmers led to its closure around 1998 and in 2003 it houses the Greenman Insurance Company.

Taking its name from Admiral Sir John Talbot, the Talbot Arms, like The Black Dog, was certainly in existence as early as 1840 and it is almost certainly much older than that, probably being eighteenth century in origin. The existing building dates from the 1926 rebuilding after a fire partially destroyed it, and if pictures of the pre-1926 building are to be believed, it was certainly not the original building. During the 1970s the interior was much altered, the public and lounge bars, along with a small private room, made into a large bar.

In the pre-Village Hall days the Talbot Arms was the centre of the village's social life with the field behind (Hacker's Mead) being used for its high days. The annual club meeting in May was one such day when, after a church service, everyone adjourned to the pub for the official business and to sports, games and tea in the field. The cricket club held all its meetings there until it built its own clubhouse, complete with a bar. That would have been handy for probably the most remembered of pre-war landlords, Tom Sloman, who was more than useful with both bat and ball.

A postwar landlord who was always ready to help the cricket club, and anyone or anything else in the village come to that, was Doug Leaver who, with his wife Betty, finally moved to the Blue Boy at Clapton near Crewkerne. The sporting connection is continued with the landlord at the time of writing, Andy Snowsill, who took over in 2003 and is an active member of Uplyme football club.

The Black Dog just before it burnt down in 1905. It was rebuilt in 1916. In the 1840s the landlord was Robert Hayball, a millwright and gunsmith. Later Victorian landlords included Gabriel Hellier and George Hayball, presumably Robert Hayball's son. At the far end of the building were stables where one could hire horses, a carriage and pair and even three donkeys and a donkey chair to take old ladies to church.

Bill Cross, barman at the Talbot Arms in 1940, with Cinders, the barmaid, ready to serve customers in the old public bar to the left of what is the main door in 2003. Bill was carter to Billy Manfield of Court Hall Farm. Bill's prowess on the dartboard was legendary.

The Rhode Hill Fruit Company. Seven of the greenhouses at Rhode Hill in which the Rhode Hill Fruit Company grew peaches, nectarines, tomatoes and other plants. Their retail outlet was in Broad Street, Lyme Regis, where they advertised, among other things, bouquets, wreaths and all house, table and church decorations. They were one of the leading suppliers of floral decorations for garden parties, hunt balls and other big occasions.

Little Winters before it burnt down in 1931. Mrs Bacchus is in her garden with Colonel Bacchus and Sandy. Whitty Down can be seen in the background where Thomas Whitty collected the dyes for his celebrated Axminster carpets in the eighteenth century.

Chapter 13

FLORA & FAUNA

FLORA

One can well understand the sense of excitement that follows the discovery of a rare bird or flower. The bush telegraph that brings dozens of twitchers together to watch the mundane behaviour of a shore lark is but one example. Usually, the species verges on dowdy in appearance, but it is one more to be ticked off a personal list, rather like a train-spotter at Axminster Station.

It is much the same with flowers. See a bee orchid and the discoverer purrs with excited satisfaction. See a dandelion, or a celandine, especially in your own garden, and the first reaction is to get the trowel and root the wretched thing out. But the dandelion is far prettier than the bee orchid – it just happens to be far more common, and a weed – and thus overlooked.

Happily the parish of Uplyme, for the same reasons as for its richness in bird life, has so many different varieties of flowers that it would be almost impossible to list them all. Indeed there are said to be over 400 to be found in the Landslip alone.

Diana Shervington with, as she says, help from Tiggy Thomas, has listed those she had found in the churchyard of St Peter and St Paul's Church, a list she shared with the village in the April 2003 edition of Uplyme's *Parish News*. A point that might have passed the uninitiated by, but is shrewdly pointed out by Diana, is that the churchyard has not been ploughed for centuries, neither has it suffered the doubtful benefit of an introduction to Mr Fison.

The list is impressive: agrimony, alkanet, bibwort, bitter cress, black medick, blackthorn, bluebell, bog arum (Lords and Ladies), bramble, broad-leaved dock, bugle, bulbous buttercup, celandine, cleaver, common cat's-ear, common figwort, common hemp-nettle, common vetch, cow parsley, cowslip, creeping cinquefoil, creeping thistle, daisy, dandelion, dog rose, dog violet, changing forget-me-not, early forget-me-not, elder, field speedwell, germander speedwell, great plantain, ground ivy, groundsel, hairy bitter-cress, hartstongue, hawkweed, hedge woundwort,

An albino sparrow.

hemlock, herb robert, honeysuckle, ivy-leaved toad-flax, lady's bedstraw, lady's smock, lesser chickweed, lesser knapweed, little robin, mallow, ox-eye daisy, pearlwort, pignut, primrose, prickly sow-thistle, pussy willow, ransom, red campion, red clover, red deadnettle, rosebay willowherb, rosemary, rough chervil, rough mallow, scarlet pimpernel, shepherd's purse, smooth sow-thistle, snowdrop, sorrel, spear thistle, spotted orchid, stalata, St John's wort, tallima, thyme, water dropwort, valerian, white clover, wild madder, wood speedwell and yarrow; as many as 83 different flowers and shrubs in all.

As far as its flowers go, the churchyard is Uplyme in cameo with all those flowers, and many more, to be found around the parish. They include the blue-bell and the cowslip. The former is one of our more common flowers, especially in the woodlands and hedges where it gets that little bit of shade that it thrives on. Then it is capable of excelling any other flower when it comes to putting on a show of riotous colour if the conditions are right for it. They were in 2002 when it seemed as if all of England's woods were awash with blue and the bluebell gave an almost-as-good repeat performance in 2003. Then they were seen at their best in Uplyme in the woods below St Mary's where the tiny lane turns dog-leg and runs on towards the top of Woodhouse Hill. The cowslip is getting scarcer – another victim of modern farming methods and pesticides – but it thrives happily in the Quarry Lane area.

FAUNA

Uplyme may be a small village, but it is far from being a small parish, which does mean that the considerable variations in its environment attract far more species of the natural world to its doorstep than many other towns and villages.

Uplyme has fields and woods, hills, gorse and bracken-covered commons, ditches and ponds, tiny streams and a small river, hedgerows and banks, a stretch of the Landslip (wrongly called the Undercliff

Many cities and large towns have their urban foxes. The housing estate at Whalley Lane had its own 'rural' vixen who visited most houses in search of food for five months in 2002. She was so tame that she would take food from people's hands. She must also have been confused; depending on which house she was in at the time she was called, among many other names, Bob, Foxie, Fred and Fergol.

by a modern generation) and, last but far from least, our own small run of the English Channel. Because of that coastline, Uplyme is a convenient landfall and departure point for the spring and autumn migration of birds to and from Africa and the continent of Europe.

Such a habitat attracts a considerable variety of species of flora and fauna. This sheer variety provides the bird-watcher with the chance of always seeing something of interest when out for a walk, and not just the common birds. If you take the trouble to look you will find many of our rare birds in your midst. The common herd ranges from the tiny wren with its strident voice, to the buzzard that rides the thermal currents high above the village; from the indomitable robin, which is far from being as pleasant as its Christmas-card image suggests, to the gregarious and lovable rook. Most of the latter live in the rookery on the main Sidmouth road at Pinhay, but, throughout the year, they spend their days foraging and cawing all over the village. Around the turn of the twenty-first century a pair made their home in trees in the grounds of the Devon Hotel that look down into the Post Office car park. In the spring of 2003 there were three nests there, but the development of the grounds of the former hotel and rectory will put an end to the embryonic rookery. Most of the rook's crow-family cousins can be found in Uplyme. The carrion crow and the magpie are seen everywhere, as indeed they can be all over England. Less obvious is the jay, the most

attractive of the family, and the shiest, which creeps into our gardens in search of food but is gone in a flash at the first hint of danger.

We have mentioned the buzzard. They make their homes in the trees above Whalley Lane, in the Landslip, and around St Mary's, but can often be seen using the telegraph poles on the main road to Rousdon as a vantage spot when looking for breakfast. They share these poles with the kestrel, the daintiest of our falcons and one that is sadly in decline. The sparrowhawks became the victim of accidental pesticide poisoning when their food, small birds of every kind, ate the seed and corn that had been impregnated with various pesticides. Those small birds were immune to the poison; the sparrowhawks were not. The species virtually vanished in agricultural areas such as East Devon, but is making a comeback and, unusually for such a shy bird, has even recently been seen in residential areas, such as Whalley Lane, hawking for food. The song thrush suffers much the same by eating slugs and snails that have been killed by slug pellets. It was in definite decline a decade or two ago but seems to be making a slow recovery.

Two other birds that are on the decline in Uplyme are the barn owl and the woodcock. Once the beautiful barn owl was a familiar sight around the village – now it is only occasionally seen in car headlights. Because Uplyme is not short of woodlands or rough grassland, perhaps it is the conversion of old buildings that is the main reason for our loss of barn owls. Woodcock used to be seen in the vicinity of the Old Mill and in the fields opposite the Old Dairy House, but sadly not any more.

Although it is not very big, the River Lym is clean and in places fairly fast, making it a suitable habitat for our resident species of river birds – the grey wagtail and the dipper. From that muddy estuary of the River Axe a rare (for Uplyme) visitor is the little egret that was seen at the lake at Amherst in 2003. Other regular visitors from Axmouth are herons, from the heronry at Stedcombe, who are often seen fishing in secluded and favourite positions along the Lym. The River Lym has a small but thriving population of dippers which can be seen on the stretch from Church Street to Horn Bridge.

The grey wagtail nests in holes or cavities in riverbanks, bridges and riverside buildings. However, in the early years of the twenty-first century a pair nested and successfully reared a brood in a hanging flower basket on the patio of Jericho, a house in Woodhouse Fields. The nest of dried grasses and vegetation was lined with the hair of the family dog!

No longer seen on the river is the kingfisher, which was once regularly observed flying along the river between the Old Mill and Middle Mill. It was last spotted there in 1998. Although it is mainly a river bird, a kingfisher has been known to raid the fish-pond in the garden of Jericho in Woodhouse

Fields. Kingfishers have also been seen on a number of occasions at Amherst.

There must be something in the water at Whalley Lane. Herring gulls, our 'seagulls', have long since given up their role as true sea birds. They range far inland in search of food and are a familiar sight following the ploughman and at refuge disposal sites throughout the United Kingdom. They have also become a pest in such seaside towns as Lyme Regis, where they nest on the rooftops in almost every street. Now they have reached Uplyme, a pair recently raising its young on the chimney of Sandra Furzey's Whalley Lane home. And it was in Whalley Lane that a wryneck honoured the village with a four-day visit in 2002. A cousin of the green woodpecker, with whom it shares an almost gourmet love of ants, the wryneck (*Jynx torquilla*) was once found on the extreme eastern side of England, but has been in decline for some years, even on the Continent where it was once widespread. Visits to the South West are rare indeed. Among other rare birds that have visited the parish are Dartford warblers that have nested on Trinity Hill, where the ring ouzel and the stonechat (both thrushes) can also be seen.

In the colder winters two other members of the thrush family, the fieldfare and the redwing, are driven south. The fieldfare is not unlike its cousin, the mistle thrush; the redwing is often mistaken for a song thrush until it flies away, then the distinctive red feathers under its wings can be plainly seen.

The warbler family is well represented, although it is often hard to distinguish which member of that shy family one has just seen because of their habit of skulking in the undergrowth. One that is easy to identify is the blackcap with its black upper head (brown in the female) that gives it its name. Otherwise, expect to see the garden warbler, the whitethroat and lesser whitethroat, the willow warbler, the chiffchaff and the grasshopper warbler, among others. But, because of the lack of ideal nesting places, the common-enough sedge and reed warblers are rarely, if ever, seen in Uplyme, although both are plentiful a few miles away on the River Axe and Seaton Marsh.

The two authors are both dedicated bird-watchers – but not twitchers. Between them, together with Bill Tivenan and John Wood, they have recorded as many as 117 species, both resident and migrant, within the boundaries of the parish. They are: barn owl, blackbird, blackcap, black-headed gull, black redstart, black kite, blue tit, bullfinch, buzzard, brambling, Canada goose, carrion crow, coal tit, collared dove, cormorant, crossbill, chaffinch, chiffchaff, cirl bunting, cuckoo, Dartford warbler, dipper, dunnock (hedge sparrow), fieldfare, firecrest, gannet, garden warbler, goldcrest, goldfinch, goshawk, grasshopper warbler, great black-backed gull, great-spotted woodpecker, great tit, greenfinch, green woodpecker, greylag goose, grey wagtail, heron, herring gull, hobby, honey buzzard, hoopoe, house martin, house sparrow, jackdaw, jay, kestrel, kingfisher, lapwing, lesser black-backed gull, lesser-spotted woodpecker, lesser whitethroat, linnet, little egret, little owl, long-eared owl, long-tailed tit, magpie, mallard, marsh tit, meadow pipit, mistle thrush, moorhen, mute swan, nightingale, nightjar, nuthatch, osprey, partridge, peregrine falcon, pheasant, pied flycatcher, pied wagtail, raven, red kite, redpoll, redstart, redwing, reed bunting, ring ouzel, robin, rock pipit, rook, sand martin, sedge warbler, siskin, skylark, shelduck, snipe, song thrush, sparrowhawk, spotted flycatcher, starling, stock dove, stonechat, swallow, swift, tawny owl, teal, treecreeper, tree pipit, tree sparrow, turtle dove, water rail, wheatear, whimbrel, whinchat, whitethroat, woodcock, wood lark, woodpigeon, woodcock, wood warbler, wren, wryneck, yellowhammer and yellow wagtail.

We have two kinds of snakes in Uplyme, the adder (or viper) and the grass snake, which is equally at home in water. Other reptiles include the frog, the toad, lizards and the slow worm, which is actually a legless lizard and equally at home in the garden, especially if it is not too well maintained, as in or on the hedges and banks.

Probably the commonest mammal to be found in the parish is the badger, even if it is not seen very often unless it has been on the receiving end of a motor car. But there are literally dozens of sets to be seen. Foxes are more plentiful than one might imagine but, like the badger, are creatures of the night and not often seen. Happily, for the foxes at least, Uplyme is not regular hunting country. There was a thriving community of dormice in Barnes Meadow and, before planning permission was finally given for the controversial building, their habitat had to be respected. The developers did what the cats of Whalley Lane had been unable to do for many years and our dormice are no longer with us. Along the same lines, the Devon Hotel has a colony of the far-from-common lesser-horseshoe bats. What will become of them as the developers are busy gutting the place does not bear thinking about.

Hedgehogs are not as common as they used to be but the rabbits, although not as plentiful as they were in pre-myxomatosis days, are making a come-back, and other mammals to be found include the roe deer, which lives in the woods around the village but often comes quietly close to our gardens, and the muntjac, which visits occasionally. The grey squirrel is everywhere but vanishes at the first hint of danger. And, if you are lucky, you can still spot a hare in the bigger fields on and around Trinity Common.

At Amherst, evidence of an otter was noted in the winter of 2002/03, two trout having been taken from the lakes and consumed on the banks. Fishermen have seen the animals and they have also been spotted at Cathole Farm. We also have weasels, stoats, rats, mice and shrews.

A dipper, a frequent visitor to
the River Lym.

A grey heron.

A lapwing.

A hobby.

A Dartford warbler which has been seen at the Trinity Hill Local Nature Reserve.

A pied wagtail.

What of the 'Beast of Uplyme?' Jan Fowler claims that one morning in 2002:

I drew back the curtains of my home in Wadley Hill and quite clearly saw a big cat in the field opposite. I would say it was a black panther. We once had a black retriever and it was about the same size as that. On another occasion my son Gavin saw a black cat at Rocombe that ran down the road in front of his car; it looked more like a lynx with its pointed ears.

There are bugs of every sort, plus bees, bumble or otherwise, wasps and hornets, flies, butterflies (sadly in decline), and moths, including the delightful humming-bird moth which is on the increase. Ants, earwigs, centipedes... Uplyme has them all.

WILDLIFE IN CROGG LANE
By Molly Matthews (written in 1991)

Crogg Lane is not an important thoroughfare. There may be inhabitants of Uplyme who have never even heard of it. It is a small, steep, shady lane, barely 200 yards long, that winds down from the main road through Uplyme opposite the New Inn and Stafford Mount gardens to Springhead Road at the bottom.

It is one-way only and just wide enough for a car to pass down it and not hit a pedestrian if he or she cowers close to the bank. In late summer the de-control signs are totally obliterated by lush foliage. But even if drivers could see the signs, there would be no danger. Few cars come this way and those that do proceed cautiously.

I walk up and down this lane very often on my way to the village shops. Last summer I began to amuse myself by counting the different species of wild flowers and other growing things that cram its Devon banks. Not that Crogg Lane is especially flowery. It is just a very ordinary lane, chosen only because I happen to go that way. But I find it amazing that there is so much variety in such a small space. There seems to be a bit of everything, the smallest flowers just managing to show their faces among the bigger, bolder greenery. I decided to count everything from the big oak tree down to the moss on the stones and to take a whole year so as to have the full range of seasons.

Then of course I wanted to count the birds too and any other wild creatures that I might see. That meant I had to include insects which made it much harder for me.

I am not an expert naturalist but I am pretty fair on birds, not bad on wild flowers (with the help of books) but poor on insects. Because of the late wet spring, butterflies have been late in appearing and where are all the ladybirds?

Any bird that I can see above the crowning foliage can be counted, like seagulls, for example, or a hovering kestrel.

At the top of the lane one emerges into sunlight. On either side where Crogg Lane meets the main road there are houses, each with its well-kept garden. My count stops short of these because they belong to another world. I am counting the wild things that nature has provided to clothe the lane and the wild creatures that inhabitant it. But the garden flowers at the top attract insects that I do not see in the darker, more shadowed lane below. These last few yards provide a different habitat.

However, I cannot altogether exclude the works of man, of which the lane itself is an example. Crogg Lane probably came into being hundreds of years ago simply by people going that way habitually and piling up rocks, stones and other obstructions on either side to get them out of the way. Only a very old lane is so deeply sunk between the fields, as indeed most of the Devon lanes are. They are part of an ancient network.

I must thank men too, or perhaps one special benefactor, for some of the trees that line the lane. There are two beautiful Norway maples and a copper beech that must have been deliberately planted early in this century. But the biggest and oldest of the trees are natives, self-sown on the very top of the rocky Devon bank, where an acorn, beech nut or winged sycamore seed lodged long ago and found something good to nourish it among the stones. There are other seedling trees now, poking their heads up all along the bank. Most of them will come to nothing for lack of space.

In the early spring a clump of daffodils thrusts itself out from the bank halfway down. They must have come by chance from a garden for they are not our native variety. But even if they were once cultivated, they are wild now and a welcome addition to the natural scene.

And so to my list, which begins with the vegetable kingdom.

Trees and Bushes: Oak, Sycamore, Beech, Copper Beech, Scots Pine, Chestnut, Fir, Elm, Norway Maple, Field Maple, Ash, Hazel, Holly, Box, Willow, Elder, Hawthorn, Dogwood, Blackthorn, Ivy, Dog Rose, Bramble.

Smaller Vegetation: Primroses, Violets, Celandine (lesser and greater), Golden Saxifrage, Buttercups, Red Campion, Herb Robert, Daffodils, Bluebells, Stitchwort, Chickweed, Speedwell, Dandelions, Wood Garlic, Wild Strawberry, Shepherd's Purse, Docks, Dog's Mercury, Groundsel, Plantain, Fat Hen, Hawksbeard, Hawkbit, Lords-and-Ladies, Ground Elder, Ground Ivy, White Clover, Lesser Trefoil, Wood Vetch, Horseshoe Vetch, Stinging Nettle, White Dead Nettle, Yellow Archangel, Cow Parsley, Bindweed, Hedge Bedstraw, Goose Grass, Scotch Thistle, Woundwort, Nipplewort, Pennywort, Creeping Toadflax, Herb Bennet, Camomile, Knotgrass, Meadowsweet, Willow Herb, Garlic Mustard, Sowthistle, St John's Wort, Red Cranesbill, Hogweed, Horsetail, Moss.

Grasses: Rye Grass, Common Bent, Wild Oats, Annual Meadow Grass, Meadow Fescue, Couch Grass (and probably several more).

Ferns: Hart's Tongue, Lady-Fern, Spleenwort
Fungi: Puffballs, Beech Tuft, Grisette
Total 88

The Animal Kingdom

Birds: Robins, Wrens, Sparrows, Dunnocks, Starlings, Great Tits, Blue Tits, Cole Tits, Willow Warblers, Chaffinches, Goldfinches, Greenfinches, Bullfinches, Blackbirds, Song Thrushes, Redwings, Swallows, Magpies, Jackdaws, Rooks, Woodpigeons, Seagulls and a Kestrel.

Insects: Butterflies: Tortoiseshell, Peacock, Speckled Wood, Comma, Adonis Blue, Gatekeeper, Large White, Small White.

Other insects: Bumble Bees, Honey Bees, Hover Flies, House Flies, Bluebottles, Greenbottles, Crane-Flies, Wasps, Dragonflies, Lacewings, Mosquitoes, Rose Chafers, Midges, Moths, Ants.
Other Small Creatures

Mammals

A fox which crossed the lane just in front of me, jumping down on one side and up the other, a mole that tumbled out of a hole in the bank and scrambled back as fast as he could, hedgehogs, squirrels. I might add people, dogs and horses but I think those are not wild enough.
Total for the Animal Kingdom: 58

Altogether my grand total for all living things is 146 – not bad for this short little strip of roadway. Of course a real naturalist would find many more.

The dawn redwood in Venlake End.

THE GARDENS OF UPLYME

Uplyme possesses four or five large and interesting gardens. Rhode Hill, Harcombe, White Ley, The Moorings and Pitt White all have horticultural splendours to offer while Woodhouse with its pinetum and Ware House with its spectacular rare trees and shrubs are worthy of mention.

Harcombe garden and woods were created in a damp peaty area in 1919 by Captain F.J. Francillon, who worked for the Bombay and Burma Trading Corporation. He had travelled widely through the forests of Laos and Thailand where he procured seeds, which formed the basis of his very beautiful woodland garden up at Harcombe. He planted 90 species of primula and grew from seed very many rhododendrons, some of which had not begun to bloom before he died in 1936. But the blaze of azaleas and rhododendrons in springtime is a tribute to a great gardener who planted not only for his own pleasure but also for posterity.

At Woodhouse Dr Baker and Revd E. Rhodes established the pinetum which they planted between 1840 and 1866. Because at that time trees were brought direct from their country of origin, we find rare species such as the Handkerchief tree (*Davidia*). There are several cedars (*Cedrus atlantica*), natives of the Atlas Mountains of North Africa, first introduced into Britain in 1845. It is worth visiting the pinetum merely to see one tree, the Wellingtonia (*Sequoiadendron giganteum*), which is one of the oldest and largest species of tree in the world. This tree is alleged to be the second-highest tree in the British Isles; certainly it is immensely tall. The redwoods (*Sequoia sempervirens*) are natives of North California and South-West Oregon, where they can reach a height of over 300 feet and live for upwards of 2,000 years! Their name derives from an Indian chief, Sequoyah. The tree was introduced into Britain via Russia in 1843. Our splendid specimen in the pinetum must therefore be about 150 years old, with only a mere 1,850 years to live! One of the *sempervirens* in the pinetum has split into four separate trunks (possibly caused by lightning or fire), all of which are growing vigorously and are already very tall. Other rare or unusual trees worth mentioning are a fir (*Abies nobilis*), native of Oregon, and japonica (*Cryptomeria japonica*) from Japan or China. There is a very tall *araucaria*, better known as a monkey-puzzle tree; then there are Douglas firs, an eastern hemlock (*Tsuga canadensis*), sweet chestnuts, oaks, beeches, lodgepole pine (*Pinus contorta*) and many other trees, as well as rhododendron species and old hardy hybrids. The Prescott pinetum was donated

The Moorings at the junction of Lower Rocombe Road and Springhead Road, 1934. Tom Crichard is pictured with his mother and an unknown girl.

The Wellingtonia and a redwood in the Prescott pinetum.

by Captain John Prescott, RN, in 1976 in memory of his father, Colonel John Addington Prescott, Grenadier Guards. It is managed at the time of writing by the Woodlands Trust. It is of course open to the public all the year round; access is just off the Woodhouse Hill at the back entrance to Old Woodhouse. As a tiny footnote, it is perhaps unfortunate that the parish map managed to avoid mentioning the pinetum.

At White Ley, General Sir David Mostyn has a fine collection of over 150 roses in his garden. He has a magnificent oak which may well be 400 years old with a span the length of a cricket pitch. In 1964 he made a tree house in the oak for his children, renovating it in 1984 for his grandchildren. In the great gale of January 1990 he lost 360 trees (beech, ash, oak and sycamore) from his estate on Springhead and Pond Wood. Some of the roots of the trees had been undermined by badgers!

Rhode Hill possesses two mature Wellingtonias and three tree rhododendrons (*Rhododendron arboretum*), which produce a blaze of red in late spring.

At Ware House there is a wonderful collection of trees including gingko and a katsura (*Cercidiphyllum*), a native of East Asia. In the autumn the katsura puts forth tiny pale-yellow or smoky-pink leaves which possess a pungent scent like burnt sugar. Ware House also has a lucombe oak. In 1765 a remarkable hybrid between a turkey oak and a cork oak was raised by an Exeter nurseryman named Lucombe. The lucombe oak in Ware House garden is a magnificent park tree, with dark green leaves and a grey, corky bark.

Dr Mutch created the garden at Pitt White alongside the River Lym that contains a collection of hardy bamboos unrivalled in Europe. He also planted the Norwegian maples in Crogg Lane.

At Church Acre in Rhode Lane there is a splendid *Paulownia*, a Chinese tree which produces handsome, fragrant purple flowers. There is also a variegated tulip tree (*Liriodendron tulipfera*), which hails from North America with flowers like large greenish-yellow tulips and soft white wood, and a medlar tree (*Mespilus germanica*) bearing fruit like small brown apples that are eaten when decayed.

The garden of two and three quarter acres at The Moorings was created in 1963 by Tony and Enid Marriage. The land was then three rough grazing fields with patches of scrub, brambles and bracken. It stood on a steep slope on the southern side of Springhead above the Rocombe road. Tree and shrub planting began in 1963 and is still continuing at the time of writing. The broad paths were made by bulldozers in 1969. There are 20 species of eucalyptus, 10 of pine, 5 South American beeches (*Notophagus*), and many other trees such as Bhutan pine, a balsam

poplar, a Mexican cypress, an hibiscus, a crazy hazel, *Sequoia*, red cedar, silver maple, roble beech, poplar (*Populus robusta*), Norway maple, a deodar (*Cedrus deodora*) from the Himalayas, and others. The garden, which suffered a great deal of damage from the terrible frost of 1987 and the violent storms of 1990, is open to the public under the National Garden Scheme a couple of times in the spring, when the snowdrops and bluebells are at their spectacular best, and one day in November for the autumn colours. The snowdrops which are sensational in February are worth a visit, but John Marriage believes the real stars of the garden are the eucalyptus trees. Something like 150 people each year visit this rather secret but special garden. Many, many more would be rewarded and delighted if they explored its hidden treasures.

In the cemetery there are three silver birches up the path on the left as you face the cemetery from the road. Four *Prunus* flank the circle halfway up the path. There are small-leaved lime trees, a mountain ash, flowering cherries and, most especial of all, a ginkgo which can truly claim to be a native of Britain and to have flourished here more than 300 million years ago.

One other tree in another part of Uplyme is worthy of mention. In Venlake End, Marjorie Duke planted a dawn redwood (*Metsequoia glyptostroboides*) in the 1970s. This tree, which was thought to be extinct and known to scientists only as a fossil, was rediscovered in 1941 by a Chinese botanist. The fossil tree, as it has been called, grows naturally only in isolated areas of East Szechwan and West Hupeh, China, where it thrives best in shady moist localities such as ravines and the banks of streams. Yet, surprise, surprise, here it is flourishing in the suburban environment of Venlake End in the heart of Uplyme, quite a far cry from China. Seedlings were sent from China in 1948 to the Arnold Arboretum, USA, who presented more than 600 packets of seeds to botanic gardens around the world. Marjorie acquired a seedling 6 inches high in the spring of 1971 from a nurseryman at Blackpool Corner. The tree is growing splendidly, has attained a considerable height and proves a welcome and fascinating visitor with its spring and summer foliage and autumnal tints.

And talking of hidden treasures, besides all these arboreal delights, there is still the Trinity Hill Local Nature Reserve to mention, created in 1990. Fifty acres in size, at the very top of Uplyme in the north, the reserve is heathland with a mixture of birch, pine, mountain ash, alder buckthorn and (surprisingly) crab apple, with plenty of heather, gorse and low scrub. There you may find birds, mammals and invertebrates such as the bog-bush cricket, the green tiger beetle and a host of rare spiders, wasps and beetles.

In 1926 the Talbot Arms mysteriously caught fire on consecutive Thursdays in July. Both fires started in the garage. On the second Thursday the building was gutted. The Exeter fire-engine came down the hill from Yawl so fast that it failed to stop until it had reached the Rectory (now the Devon Hotel)! The firemen were helped by a chain of villagers, some in their nightwear, who brought water from the River Lym.

The Landslip, 25 April 1857. This is one of a collection of wood-cut views published as a book by the nineteenth-century Lyme Regis bookseller and publisher Dunster. Drawn only 18 years after the slip it has to be the oldest surviving picture of the event. It shows the chasm between the 'mainland' and the area, some 20 acres in all that slipped away before it was 'clothed' in the trees and bushes.

Chapter 14

FIRES & NATURAL DISASTERS

THE LANDSLIP

The coastline between Charmouth and Beer Head has a considerable history of instability, with falls being recorded as far back as the fifteenth century. By far the biggest occurred during the Christmas of 1839 when some 20 acres consisting of 8 million tons of rock and soil slid down towards the beach and sea between the Devon-Dorset boundary and Rousdon.

The first signs that something was seriously amiss were discovered by the Crichard family who came home from work on Christmas Eve to encounter great difficulty in walking along the path to their cottage on the edge of the cliffs near Downlands Farm. The path itself was sinking and cracks were beginning to run across their garden. Inside their little home they discovered that the movement of the earth was causing the floors to warp alarmingly.

In great panic they rushed to Downlands Farm and borrowed a cart to carry their meagre belongings to safety. But before they could reach their home again, a new path had to be cut to enable the horses to pull the cart close enough to the house to load it and then drive it out again. They spent Christmas Eve in a barn at Downlands Farm and awoke the following morning to find that the disturbances had ceased. An ominous calm lasted throughout Christmas Day, although any thoughts that the problems had gone away were soon proved false. That night a coast-guard from the station at Axmouth was patrolling the cliffs near Downlands (smugglers often took advantage of holidays such as Christmas and Easter to go about their nefarious business) and he was startled to discover the ground beneath his feet was moving up and down as ridges ran across the fields. The great cracks appeared and awe-inspiring noises rumbled around. Although there was some moonlight, it was still dark enough to add to the terror that had gripped the man. He quickly moved to a place of safety to watch unbelievable scenes as what must have seemed like the entire world slid towards the sea and forced a huge ridge to rear up out of the water.

The real extent of the convulsions was not apparent until daylight when it was seen that a huge chasm ran for well over a mile, more or less parallel to the sea, and the fields that had once flourished above it had slipped to one side and were, in some places, still intact with their hedges and trees undisturbed. The winter corn had already been sown and it was reaped seven or eight months later.

Naturally enough, in an age when the church had a firmer grip on the minds and souls of people than it does today, the landslip was quickly attributed to an act of a wrathful God, and it was firmly believed that the disaster was the beginning of the fulfilment of the Book of Revelations.

But the truth was far more mundane. The cliffs here came in two layers. Cretaceous period greensand porous chalk sat on top of Keuper marl, which acted as a barrier to the rain that easily found its way through the top layer. Once the water reached the marl it stayed on top of it and spread its way along it to form what in effect was a well-oiled slide. Any movement that was going to take place would inevitably go towards the sea, the direction that the slide took. An abnormally wet winter had not helped.

The ridge that had thrust itself up from the sea was soon washed away but the landslip is with us still. Landslip is its correct name, despite the modern term Undercliff that is nothing other than change for change's sake. You might as well try to call it the Overbeach. Although it took its time, nature clothed the chasm, so much so in fact that it is not easy to see the extent of the slip except from old prints.

The South West Way follows the old public footpath through the Landslip from Seaton to Lyme. It is a tough, seven-mile-plus hike, much of it through dense woodland, but well worth the effort if only to see some of the 400 different flowers that are said to grow there. It acts as a magnet to bird and animal life but the dense undergrowth does not really afford too many chances of glimpsing them.

Before the Second World War a small cottage run by a Mrs Peach was well known for its cream teas and it was a treat to be taken there at the weekend to be regaled with real Devonshire cream, home-made scones and jam. And, if you think it was a long way to take an eight-year-old from Seaton just for that, you are right – but well worth it, claims Gerald.

Almost inevitably legends have grown up about the Landslip. Most of them centre on a bag of gold coins that one of the cottagers risked his life to go back into his home for, just before the building went down over the edge. One version claims that he was

The height of the fire at Brookside Cottage.

The ruins of Brookside Cottage after the fire.

reluctant to give up his treasure and, as he jumped the widening chasm, the weight of the money dragged him, and the bag of coins, down into the slithering soil where both were buried forever. Another version has him coming to his senses and abandoning the bag altogether. The real flaw in the story, however, is that a humble farm labourer is hardly likely to have been in a position to possess a bag of gold coins in the first place.

Among his many West Country novels Sabine Baring Gould wrote *Winefred* (published in 1900 by Methuen), a novel based on the Landslip and probably much of its chapter dealing with the landslide is based on fact. Happily, Praxis Books brought out a limited reprint in 1994 and it is a good read for anyone interested in the story of the event.

THIRD DEVON FIRE IN TWO DAYS

FIRES

Like all towns and villages Uplyme has had its fair share of fires, although not like those that devastated nearby Axminster, Chard, Honiton and Ottery St Mary. Individual fires were almost, if not totally, accepted as being in the natural order of things in Victorian England. Uplyme, not necessarily with fires in mind, had its first piped water-supply on 7 January 1896; two of the points of supply can still be seen opposite the top of Tapper's Knapp and at Venlake Cross. A third was outside Eddie Wheadon's butcher's shop. Two years later five standpipes were placed in the village, this time with fires in mind. By 1911 it was possible to have water piped into your cottage if you could afford the 30s. (£1.50p) installation charge and the subsequent annual charge of 2s.

On a different note, oil-lamps, first mooted in 1904, arrived in Uplyme in 1906 and a man was employed at 16s. (£0.80) a week to light them (and douse them in the morning).

The village's most memorable fire, but not necessarily the worst, broke out in a garage next to the Talbot Arms in Uplyme in June 1926. It not only completely destroyed the garage and Mr Larcombe's lorry that was inside, it also spread to the inn where considerable damaged was caused.

The landlord, Mr Tomlin, and several locals dragged most of the furniture to safety. But both they and the firemen, who were eventually reinforced by the brigades from Exeter and Axminster, were in great danger from the aerated water siphons that were exploding in the cellar. When the Exeter brigade arrived it was going so fast that it was unable to halt the horses until the Devon Hotel (then the Rectory) was almost reached. The extreme heat generated led to the men having to dodge the corks that began popping out of the bottles. With some ingenuity, and not a few wistful looks from his helpers, Mr Tomlin eventually saved the day when he turned on the taps of all the beer and cider barrels and that beat the advancing flames. Something along the lines of

'greater love hath no man' springs to mind!

A few yards away at Venlake Cross, Crossways, the home of Mr and Mrs Charles Lawes, was destroyed by fire in around 1930. Said to have been the oldest cottage in the village and thatched and tinder dry, it blazed merrily. Mr Lawes was awakened by a passing motorist and found oak beams above the fireplace well alight. He brought his wife and 73-year-old father-in-law Charles Norman to safety just before the staircase collapsed. A modern bungalow was built on the site from where the Lawes family ran a small sweet shop after the Second World War.

As previously noted, Crossways was rebuilt. But Hermitage House never was after it was destroyed by fire and, in 2003, we cannot even be certain where it was. It was the home of George Pulman (see Chapter 21) and his wife, the latter living there until her death in 1901. Bought by Revd F.C. Bosanquet, the house was rented to a Colonel Scott.

The origin of the fire was unknown but at around 4.30 on the afternoon of 29 April 1902, neighbours saw smoke coming through the thatched roof and flames soon followed. The Lyme Regis Fire Brigade was soon on the scene and later, the Axminster Fire Brigade, who had a steam fire-engine, was informed by telegraph. But when they arrived two hours after the fire only the bare walls remained and what was said to be 'one of the prettiest houses in Uplyme' was just a pile of smoking ruins. The Scott family and their neighbours dragged much of the furniture and the family's belonging to safety; later they were stored at the Rectory.

The Axminster Fire Brigade was not dilatory – far from it. They were not informed until 5p.m. and, it being fair day in Axminster, it took some time to get some horses and then, their station being in West Street, they would have had to force their way through Trinity Square, which was crowded with animals and bystanders. Making matters worse, the nearest water was 300 yards away (probably the River Lym at Waterside). As we said, it is not known for certain where Hermitage House was. But in the 1930s a Mrs Bosanquet was living in a house opposite The Black Dog that is now called Lydwell House – probably built on the site of

Hermitage – and that is about 300 yards from Waterside.

After the fire the unsafe walls stuck out into the road and traffic had to be diverted until the following day, which also suggests Lydwell House because the road was widened there in the interests of traffic safety well before the Second World War.

A contemporary newspaper account from 1866 of the fire that destroyed the cloth factory belonging to Mr James Boon on the site that is now Pitt White in Mill Lane tells us that:

Flames were discovered issuing from the roof of the cloth factory at two o'clock... the fire raged with tremendous fury. The roof fell in with a tremendous crash, burying all the valuable machinery, manufactured goods and other contents. More terrible consequences would doubtless have resulted had not the engineer had the presence of mind to knock the taps out of the steam boiler, which, but for this would probably have burst. The greatest alarm was spread throughout the neighbourhood and people soon came pouring to the spot from Lyme and the rest of the surrounding districts. The factory is completely levelled. All the complicated and valuable machinery lies a wreck. The origin of the fire is as yet a mystery.

Over a century later (16 July 1996), Brookside, a six-room listed building, which was built in the mid-seventeenth century beside the River Lym and next to Pitt White in Mill Lane, was also destroyed by fire. It all happened suddenly; Patrick Hepherd, a retired Royal Navy officer, and his wife Shirley were just finishing lunch when she smelt something like burning plastic. Investigation found that flames were shooting out from the bottom of the wall in the study. Less than a week earlier they had bought a video recorder in a bargain sale. It was set to record a programme later that day and, for no apparent reason, it had suddenly burst into flames. It was already impossible to reach the telephone; no one was home at neighbouring Pitt White and Mrs Hepherd raced to The Roost where Imogen Thomas dialled for the fire brigade.

The smoke went vertically up into the sky for hundreds of feet and, although six fire appliances fought the fire with water from the River Lym, the cottage was doomed. Almost everything was destroyed – furniture, fittings, mementoes, photograph albums and, finally, all the handsome thatch so lovingly collected from Turkey and expertly laid by a master thatcher. But what the fire-fighters did succeed in doing was confining the fire to Brookside alone. Amazingly, no damage was done either to neighbouring Pitt White or to the trees in Mill Lane.

Within two hours it was all over. Brookside was a smouldering heap of ashes. The Hepherds had escaped with their lives, the clothes they were wearing, their dogs and a few sticks of furniture. So intense had been the heat of the fire that the two knobs on the taps in the kitchen were reduced to two blobs of foam! What had been a beautiful and historic home was now a hideous smoking pile of black ashes.

Brookside rebuilt.

Mona House at the top of Tapper's Knapp in the 1930s, which was used as a receiving house, private premises that took letters for collection by a country postman. It is therefore thought to be most likely that it was Uplyme's first Post Office, kept by one Job Fowler who died in 1831. Mona House was partially destroyed by a fire at the end of 2002. Mona House was originally called St Leonards and sold groceries and ironmongery.

Mona House after the fire.

The 200-year old cottage, the Venlake home of Mr and Mrs Charles Lawes and said to be Uplyme's oldest, after it had been destroyed by fire in around 1930.

Venlake in 1880, with the debris left after what was described at the time as 'a remarkable flood, which altered the entire configuration of the land.' The picture was used in evidence in the re-examination of Harry Stocker in the case of 'Cartwright v Axminster RDC', before Mr Justice Sargant in the High Court of Justice Chancery Division during the summer of 1915. Mr George Cartwright of Nottingham, and the owner of Hook Farm (above Venlake) was seeking to restrain Axminster RDC from alleged trespass in a field on the farm known as Venlake Field. The case centred on proving that a footpath existed across the field. This picture was introduced to support Harry Stocker's testimony that a fence and stile, parts of which appear on the right of the picture, did exist. The RDC won the day.

A bulldozer belonging to the Devon County Council contractor is hard at work clearing the snow on Uplyme's main B3165 road outside the New Inn after an overnight blizzard in January 1972.

SNOW AND RAIN

Uplyme's position in a valley surrounded by hills on almost every side might make it difficult to escape from during the happily rare blizzards that occur. But the proximity of the sea and its salt air usually counteracts that. One occasion when it did not was on the last Saturday night of 1962 when the worst blizzard since the 1880s buried much of East Devon beneath four to six feet of snow with drifts, in places, of over 20 feet. The road to Axminster was impassable at Hunters Lodge, almost always the worst place in the parish when there is snow, until the County Council workforce had cut a path through the road after working non-stop for 36 hours.

The same workers eventually cut paths through most main roads but, two weeks later, a second blizzard that raged for the best part of a day negated much of their efforts. Even when the roads were again freed, in most places traffic was driving on a foot of packed ice. Firms delivering feedstuffs to farms were able to call on the Army for help in the shape of lorries and drivers. Uplyme remained fairly accessible to traffic, unlike nearby Stockland, which was cut off for ten days before a lorry belonging to Morrish & Son, carrying over twice its advertised load weight and many prescription medicines, reached it. It would be nine weeks before the great freeze ended and, if not overnight, the snow vanished quickly and without the flooding that the pessimistic had predicted.

Despite its surrounding hills, Uplyme is not liable to much in the way of serious flooding; much of the rain that flows readily down Gore Lane, Whalley Lane and the main B3165, is channelled – or channels itself – into the River Lym. But, in 1880 at Venlake, there was what was described at the time as 'a remarkable flood, which altered the entire configuration of the land', and left a considerable amount of debris along the road.

Before the re-cutting of the small stream around the Village Hall car park the water from the B3165 would sometimes prove too much for it and it overflowed on to the cricket field. When the River Lym did the same on the other side of the field the whole pitch would be under water.

Another element which affected the village in the 1980s was the ultra-gale-force wind that wreaked havoc along the South Coast, destroying in a moment entire avenues of trees, many the work of a century or more. Uplyme was on the edge of the storm's area and there was not much damage to its trees. But many houses lost slates, tiles and chimneys, including Hook Farm, the home of Dennis and Betty Howlett at the time, where an entire roof was lifted off and dropped neatly beside the house, without much obvious damage having been done to either.

Left: *Uplyme Village Hall in 1923 in all its pristine glory. Behind stands Mrs Ethelston's Primary School, much smaller than it is in 2003.*

Above: *The Furzey family outside the Village Hall on the occasion of the diamond wedding celebrations of the head of the family, John, and his wife Anne. Included in the picture are, left to right, front row: Walt, Oliver, John, Anne, Rose (Mrs Honeybun), George.*

Left: *An Uplyme tug-of-war team with its rope in front, from the 1920s. Jim Copp is extreme left, back row, and Bill Cross is kneeling on the right of the front row.*

Uplyme Tennis Club, c.1924. The picture includes: *Mrs Stanning, Mrs Budge senr, Mrs Budge junr and Maggie Symonds.*

Chapter 15

LEISURE

THE VILLAGE HALL AND THE KING GEORGE V PLAYING-FIELD

Uplyme is not unique in having a fine community spirit, which is something that is indelibly built into the English way of life. But Uplyme, where that spirit was nurtured over centuries, survived the influx of newcomers who arrived after the Second World War. Then it became increasingly easier to retire to the countryside, or go there because the countryside was an attractive dormitory 'town' when cars became the norm. Most of the newcomers quickly felt that they belonged – and, even more important, the locals felt that they did as well.

The assimilation of the new villagers is perhaps nowhere better illustrated than in the building of the new Village Hall. Almost everyone in the community did something. They worked on the fund-raising committee, organised events to raise the cash, or spent their money at those events. The outcome? Uplyme has a village hall that its inhabitants can be proud of.

The story of a village hall beside the cricket field started in 1920 when *Pulman's Weekly News* reported that the rector, Revd Ernest Bramwell, chaired a well-attended meeting called by the village's devotees of dancing and whist drives. They wanted somewhere large enough for their own particular recreation. The figure of £500 was mentioned when the question of cost was raised and most people seemed to agree that a building of galvanised iron measuring around 60 by 30 feet would be ideal.

Like those of God and of justice, the wheels of village communities often grind exceedingly slowly at first. And, although a building committee was formed, it was not until 19 April 1923 that they told a public meeting that a site by the entrance to the cricket field had been purchased, and that a contract had been signed with a local builder, Mr A.E. Hillman, for the erection of an asbestos building at a cost of £850. Those three years had not been idle ones. Already the sum of £459 had been raised, the rector had made a loan of £100, and the meeting quickly agreed that the committee could borrow the £300 still required.

The management committee consisted of Revd Bramwell, chairman (Uplyme's rector was expected to take the chair on most village committees), Mrs

Bramwell, Mr Alban Woodroffe, Mr H. Budgett, Mr H. Jewell and Mr W.D. Saunders. In 2004 it might seem a question of caste that Mr C. Marchant and Mr G.W. Tolman were added, 'with a view to include representatives of the working classes', but it was still the 1920s and it would take the Second World War to break down the class barriers, something the First World War had singularly failed to do.

Pulman's Weekly News attributed the suggestion that some members of the working classes were needed on the committee to a Mr Moss. But that same paper later quoted Mr Moss as saying that 'he most certainly had not made the suggestion.' Later Charlie Marchant, who 'got the blame', quickly issued a denial. Whoever made the suggestion, it was taken up.

Just over six months later Uplyme had its Village Hall. Earlier, on 5 May 1923, a foundation-stone-laying ceremony was performed by John Doble of Wadley Hill in front of almost the entire village and a guard of honour of the 1st Uplyme Scout Troop under A.S.M. Martin. Mr Doble was standing in for his wife who, as the village's oldest inhabitant at the time, had been selected to 'lay the stone', but was unable to attend through illness. She was not forgotten – a bottle of sherry was sent to her – and, no doubt, she talked her husband into giving her the silver trowel that he had used to lay the stone and been presented with after the ceremony.

Happily, the foundation-stone was preserved when the hall was finally demolished in February 1995 after 71 years of service to the village. It is incorporated in the foyer of the new hall. Sadly, however, the whereabouts of that silver trowel used to lay the stone are not known.

On 8 November 1923 the hall was opened with a dance and entertainment organised by the rector. A sum of £30.11s.0d. (£30.55p) was raised towards hall

The cricket pavilion and the Village Hall.

Left: *The 93-year-old John Doble, deputising for his wife who was ill, laying the foundation-stone of the new Village Hall in 1923. Mrs Doble, Uplyme's oldest inhabitant, had been chosen to perform the ceremony. She was not forgotten – a bottle of sherry was sent to her home in Wadley Hill, sometimes referred to even in 2004 as Doble's Hill. Sadly, the silver trowel John Doble used is no longer with us but the foundation-stone, bearing the date 1923, has been incorporated into Uplyme's new Village Hall, built in 1994. The nearest Scout is Leslie 'Punch' Tolman. One of his fellow Scouts on that day was Will Crabbe.*

Uplyme's original Village Hall, an old, tried and trusted friend, awaits its demolition in 1994.

Left: *Village Hall Management Committee chairman Carl Holland (left) exchanges contracts with Bob Quick, director of East Devon building firm, T.C. Kingdon Ltd, outside the old Village Hall in 1993. Tom Edwards, committee member, is behind with Peter Baldwin, the architect, on the right.*

funds, the first of untold thousands of pounds that have since been raised in the hall to help local organisations.

The first hall was 70 by 30 feet in size, had a stage, toilet facilities and a small kitchen. Even more so then than the new hall is today, it was the hub of Uplyme's social life. That is not to denigrate the present Village Hall. Times just change. The Men's Club died a death; the cricket club now has its own pavilion and members take their teas there; and whist drives, and now even bingo, seem to have gone out of fashion. The ubiquitous jumble sale still holds its place as the queen of the fund-raising circuit. But 'outside' events have helped to fill the vacuum. Such modern-day things as antique fairs prove popular and, St Peter and St Paul's being a popular venue for 'outside' weddings, the hall is an ideal setting for receptions. Its ample car-parking facilities (recently enlarged) prove an added attraction.

They all met there. The cricket club, the football club, the British Legion (now the Royal British Legion), the rifle club, the WVS, the flower show, the Scouts and Guides and the Mothers' Union. If it met in Uplyme, it met in the Village Hall. Dancers danced there, partygoers partied there, playschool played there and prospective MPs came there looking for the votes that the voters would later cast in the hall. The Parish Council met there; for a short spell it served as a doctor's surgery; and, in the 1930s, it acted as a branch of the Devon County Library.

Between 1939–45 it was Uplyme's wartime HQ where hundreds of pounds were raised to back the men at the Front or to send comforts to them. It began its wartime service as the reception point for the evacuees and a distribution centre for ration books and gas masks, although the latter were also fitted at Mrs Ethelston's School. Formed in 1940 as the LDV (Local Defence Volunteers), and quickly renamed the Home Guard (and immortalised by the TV series as 'Dad's Army'), the group met there until their stand-down on 31 December 1944 when danger from invasion, long since obvious to the layman, became obvious to the authorities as well. Admiral and Lady Jackson ran a canteen for troops at the hall and the weekly dance that, besides being a source of revenue, also helped to take villagers' minds off the worries of the war.

Among other events that took place in the hall during the war years were socials for the Land Girls, a dance to raise money for the Aid to China Funds, dances organised by the locally stationed American soldiers and a Red Cross fête. Camouflage netting was made there, most likely by outworkers of Axminster Carpets Ltd who had switched from carpet manufacture to war work. And where else could (or rather would) Uplyme hold its Welcome Home Party for its men and women when the war was over?

It is of more than passing interest that the 1925 balance sheet of the 1st Uplyme Boy Scout Troop lists

a payment of £1.6s.0d. (£1.30p) for 'payment for Hall for Dance on 22 October.'

It is probably impossible to say just what the record for the size of an attendance in the old hall was and the modern safety regulations dictate what its successor can hold. What is known, however, is that there were over 400 people inside to watch the local Scout troop's annual entertainment in 1934 – *Pulman's Weekly News* reported that: 'In anticipation of an excellent evening's amusement patrons came early to claim their seats in the hall... which was crowded before the programme began.' The newspaper also reported that, with £30.11s.0d. profit at the very first function in the hall in November 1923, at sixpence (2$^1/_2$p) per head, 1,222 people were present. Which is nonsense, of course. That £30 must have also included the profit from the teas and a raffle. Even so, between 400 and 500 people must have been present in a hall that was much smaller than its successor.

But village halls, like cars, pots, pans and people, wear out. The question of a replacement was first raised as far back as 1973. It was not until 1984 that the decision was made to build a new hall on the land to the rear of the old hall that had been given as a car park overflow by Lawrie and Jean Masters some years earlier. It was opened on 1 October 1994. In between those two rather perfunctory statements there were, if not blood, certainly a lot of tears, toil and sweat.

At first it was believed that the new hall would cost £100,000, with £66,000 coming in grants. By 1993 the cost had doubled but the grant was still £66,000 and, in the event, Uplyme had to raise £125,000. It did – with a lot of hard work.

We started by saying that everyone helped. Obviously some did more than others, none more so than Sandra Furzey. If she ever had to give evidence in court, and was asked where she had been on a certain evening between 1984–94, she would almost certainly be able to answer: 'Raising money for the new Village Hall.' Those who know her swear that

One of the many bingo evenings held in the old Village Hall to raise money for the building of the new hall. The caller is Paul Stoke Faires with Fay Richards about to collect a raffle prize. Seated facing the camera are Tony Hicks (left) and Violet Gosling.

when she goes to heaven she will immediately start selling draw tickets there.

Another name that will always be associated with the building of the new hall is that of Adrian Pearson, who was asked to become the chairman of the fund-raising committee in late 1987. It was, he confessed, 'a job I took on with some trepidation the following April, along with the position of treasurer.'

Obviously there were others. Carl Holland and Tom Edwards led the sub-committee that dealt with planning applications, tenders and a mass of other paperwork. No fund-raising function took place in the old hall without the inevitable cuppa and biscuit supplied by Joy Bennett, Violet Gosling (also hall secretary for 13 years) and Barbara Pearson – so much so that newcomers to Uplyme were said to have thought that the three of them lived in that tiny tearoom. Another stalwart was the late John Ball who called the profitable weekly bingo sessions in the hall for many years. A sad loss was that of Andrew Fisher, a founder member of the fund-raising committee, who died suddenly halfway through the work. He was a great loss – and not just to the Village Hall and its fund-raising committee. Adrian Pearson's admirable *A Brief History of Uplyme Village Hall* lists the sources that helped towards that magnificent final quarter-of-a-million pound plus. Some of them were:

12 annual village fêtes £8,372.
22 jumble sales £6,786.
12 major raffles £4,235.
6 boundary walks £2,363.
12 car-boot sales £1,931.
7 mini-markets £1,221.
3 plant fairs £704
Auctions £2,772
Carol singing £687.
Skittle nights £435.
3 harvest homes £582.
Sponsored knit £2.
Cabaret night £157.
2 name-the-doll contests £56.
2 guess-the-cake-weight contests £52.
The rector's sponsored bell peal £475.
2 balloon races £695.
Celebration event £695.
Flower festival £589.
Black Dog cream teas £167.
'Big Ted's' raffle £167.
Clive Pig £115.
Turf-turning £153.
Roy Van Duke £88.
Foundation-stone laying day £146.
Cliff Richard raffle £87.
Bedlam Theatre show £131.
Dog show £53.
A Horrible Hour Show £100.
Sykes and Nancy £34.

Beauty and the Beast from Mars £130.
2 for the 1/9s £31.
A Summer Evening of Opera £31.
Village Sign Prize £150.
Miss Wilson's slim £59.
Young Farmers' Concerts £258.
Mr Gosling's Quiz Nights £882.
Abbotswell cream teas £53.
Collecting jars £284.
Mr Mason's trolley dash £50.
In Memory: of Andrew Fisher £380.
  of Tom Ingoldby £145.
  of Charles Bowen £5.
Ladies' tennis £41.
New Inn pools £25.
Firdene Coffee Morning £156.
Bell-ringing event £18.
Progressive lunches £135.
Mr and Mrs Thomas' Quiz £184.
Yawl Farm coffee mornings £239.
Applegarth Singers concerts £281.
Variety night £81.
Fireworks £55.
Pear Tree quiz £36.
Mrs Jones's ploughman's £110.
Webb Ivory prize £100.
Fisher family fun run £25.
Mark Bailey's run £16.
Mrs Furzey's slim £91.
Lyme Regis Dramatic Society concert £364.
Shell 'Better Britain' £400.
Old Uplyme Slide Shows £1,500.
In appreciation of Mr Marshall's piano playing £497.

And not forgetting that there was interest of £16,502.

The Uplyme cricket club did not move to the field opposite the Talbot Arms, George V Field, until around the end of the nineteenth century. Before that they had played at Yawl Hill or Ware and the village's high days, the annual club day and suchlike, took place on the field behind the Talbot Arms known as Hacker's Mead.

What is now the King George Playing-Field may have been glebe land during Charles Wickstead Ethelston's time as rector, but it is possible that he (or the family) purchased it because, in 1915, H.W.E. Ethelston, who was killed in action in France, is said to have been 'the last member of the family to have owned the playing-field in Uplyme.' What is certain is that Revd Ernest Bramwell purchased the field (and the allotments) in 1921 for the sum of £500 and conveyed a small portion of the field to 'certain persons' as a site for the Village Hall. As he was the chairman of the committee that was responsible for the raising of funds and the building of the hall, one of those 'certain persons' was himself.

In 1927 Revd Bramwell offered the rest of the field to the Parish Council for the sum of £750 but his offer was refused at a public meeting of ratepayers. A year later a private limited company, the Uplyme Cricket and Lawn Tennis Club, was formed to purchase the field and sublet it to the cricket club. It seems that debts were accrued – in 1934 the field was still in debt and finally, in 1938, the field was conveyed to the National Playing Fields Association who paid off the outstanding amount.

The field was registered under the King George Fields Foundation, which was a national scheme set up to commemorate the life of King George V. The trust deed states, 'The field will be used in perpetuity as a cricket field and a recreational ground for the benefit of the inhabitants of Uplyme in the County of Devon.' Trustees administer the field under the umbrella of the National Playing Fields Association. No funds are available from the Association for maintenance work and the Trustees are dependent on revenue from the tennis-court to maintain the field, although the cricket club contribute a great deal in cutting and maintaining the playing area.

In 1952 the Parish Council established a children's play area on the west side of the field that, in recent years, has been moved to a more appropriate location and refurbished. The tennis-court has been resurfaced and a basketball area, by courtesy of the English Basketball Association, established. In one corner of the field is a croquet court and in 2002 an all-weather strip was added to the cricket square by courtesy of the Lord's Taverners. One of the aims behind this was to encourage young cricketers to come for tuition; another was to provide established players with better practice sessions.

Some villagers may not be aware that the National Playing Fields Association owns the entrance from the highway and part of the Village Hall car park; the latter is let to the Village Hall for a peppercorn rent of five pence per annum.

For a spell during the 1950s the village football club played its home games on the lower end of the outfield. But, as many other towns and villages have discovered, cricket and football, like oil and water, seldom mix successfully, and the footballers now play in an adjoining field. Towards the turn of the twentieth century they acquired changing facilities at the Village Hall, the funding of which was in no small way due to Lottery monies.

During the summer the King George V Field stages the village fête and then the flower show. Both bodies, along with the many local residents and visitors who attend, and all the other users of the field, must appreciate that Uplyme is so fortunate to have such a beautiful field in its idyllic setting amidst the backdrop of the hills – and all without any cost to the council-tax payers.

Left: *The Village Hall has witnessed many happy events, including the diamond wedding celebrations of John and Anne Furzey, pictured here cutting the cake, on 11 October, 1956.*

Right: *Guests begin to arrive at the official opening of Uplyme's new Village Hall on 1 October 1994. The old hall, soon to be demolished and its site taken into the new car park, is on the right. Taking a well-earned rest (from selling draw tickets with Sandra Furzey) is Charlie Bachelor.*

The 1st Uplyme Troop of Boy Scouts was founded by Alban Woodroffe in 1912. The troop poses for its photograph in the 1920s in the garden of Ware House. Left to right, back row: Cyril Tolman, Frank Bowditch, Rex Woodroffe, Tom Stocker, Wilfie Austin, ?, Billy Dark; middle row: Arthur Gudge, George Bastin, Jack Bowditch, Alban Woodroffe, Jack Dark, Will Crabbe, ?, Mr Woodroffe's pageboy; front row: Fido Crabbe, ?, Alfie Bastin, Freddie Restic, ? Beer, Freddie Ash, ?, ? Tolman, ? Tolman.

Left: *In 1914 Jack Irish was made a King's Scout and is seen here proudly carrying his patrol flag with his brother Len beside him. Sitting on the new saddlestone seat in what became the car park of the New Inn are, left to right: Fred Larcombe, ? Forsey, Harry Irish, landlord of the New Inn, Tommy Gay, ?. Tommy Gay always spoke with a rich Devon accent and invariably began his conversation with 'Ow be e?'*

Right: *The Peach brothers, patrol leader Tom and Scout Gilbert, in 1916.*

Chapter 16

SCOUTS & GUIDES

SCOUTS

Like so many other good ideas, the Scout and Guide movement was born in Great Britain and all that was said to be good was embodied in the ideals of the movement. Formed in 1908 by Lord Robert Baden-Powell at a camp on Brownsea Island in Poole Harbour, Scouting spread like wildfire across the United Kingdom and then the world – so much so that by the 1990s there were around 14,000,000 members in over 100 countries.

That 'fire' reached Uplyme in 1913 when the enrolment of the 1st Ware Uplyme Scout Troop took place in the new Scout Room at Ware House, the home of Mr Alban Woodroffe. He was a local JP and the Boy Scout Commissioner for East Devon, and the new troop's first Scoutmaster. There is evidence to suggest that prior to 1913 some Uplyme boys had been enrolled in the Lyme Regis Troop and it is more than likely that they were among the 14 Scouts who were the first members of the new troop at Uplyme.

Alban Woodroffe provided the 1st Uplyme Troop with its new home, a 30ft by 17ft electrically lit building at Ware. Among those present at the opening ceremony were Mrs Woodroffe, Revd A.W. Parke (the troop's first chaplain), Mrs Parke, Miss Gladys Allhusen and several of the parents of the Scouts.

Scout Wilfred Crabbe, 1920.

The troop would quickly build an outstanding reputation for itself. With the District Commissioner as its Scoutmaster it probably had no other choice. But there was never any suggestion that Mr Woodroffe was ever a martinet. Rather, that he was a man with an unfailing zest to do something for the betterment and welfare of the young men of Uplyme. With that in mind he applied the same energy and enthusiasm to Scouting as he did to the drive and leadership that he gave to the many other local bodies and organisations on which he served.

By 1925 that drive and leadership had been the catalyst that brought no less than seven King Scout badges to the troop. A few years later there were 11 King Scouts at Uplyme, an outstanding achievement for a tiny village troop of five Rover Scouts and 17 Boy Scouts. Many King Scouts attended the annual St George's Day Rally at Windsor Castle to receive their badges from the Monarch; among Uplyme Scouts who are known to have done so was Roy Stapleforth in 1939. Within a few years he would be killed in action flying Spitfires out of Gibraltar.

In Rover Mate Tom Stocker, the Uplyme Troop had the first Rover King Scout in the whole country (and thus the first in the whole world). Another achievement of the 1st Uplyme Troop was to produce the first person to win the Silver Wolf, the troop minute book for 30 May 1929 reporting that: 'Mr Arthur Chapman, a former Scouter of this troop and the first British Scout to receive the Silver Fox visited the Scout room.' Alban Woodroffe was later to receive the Silver Wolf.

So efficient would the 1st Uplyme Troop become that it won the county banner (for the best troop) three years running and in competition with troops from such cities as Exeter and Plymouth. It was that achievement that led to their being presented with a special standard to mark their 25th anniversary in 1938 by a French countess, the Countess de Latinay de Lissac, who had formerly resided in Lyme Regis.

Starting in 1920 the Uplyme Troop brought out an annual magazine that listed its activities of the past 12 months. It was almost certainly paid for by Mr Woodroffe and given away, because no mention is made of its cost or of any sales figures in the balance sheet that was included in each edition. Two such magazines (for 1920 and 1925) are in the hands of the 1st Lym Valley Scout Group at the time of writing.

The troop would almost certainly have had a visit from the Chief Scout. Lord Baden-Powell was a personal friend of Alban Woodroffe and it is known that he visited him at both Ware and Rhode Hill on at

Above: *Patrol Leader W. Austin, 1916.*

Above left: *Scout Arthur Gudge, 1920.*

King's Scout John Irish, 1928.

Rover Scout Frank Bowditch, 1924.

Above: *As any old Scout will tell you, the highlight of the scouting year was the annual camp. Of all the many facets of local life in which Alban Woodroffe served both Uplyme and Lyme Regis, Scouting was almost certainly the one that gave him most pleasure. That meant his annual highlight was also the annual camp; not even the 76 years that have passed since this photograph was taken at the 1st Uplyme Troop's camp at Ringstead Bay in 1928 can hide the look of quiet enjoyment of his face.*

Above right: *Patrol leader Percy Wiscombe, 1916.*

Right: *Cyril Tolman, pictured here, as a Boy Scout in 1916, was an active committee member of Uplyme AFC between the two wars. He lived in Whalley Lane and served as a submariner during the Second World War, despite having lost an eye in an accident in his younger days.*

The certificate personally signed by Robert Baden-Powell awarding the highly coveted Silver Fox to Alban Woodroffe in recognition of his services to the Scout Movement.

The 1st Lym Valley Scouts with their awards after completing the Exmoor Challenge in 1992. Left to right, back row: James Booth, Matthew Wyon-Brown, ?, Dominic Holland; front: William Booth, James Marsh, Christopher Wyon-Brown, Adrian Furzey.

least two occasions. It is inconceivable that the Chief Scout would have left Uplyme without visiting his friend's troop, although there is no reference that he ever did. It is known for certain, however, that in 1929 the Uplyme Troop took part in the Dorset County Rally at Blandford and marched past the Chief Scout and Lady Baden-Powell, the Chief Guide. Then, no doubt, BP would have certainly greeted his old friend and spent a few minutes with his troop.

A move from Ware to Rhode Hill must have been made before 1929; the first entry in the *Troop's History* (maintained in Alban Woodroffe's own handwriting), in January of that year begins 'Headquarters, Rhode Hill, Uplyme, Devon'. The history of the troop for the years 1913–28, if they existed, has vanished.

It was at Rhode Hill in 1934 that the troop celebrated its 21st birthday and Assistant Scoutmaster Wilfred Austin presented a scroll to Mr Woodroffe, commemorating his service to them during that time on behalf of 109 past and present members. Wilfred Austin was the rock on which Mr Woodroffe depended to run the troop during his frequent absences at home and abroad on business trips. It was fitting that he returned the compliment later that year when he presented his assistant with a writing case in recognition of his 21 years of service to the Uplyme Troop.

Like all Scout troops throughout the country, the 1st Uplyme Troop did its bit during the Second World War. It helped with the organisation of the local ARP, with the arrangements for the arrival of the evacuees and the collection of waste paper. Four former Uplyme Scouts – Horace Holman, Arthur Hutchings, Gilbert Marks (from Monkton Wyld) and Roy Stapleforth – were killed in action while serving with the Royal Air Force, and Sid Henderson, also serving in the Royal Air Force, was killed when he was knocked down by an Army lorry in North Africa.

In 1942 Alban Woodroffe gave a site for new headquarters and a sub-committee was formed to raise

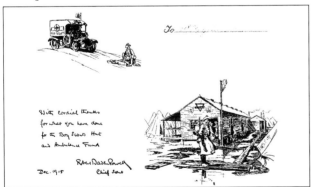

Among the many Uplyme residents who helped out on the Home Front during the First World War was the 1st Uplyme Boy Scout Troop. It was sent this certificate by the Chief Scout, Lord Baden-Powell, for raising money for the Ambulance Fund. The mention of 'for what you have done for the Boy Scouts Hut' suggests that their HQ at Ware House was used by the military.

money to build a new hall. Mrs Francillon was the chairperson and also the appeals secretary and treasurer, with Mrs Bowditch, Mrs Bosanquet and Miss Allhusen as committee members. It was said that £600 would be needed to build the new hall. By July 1943 as much as £434 had been raised. Of this £283 was the result of subscriptions and £151 came from a fête at Harcombe House. The latter, being a remarkable amount in peacetime, was all the more remarkable because there was a war on, and that meant that there were many national (and far more pressing) fund-raising activities to support. For the time being that £434 was invested in War Bonds. The war also meant that building materials were virtually unobtainable and it was not until 5 May 1948 that the new hall was officially opened on a strip of land at Church Acre by the County Commissioner, Lieut Gen. Sir Edmond Schrieber, in the presence of a large gathering. The new, prefabricated building, which was erected by the Lyme Regis firm of Stratton & Monday, was 69 feet long and 24 feet wide. By then the £600 estimate had risen to £1,500, which included the new hot-air heating system, the approach driveway and the architect's fees. It left the troop £300 in debt. But, a month after the opening ceremony, Miss M. Wood held a garden party, which brought in £130, and other events ensured that the debt was cleared by 1950.

Alban Woodroffe's son Rex, who had followed his father as Scoutmaster at Uplyme, died in 1949 in Argentina where he had gone to work and live. He was brought home and buried in Uplyme cemetery in the presence of many old Scouts.

An unusual occurrence took place in 1950 when a patrol was formed of boarders at St Andrews when it opened as a boarding-house to the Woodroffe School. The patrol called itself the Andrew Patrol for a while, although that name was soon changed to the Curlew Patrol, as Scout patrols are almost always named after birds or animals. Uplyme had had its Woodpecker, Lion, Fox and Horse Patrols.

By the 1950s Alban Woodroffe was a sick man and Scouting was at a low ebb in Uplyme. There were no more entries in Alban Woodroffe's *Troop History* for four years. Then, in 1955, Mr N.W.J. Adams wrote that he had become the new Scoutmaster in September, taking over a troop of 18 Scouts in four patrols. It is the last note in the history, the next surviving written records of the troop being found in the minute book of the Group Council, which dates back to 1936.

By 1960 there was a chronic shortage of funds. The troop was down to ten Scouts and it had 10s.7d. (53p) in the bank and was faced with expenditure of £250 for seating and sanitation at the Scout Hut, although a grant of 75 per cent was available.

Mr E. Barber became Group Scoutmaster in 1959 and, backed by a hard-working management committee, put the troop back on an even keel, so much so that by 1967 there was £70 at the bank and were 28 Scouts in the troop. Two years later the troop

Above: *The 1st Lym Valley Scout Group's sponsored bounce in May 1992. Left to right, back row: Sam Wakeman, Leonie Wakeman, ?, Mark Bailey;* front: *Matthew Wyon-Brown, James Booth, Christopher Wyon-Brown, William Booth, Lois Wakeman, Teresa Smith.*

Left: *The front cover of the September edition of* Pathfinding, *the Official Organ of the 1st Uplyme Troop of Boy Scouts, includes RBP (Robert Baden Powell) towards the foot of the picture. This suggests that it was an original drawing by the Chief Scout; there is also a possibility that he drew it especially for the troop and its Scoutmaster, his close friend Alban Woodroffe.*

Above: *James Booth (left) and Matthew Wyon-Brown raise funds for the 1st Lym Valley Scouts by washing car screens at Uplyme Filling Station in 1992.*

Right: *The 1st Uplyme Troop of Boy Scouts in 1925.*

had acquired its own van. But numbers fluctuated – there were 12 members in 1970 when Mr Barber left the district and Mr Pratt became Scout Leader, helped by Carl Holland.

The troop's 'great days' between the two world wars, when they had 11 King Scouts, were remembered in 1966 when two members of the Uplyme troop, Norman Taylor and Michael Denham, received their King's Scout badges.

Mrs Barbara Kidson became the Cub Mistress in 1967 and was joined by her husband Ken as Venture Scout Leader. Later Mr David Smee became Scout Leader.

In 2003, over half a century later, the local Scout movement is busy raising funds for its hut's refurbishment. Like its predecessors the troop has known times of hardship but, like those predecessors, it is in good hands.

WOLF CUBS

In 1930 the Cub Master was Miss M. Williams, her assistant (later Cub Master) was George Bastin and, by 1939, there were 21 Cubs in the pack. In 1960 Mrs W.E. Taylor was Cub Master with a pack of 16. She handed in her warrant in 1967 after many years of service. Numbers had dropped dramatically but, after a small interregnum when Mrs Barbara Kidson succeeded her, they had risen from five to 12 by 1969, and 18 in 1972. Mrs Rita Ellis, then Mr Ellis, were

Uplyme Guides at High Wych in around 1954.
Left to right: *Gwyneth Cary, June Cawley (captain), June Cary, Anne Wilkins.*

Uplyme Cubs on a visit to the Eden Project in Cornwall around 1997.

Cub Leaders, Mrs Ellis taking over as Guide Leader.

One of many to-be-lamented and minor irritations of this modern age is changing for change's sake the names of various positions and institutions. A football linesman is now a referee's assistant; even worse is the Wolf Cub who has become a Cub Scout.

GIRL GUIDES

There was a Girl Guide Company in Uplyme certainly as early as the 1920s with the Guide Mistress being Lieut Gladys Stapleforth. They met at the then Rectory (later the Devon Hotel). But, by the outbreak of the Second World War, this company seems to have disbanded, probably due to a lack of numbers.

Interest was rekindled after the war and, on 16 February 1949 at a meeting held at Woodhouse, at which it was said that nearly 20 girls were keen to join, the decision was made to restart the company. Those present at the meeting were Miss Cartwright, Mrs Symondson, Miss Jacob, Miss Drummond, Miss Blathwaite and Mrs Sykes. Mrs Payne became the Captain and, because she was not yet a Guide, 'it was agreed that she should go to Seaton to learn something of the work.'

The first meeting of the company was held in the Village Hall on 28 March where the girls were told that their uniforms would be bought for them but they would have to repay the cost at 3d. (1$\frac{1}{4}$p) a week. The Captain and the Lieutenant (Mrs Housdon) had their uniforms provided but, unlike the Guides uniforms, they remained the property of the company. Five years later a change in the pattern of the uniforms meant that the company had to be refitted, with the same financial agreement. Another problem with uniforms would be that Guides would grow out of them but, although no mention can be found in the minute books that it actually happened, no doubt this would have been solved by selling them on to younger girls.

The specially reduced fee for using the Village Hall was two pounds per annum, but the Guides

The Uplyme Brownies Thinking Day in 1969. Those present include: Jane Brigden, Karin and Tina Christopher, Sarah Gosling, Kathryn Jones, Julie Paull, June Powell, Teresa Powell, Jane Smith, Karen Walker and Katie Price.

Brown Owl Pam Morrish with some of her pack, c.1960.

would have to give way if a superior booking was available. Funds were augmented by the formation of a local Guides Association; it met once a year, usually in the form of a garden party, and the mother of a Guide could join at an annual fee of two shillings and six pence (12¹/₂p). There were 16 members at the end of the first year, their subscriptions, totalling exactly two pounds, paid the hall rental.

Although the early minute books pay considerable attention to funds and the need to economise wherever possible, the company was certainly solvent with a £17 balance in 1951, increasing to £23 in 1952 and rising above £30 a few years later. The increase was due in no small way to the fund-raising events that the Guides organised, including a profit of £20 on a jumble sale.

By the 1950s Miss W.H. Baker of St Mary's was the District Commissioner of Girl Guides and took a great interest in the Uplyme Guides. It was at this time (1954) that Miss Payne stood down as Captain and was replaced by Mrs Evans.

The Guides moved from the Village Hall to the Scout Hut in 1959, the reason being that the last part of their activities at the hall were always disturbed by the early arrival of people attending any functions that followed their own meetings, including, on one occasion, when the company arrived to find that the British Legion had already put a Magic Lantern in place in readiness for their own meeting that followed. They were also not allowed to put their own decorations and equipment on the walls.

Numbers remained good but the eventual formation of two other companies – the 2nd Uplyme and 3rd Uplyme – may have played a part in the disbandment of the 1st Uplyme Company, the village company, in 1954. Both the new companies were formed in around 1956; the 2nd Uplyme Company at High Wych School where there had been a Brownie pack since 1954; and the 3rd Uplyme Company at

Miss Pam Morrish, who founded the 1st Uplyme Brownies pack in 1950, seen in 1990 with Dorothy Grabham, a member of that original pack (left) *and Kathy Summers, Brown Owl 1985–91.*

Rhode Hill, the boarding-house for girls attending the Woodroffe School in Lyme Regis. In 1956 there were 13 Guides in the 2nd Uplyme and 21 in the 3rd Uplyme Company. At one stage out of 24 Brownies at High Wych there were two Lebanese members, one from Ceylon, one from India and another from Malaya. All three companies came under the care of the same committee.

Certainly by 1972 the 1st Uplyme Company was back in business and thrives in 2003. Through the years the 1st Uplyme Company has had many able Captains – Mrs Bugg, Mrs Pocock, Mrs Taylor, Rita Ellis, Wendy Smith and Christine Govier among others, and especially June Moulding (née Cawley) who had been an original member of the Brownie pack. It was under such leadership that Jane Mortimer, Jane Ward and Hilary Masters were some of many Guides to win their Queen's Guide Badges. In 1975 the Rangers were formed with four members.

BROWNIES

Miss Pam Morrish, who held the first meeting in her garage, formed the Uplyme Brownies on 30 September 1950. She was Brown Owl for 31 years and was present when the pack celebrated its 50th anniversary with a special church service and party, along with her first Pack Leader June Moulding (née Cawley), who had stood in as Captain for the Girl Guides on occasion when Mrs Payne was ill. The first Tawny Owl was Miss Hilda Hutchings.

On 7 July 1971, the pack celebrated its 21st anniversary with a party in the Village Hall. As many as 66 people were present, including three members of the original pack with three members of the then current pack using the occasion to pass their hostess badge.

There were over 80 Brownies, old and young, at the 50th birthday party, and many others who were unable to attend sent their best wishes. At that party Miss Morrish and the youngest member, seven-year-old Anna Guest of Queen's Walk, Lyme Regis, cut a special cake. For many years the people of the village would have been more likely to notice if Miss Morrish and her Brownies were not running the Treasure Hunt stall at the annual village fête, rather than noticing that the sun had failed to rise that morning.

In 1954 a 2nd Uplyme Brownies Pack was formed at High Wych School; that same year an unnamed Brownie is mentioned in the minute book as gaining the Golden Hand, the first of many such awards. Like the Scouts, Guides and Cubs, the Brownies have always been ready to serve the village in any way possible. Whether it is a fun day, like the village fête, or a more serious moment, like the Remembrance Day service, they are always smartly turned out. They do so in 2003 under the leadership of Penny Randerson.

Uplyme Cricket Club, c.1960. Back row, left to right: Derek Hallett, ?, Jim Stone, Paul Apanasewicz, Roland Howarth, Arthur Larcombe, Terry Norris, Mr Leas (chairman and umpire); front: ?, Bob Mason (captain), Janet Mason (scorer), Ted Denham, Michael Denham.

Uplyme AFC, c.1972. Back row, left to right: Keith Wiscombe (manager), Fred Smith (chairman), Graham Hayball, John Cloud, Martin Edwards, Roy Perham, Lance Turner, Mr Simpson (supporter), Steve Wiscombe, Stan Fifer, Bill Crabbe (president), Frank Bowditch, Bob Smith (assistant manager); front: Spencer Davies, Graham Turner, Steve Jones, ? Curtis.

Chapter 17

SPORT

A HAPPY MARRIAGE – THE STORY OF THE UPLYME
AND LYME REGIS CRICKET CLUBS

In 1986 the Uplyme and Lyme Regis Club celebrated its centenary with a match at Lord's and, later, a very enjoyable dinner at which the President, Dennis Applebee, said 'Apparently we are not one hundred years old after all.' He was referring to an article in the *Lyme Regis News* by Gerald Gosling, who had been asked by that paper to write a short history of the club. The club had held its centenary in 1986 because, certainly since the 1950s, each summer had seen the addition of one year to the statement on the front of the fixture card that this was the club's 69th, 70th, 71st, and so on, year. Who started the habit is not known, but successive secretaries, including Gerald Gosling, we hasten to add, simply, and understandably, continued the practice.

But, instead of any Uplyme and Lyme Regis Club having been formed in 1886, research had revealed that the Lyme Regis Club was formed in 1862, the Uplyme Club in 1877 and the two clubs amalgamated as the Uplyme and Lyme Regis Club in 1935.

In 1935 it had been reported in the *Pulman's Weekly News* that:

The newly-formed Uplyme, Lyme Regis & District cricket club came about because local sportsmen were anxious to keep the game alive in their area... once two clubs, the Uplyme cricket club and the Lyme Regis cricket club had lived together side by side... the senior of the two clubs, the Lyme Regis club, had played until the 1930 season, it had arranged fixtures for 1931 but had folded before that season got underway... the Uplyme club had become worried over the tenancy of its ground and support was not all it could be... the solution, once the availability of the ground was secure, was the formation of a new club... before that the Lyme Regis club had been running since 1862.

Between 1890 and the early 1900s the Lyme Regis Club had disbanded and, around that time, a Lyme College team had been in existence. They played mainly on Wednesdays and may also be found in the local press as St Andrew's College and, occasionally, Lyme Old Boys. Where they played is not known. Revd Edward Peek at Pyne House in Broad Street

founded the college. He himself lived at Poulett House (later the Alexandra Hotel), where he converted the stables into a private chapel – now the Peek Memorial Chapel, which was presented by Lady Peek for the church people of Lyme Regis in memory of her husband and his uncle.

Staff regularly made up the college team, H. Curgenven probably being one such member that did, although he played regularly for Uplyme as well. He is found on a regular basis in the college teams, where he was a more than useful all-rounder. A brother (?), George Curgenven, played for Lyme Regis.

Peek died in 1898 and the cricket team died with him. Apart from this passing reference, and the occasions that it may have played either the Lyme Regis Club or the Uplyme Club, it has no place in this story.

There is no record of any meeting at which the decision to form the Lyme Regis Club was taken, but it was stated that it was the 'newly-formed club' that went to Colyton in 1862, which makes the combined Uplyme and Lyme Regis Club one of the oldest in Devon and, after Sidmouth, Ottery St Mary and Exmouth, the third oldest club in East Devon, predating its neighbours at Seaton and Axminster by a dozen years.

In that first game they were dismissed for 17 on the Colyton Club's old ground at Mr Scarborough's house in Colyford. Lyme opener R. Hillman went into club history as the maker of the first duck – almost every player to follow him would tread the

Uplyme and Lyme Regis cricket team in 1947.
Included in the picture are: *Mr Newton Taylor* (front row, left), *Rex Woodroffe, captain* (third left), *Bob Mason* (second right) – *one of the most talented all-rounders the club has ever possessed.*

same path. He was a member of a well-known local building family who, in 1923, would build the Village Hall at Uplyme where later cricketers would take their tea for many years. The other opener was Mr Gordon who scored the club's first run and then took the first wicket when Colyton were dismissed for 51. The team for the historic match was: Messrs Gordon, Hillman, Hussey, Brown, Pike, Waters, Leman, Wallis, Sturman, Barnes and Board. The match was played on a Friday, starting at 11a.m., a return game being played at home to Colyton the following Monday before 'a good crowd, especially the ladies'. Maybe it was the presence of the ladies, but, this time, Lyme scored 80, Waters making 20, and then bowled Colyton out for 50. Lyme made 26 in their second innings, Colyton winning on 59–3.

Victorian village cricket pitches were nowhere near as good as those on which the modern cricketer plays, which accounts for the low scoring which was normal at the time. And 200-run totals were seldom seen on village grounds, even as late as the 1950s.

The Lyme Club played on Revd C.W. Ethelston's ground. It was not the King George V ground, although that did belong to the church, but in a field off Yawl Hill Lane on the right above Silverdale Farm, where there are three houses at the time of writing. Then, as in 2003, the part of the field that faced the lane was unfenced, and it was here that Uplyme would also play their first home games. The field is still known as the Recreation Field and cash was paid for the right to cut gorse there for animal bedding. Whether it was the rector or the cricket club that benefited from the cash is not known.

By 1869 Lyme were playing on the first of the fields they used that belonged to Mr Harris at Ware Farm. The first ground was in the farm, where it had the cliff edge beyond its southern boundary. There was no danger to life or limb, the actual boundary being some way away from the cliff. But there was the problem of lost balls – a report on the Beaminster game that year stating that 'two of the visitors were first to hit a ball over the cliffs.' Occasionally they played on another field on the farm, the home of the Pinhay Club, and moved there on a permanent basis in 1908 after amalgamating with that club. The field is still referred to as the 'cricket field' by members of the Allhusen family at the time of writing.

A curiosity is that although Lyme and Pinhay were playing at Ware on Major Allhusen's field, and Mrs Allhusen sometimes entertained them to tea, the Major was an Uplyme player and led the side that beat Lyme and Pinhay in 1890, scoring an unbeaten 27 – the only double-figure innings in the game. The Uplyme side for that game was Major Allhusen, O.T. Dussch, R.W. Coates (the Axminster brush manufacturer who lived in the village), Revd Parke, K. Wood, M. Manley, William Smallshaw, E. Cameron, L. Bushey, R. Talbot and W. Stocker.

Little is known about the Uplyme Club's early years apart from an 1877 reference in *Pulman's Weekly News* that 'a cricket club has been formed here [Uplyme].' Its earliest known officers (in 1908) were Alban Woodroffe (president), Revd A.W. Parke (chairman) and Mr H.R. Morgan (secretary-treasurer). Mr Woodroffe would remain the president until the formation of the Uplyme and Lyme Regis Club for whom he also served as president until the outbreak of the Second World War. In 1935 his son Rex was chairman with Morgan still the secretary.

Uplyme did not move to the glebe field opposite the Talbot Arms (now the King George V Field) until the end of the nineteenth century. Before that they moved around and played at Ware, Pinhay and Yawl Hill, sharing all three with the Lyme Regis Club. The glebe field was not then the centre of the village's outdoor entertainment. Prior to the turn of the new century the field behind the Talbot Arms (Hacker's Mead in 2003) seems to have been used for the village's high days. This is indicated by an 1872 report in *Pulman's Weekly News* which states that the:

... highlight of Uplyme's year was the annual Club Meeting in May. First a service, then to the Talbot Arms for the official business, and then to the field at the back of the Talbot Arms for sports and games and tea... Aunt Sally and Kiss-In-The-Ring were kept up with astonishing gusto.

In 1896 Uplyme visited Seaton where they were bowled out for 122 and beaten by 144 runs. Seaton were very much the big name in local cricket at the time, and they turned all their star players out against Uplyme, whose team was: S. Tatchell, F. Swain, W. Curgenven, Revd H.S. Travers (borrowed from the All Saints Club), Dr Padbury, R.R. Holland, Revd A.W. Parke, J. Tatchell, M. Wynch, H.R. Morgan and E. Cain.

In 1904 Colonel R. Williams, the MP for West Dorset for some 24 years, 'in addition to his subscription, sent £5 and consented to be President.'

Fund-raising tends to be a modern necessary evil. Up until the outbreak of the First World War, and possibly beyond, most players were self-sufficient as far as cash went, either with a guaranteed income from wealth handed down, or from a good income as a doctor, vicar or suchlike. Such people were well able to hand over five guineas to a cricket club.

Entertainment was staged, of course, but fund-raising came secondary to the socialising at such events, so much so that in 1906, when an al fresco dance was held by the Uplyme Club on the ground (not on the square, one trusts), 'a large company ensured that a good sum was shared between the club and the band.'

A nostalgic glimpse of a less hurried age is brought to us by the memories of the late Joe Turner who remembered that, both sides of the First World War, the cricket field was cut by a horse-drawn mower. The horse was borrowed from the Prescott family at Woodhouse and it always wore specially made leather shoes to prevent too much damage to the turf. The first machine mower is thought to have made an appearance in around 1938.

Both the Uplyme and the Lyme Regis Clubs lived happily, side-by-side, until the 1930s when a lack of support, both financial and in player numbers, led to the closure of the Lyme Regis Club in 1931. Three years later the fact that the Uplyme Club was in danger of following suit spurred local cricket lovers into action. The ground had been sold six years earlier (1928) to a syndicate of eight people who had raised the money to buy the field. That syndicate had lost some of its shareholders. Originally it had raised a quarter of the money needed for the purchase, the remainder being borrowed from the bank. It was in order to repay the interest on that loan that the Uplyme Club had held various functions, such as dances and whist drives. There were two separate committees – a Cricket Ground Committee and Cricket Club Committee – although some people served on both. The former had never been a profit-making concern and had never paid a dividend.

There was a danger that the Ground Committee might come to an end, and if so it was highly likely that the cricket club would follow suit. 'And that is the last thing we want,' Admiral Jackson told a meeting held in the Village Hall on Wednesday, 2 January 1935. Alban Woodroffe had got the bank to reduce the interest on the loan, the saving being passed on to the cricket club in the shape of a lower rent of £20 from 1 January that year (1935), although they would pay for the upkeep of the pavilion and equipment themselves.

Admiral Jackson said:

It is the birth of a NEW and, we hope, very successful cricket club. It is suggested that we call it the Uplyme and Lyme Regis Cricket Club but I think we should leave that to the new committee.

They obviously agreed.

Alban Woodroffe was invited to serve as president upon his return from Argentina. Mr Morgan was appointed secretary, Mr Teague, from Lyme Regis, as treasurer, and the committee was Rex Woodroffe, Mr S.L. Wotton (headmaster of Lyme Regis Grammar School), Tom Sloman (mine host at the Talbot Arms), H. Freeman, C. Tucker, A. Bennett, J. Reece and Mr Wyatt.

Between them the three clubs have had many very good players down the years. One of the best was Arthur Robert 'Bob' Mason, a Crewkerne man who was courting a local girl in 1939 and turned out for the local club. And, bearing in mind the runs he would go on to make, and the manner in which he made many of them, it is not surprising that his first knock for the club, a seven-boundary, unbeaten 65, was described in the press as 'a delightful innings'. It was while playing against Chard Conservative Club, who were dismissed for 110, that Mason also took 7–52 off 11 overs. Bert Scott, Chard's hard-hitting opening farmer batsman, hit Mason's first three balls to the boundary – soon afterwards he became one of Mason's seven victims, five of which came in his last two overs as he finished Chard off with a hat trick. When Uplyme and Lyme Regis (shortened to Uplyme from here on in the interests of brevity) replied with 145–3, Mason and Ward (56) added 113 for the third wicket.

Cricket began to take second place in most people's minds during that troubled summer of 1939 when Europe slid out of control and into the abyss of the Second World War. A week after Hitler's armies spilled over the Polish border, the last team to represent Uplyme for seven years took their field against Chardstock. They were: R. Bidwell, Stringfellow (junr), Dingley, Ward, A. Bidwell, Burgess, Wynes, Johnstone, Weeks, Quick and Stringfellow (senr).

Uplyme's first game after the war was at Colyton on 29 May 1946, where they were bowled out for 49 by Renfrey (5 for 21) and beaten by 25 runs after playing with only nine men. Their side was: Messrs Earle, Ford, Lovering, Thomas, Ward, Woodroffe, Russell, A. Rutherford and H. Rutherford.

It is impossible to give a ball-by-ball history of so many seasons of good sport at the KG5 down the years. Suffice to add that it is one of the most attractive grounds in Devon with its backdrop of hills and the Parish Church looking fondly down at it. But the club's most memorable game took place on another ground that, if it does not have Uplyme's serene charm, is probably the most famous in the world. That was Lord's, which takes it name from the Yorkshire man who made it. In September 1986 it was to Lord's that a 28-strong party from Uplyme and Lyme Regis CC set out for the long-awaited centenary game. Uplyme acquitted themselves well despite having to face a huge, 311–2 total after R.E. Lanchbury (176*) and A.C. Houston (65) put on 181 for the second wicket and M.J. Robinson (61*) joined Lanchbury to add another 111 unbroken runs for the third wicket. Uplyme replied with a creditable 195:

UPLYME			
M.J. Denham	c Houston	bowled Donela	100
I.J. McMurty	lbw	bowled Erico	7
M.P. Rowe		bowled Erico	20
A.R. Mason	lbw	bowled Woolston	24
D.R. Wellman	c Houston	bowled Woolston	10
J.M. Stamp	lbw	bowled Woolston	16
M.J. Spearpoint		bowled Woolston	0
R.J. Fisher	c Kidd	bowled Woolston	6
I.A. Turner		bowled Donela	4
B.J. Rattenbury	c&b	bowled Donela	2
A.E. Larcombe	not out		0
	extras		6
	total		195

Uplyme waited seven years after the formation of the East Devon Cricket League before it took the plunge and tried its hand at league cricket; it took to it like a duck to water. In 1889, its first league season, the club won the Division Two championship and, following promotion, they finished 1st, 1st, 2nd and 2nd in their first four seasons in Division One. The breakup of that very good side led to a slow decline until, at the end of the 2002 season (by then they were in Devon Cricket League circles after the East Devon League had amalgamated with that body), they were relegated. After a few years in the doldrums they won the E Division East title in 2003 and will again be playing in D Division East during 2004.

There have been characters down the years. In the 1950s and '60s the club chairman, Mr J.A. Leys, also acted as umpire. Owing to a back complaint he officiated on a shooting stick and would shout sixes and wides rather than signal them. Of a much earlier vintage was a Colonel Green who had a volatile temper and once refused to pay a local worker who bowled to him for an hour in the nets for which a shilling (5p) or two was usually forthcoming. The reason given was: 'You are there to give me something I can hit – not hit my b***** stumps!' Revd Parke, who played quite a good game, often led the team in prayers before a match. The irascible Colonel Green is said to have snorted: 'Didn't do much b***** good rector, we lost and you made a duck!'

Another old-timer story (probably apocryphal) is told of the dislike that existed between Revd Parke and Dr Padbury. This was said to have originated when the rector refused to run on the grounds that he was tired. Tired or not, the result was that the good doctor was run out. He was an inveterate slogger and got his revenge by hitting (and losing) as many balls as possible over the cliff edge at Ware. Because the rector bought all the club's cricket balls at his own expense, he stood to lose a pretty penny.

Tom Sloman, landlord of the Talbot Arms, and good with both bat and ball, was said to have always made sure that he did not go thirsty during the tea

Uplyme Cricket Club at Lord's on the occasion of their centenary match in 1986. Left to right, back row: *Richard Matthews (scorer), Dennis Applebee, John Stamp, Philip Evans, Michael Denham, Roger Fisher, Ian McMurtry, Arthur Larcombe, Jim McMurtry (umpire), Ray Lewis (president);* front: *Derek Wellman, Ian Turner, Steve Wiscombe, Mike Spearpoint, Andrew Mason, Martin Rowe, Brian Rattenbury.*

Uplyme AFC, Perry Street League Division II champions 2002–03. Left to right, back row: *Ron Matthews (committee), Rob Hamon (committee), James Salter, Spencer Davies, Andy Snowsill, Rob Thomson, Steve Gillan, Ben Salter, Phil Turner, Phil Hodder, Alan Brown (manager);* front: *Joseph Cleere (mascot), Andy Cleere, Richard Vine, Fred Smith (president), Frank Bowditch (chairman), Danny Fowler, James Skilton, Adam Bounds, Gavin Fowler. Absent were Fred Thomson, Steve Gibbard and Jon Gardner*

interval – but it was not tea that refreshed him.

A more enduring and modern memory is that of Mike Denham and Andrew Mason putting together a sizable stand under the proud gaze of the two umpires – their respective fathers, Ted and Bob.

The club is still there in 2004, still as much a part of the Uplyme scene as it has been for over a century. And, if it had a motto, what better than Still Not Out?

UPLYME FOOTBALL CLUB

Although it has not received anything like the press that cricket once received, football has been played in the village for most of the past century. The reason for its anonymity stems directly from the fact that two different classes played the respective sports. Cricket was the preserve of the middle and upper classes that had the time to make sure that reports of their games went into the local papers. Association football had been founded largely in the universities, their old-boy associations and the officers' messes, but it had been hijacked by the workers long before the end of the nineteenth century. And the workers did not have the time, or inclination, to submit reports of their games unless they had a member of the middle or upper class taking an interest in them. Which explains why mill owner Charles Small's team at his Perry Street Lace Works did appear in the press, and those of Uplyme, who only played friendly games, did not. They were certainly in existence before the First World War, although no names of players or officers survive.

It was not until 1922/23 that Uplyme joined the Perry Street and District League where they competed in the Minor (Devon and Dorset) Section. They did not set the world alight either, the final table reading (in those days clubs were a bit haphazard when it came to fulfilling their fixtures) as shown opposite.

PERRY STREET & DISTRICT LEAGUE MINOR TABLE, 1922/23

	P	W	D	L	F	A	Pts
Axminster Res	12	10	1	1	51	8	21
Dalwood	12	8	1	3	26	11	17
Rousdon	9	4	1	4	14	21	9
Lyme Rovers Res	12	3	3	6	13	13	9
All Saints	10	2	3	5	17	27	7
Uplyme	8	2	2	4	13	20	6
Musbury	11	2	0	9	11	43	4

PERRY STREET & DISTRICT LEAGUE MINOR TABLE, 1923/24

	P	W	D	L	F	A	Pts
Dalwood	16	12	3	1	40	9	27
Uplyme	15	11	2	2	51	11	24
Charmouth	15	7	4	4	38	18	18
Lyme Rovers Res	14	7	1	6	23	36	15
Axminster Res	14	6	2	6	45	28	14
Colyton Res	14	5	1	7	18	39	11
Seaton Res	13	4	2	7	28	28	10
Beer Res	12	3	1	8	18	28	7
Axmouth	14	1	2	11	19	61	4

Gates were normally around the 30–40 mark but, in 1923/24 for the visit of Axminster in a Morrison Bell Cup game when the gate was considerably swollen by a large contingent of visiting fans, around 120 people watched Uplyme lose 6–2. Their team (Uplyme's first known footballers) consisted of: Furzey, Brewer, Case, Powell, Cox, Bishop, Robinson, Joe Turner, Thomas, B. Cloud and P. Cloud. Later that season Uplyme beat Colyton Reserves 10–0.

It was surprising what difference a year made to the team, the 1923/24 season's final table being shown above.

In 1924/25, and breathe it not at Davey Fort, Uplyme beat a nine-man Lyme Rovers Reserves 15–1 at home. The Lyme men had walked to the ground and were beaten by goals from Lawes (4), Dunn (3), Miller (3), Robinson (2), Fred Irish (2) and Joe Turner.

Uplyme finished second again in 1924/25, 3rd in 1925/26, but had dropped to sixth (out of nine teams) by 1926/27 when they beat Wambrook 2–0 with the following team: Wilf Restorick, Dick Turner, Eric Brewer, Walt Keeley, C. Richards, C. Tolman, K. Wright, Maurice Brewer, L. Irish, W. Gray and A. Cox. In 1927/28 and 1928/29 Uplyme played only friendly games, a typical side in the latter season being: Sid Baker, Downing, Young, Wally Howlett, W. Denning, R. Curtis, A. Cox, Walt Keeley, A. Lawes, Cook and G. Bastin. It was in 1929/30, when Uplyme were back in the Perry Street and District League, that, during a game with Beaminster, the visitors were so late in arriving that much of the second half was played in total darkness. Despite pleas to abandon the game, the referee insisted on continuing. An Uplyme player went home and came back with a lighted candle, offer-

ing it to the official, and was booked 'for dissent'. Sadly, history does not record who the errant Uplyme player was, but Walter Keeley was playing and the late Walter was a byword for his impish behaviour.

Back for the 1930/31 season, they finished bottom; Uplyme had to rely heavily on imports at the time. In 1931/32 the Lyme Rovers correspondent in *Pulman's Weekly News*, after Lyme Bantams beat Uplyme 5–1, could not resist a dig when he called the village side, 'Uplyme in name only with eighteen of the twenty-two players on view from Lyme Regis.' At the time (1930–34) Lyme Rovers had gone into abeyance and Lyme Bantams came into being. Their origins sprang from 1922 when the Junior Training Club was formed.

In time, as far as football was concerned, they combined with the Boy Scouts and all the schools of the town except the Grammar School. Obviously there was no place for the old Rovers' established and adult players who gravitated to Uplyme.

Imports or not, Uplyme could only finish in mid table in 1933/34. One happy moment came at home to unbeaten Charmouth when Uplyme were still looking for their first win. It came by a 3–2 margin, the loss of points eventually costing the Dorset side the title. Uplyme's team, which it did its best to drink the Talbot Arms dry after the game, consisted of: Perce Ebdon, Harold Pope, H. Hallett, G. Baskin, A. Moulding, J. Crabb, L. Tolman, Vese Munday, M. Thompon and R. Hallett. Both Perce Ebdon and Vese Munday were imports from the Axminster Town Club.

Uplyme went without league football for two seasons before joining the newly started Axe Vale League in time to finish bottom in 1937/38. The final league table was as shown overleaf.

AXE VALE LEAGUE TABLE, 1937/38

	P	W	D	L	F	A	Pts
Feniton	19	16	1	2	78	24	33
Lyme Regis Res	20	14	3	3	83	35	31
Charmouth	20	14	3	5	56	35	27
Axmouth	20	11	3	6	63	34	25
Symondsbury	19	10	3	6	74	60	23
Dalwood	20	8	4	8	60	49	20
Colyton Res	18	7	2	9	43	54	16
Beer Res	20	7	1	12	47	92	15
Whitford	19	5	1	13	45	63	11
Box House	20	3	3	14	32	79	9
Uplyme	19	1	2	16	29	85	4

PERRY STREET & DISTRICT LEAGUE DIVISION 3 LEADING POSITIONS, 1970/71

	P	W	D	L	F	A	Pts
Haslebury	22	20	2	0	119	27	42
Uplyme	22	16	1	5	91	39	33
Chaffcombe	22	15	2	5	95	58	32

There was a slight improvement in the last full season (1938/39) before the Second World War started, Uplyme finishing seventh out of ten teams. They returned to the Perry Street and District League for 1939/40 but, when that league ran a severely curtailed wartime programme, mainly with teams well above Uplyme's standard, they went back to the Axe Vale League in time to see that body fold up because of the petrol restrictions that were being introduced. The club agreed to 'stand down until the end of the war.' In the event it was not until 1955/56 that an Uplyme team again took to the field. The field was the old Axmouth pitch behind the Harbour Inn where, not yet having had the time (or money) to buy a set of shirts, the Uplyme players wore their everyday shirts and lost 4–0. The *Chard and Ilminster News* gave the Axmouth keeper as G. Joslin – and he does remember that the Uplyme left-winger was called Arthur Larcombe, who wore a rather natty white shirt and equally natty plimsolls.

At that time the Perry Street League was very much 'the sick man' of local football, having lost almost all of its better teams to senior leagues, and there were not enough sides left to provide a full programme for its members. This may or may not have been the catalyst, but Uplyme again disbanded until 1968/69 when the club was reformed. It then finished sixth out of 14 teams with a league record of 13 wins and 13 losses.

The club's first-ever cup final arrived in 1970/71 when, after a 3–3 draw with Haslebury at Lyme Regis (abandoned after 71 minutes) when Uplyme were lucky, and another 3–3 draw at Lyme Regis when Haslebury were lucky, Haslebury won the third game 3–1 at Axminster.

After the final the top of the Division Three table, shown above, makes interesting reading. Keith Wiscombe's 33 goals played a large part in that second-place finish.

The first successful cup final came in 1974/75 at Drimpton where Uplyme beat Chaffcombe 3–2 in the John Fowler Cup final after one of the most sensational finishes ever in a Perry Street and District League cup final. Chaffcombe were leading 2–0 with three minutes left when Frank Bowditch scored from the penalty spot. In injury time Alan Reynolds and Clive Hayball scored within 30 seconds of each other to win the game.

The club continues to the time of writing and, in the seasons between 2001/02 and 2003/04, it has blossomed out in no uncertain style. The Perry Street and District Football League's Division Three championship in 2001/02 was followed by the Division Two championship the following season, when the Tommy Tabberer Cup was also won. Promotion to Division One followed and (in late 2003) the side is still having a very successful time, with a second team again being run.

Many people have served the club down the years, none more so than Frank Bowditch who, after a career as a more than useful player, has been linesman, manager and chairman for around 20 years. His wife Wendy has been a loyal helper as well on the fund-raising committee that worked so hard to buy the club's Venlake home in the late 1990s.

Previous chairmen include Wally Eggleston, John Tasker and Fred Smith, the president in 2003. There will always be loyal players in all football clubs – at Uplyme they are epitomised by Geoff Fisher who

Uplyme Football Club, pictured before a Morrison Bell Cup game in 1921. Captain Morrison Bell, MP for the Honiton constituency, gave the cup for competition between amateur sides in his constituency. The match was played near Pond Wood at Rhode Hill. Among the players are George Bastin (standing, extreme right) *and John Reed* (third from left in the back row).

follows a lengthy career as a rugged, no-nonsense defender by acting as first-team linesman. Likewise all clubs have loyal supporters – Uplyme's biggest stalwart being Ron Matthews who has followed them since the club restarted in 1955/56 – 48 seasons to 2003 – surely he is due a medal in 2005. Other supporters included Ron Turner, landlord of the Talbot Arms and a useful player with Axminster Town, and Bob Mason, who played for both Uplyme and the enemy (Lyme Regis). Those two also played prominent parts in the 1955 restarting of the club. There were also Cecil Harris, Jack Stamp, Mr Uglow and Mr Reed of Uplyme Filling Station.

Lym Valley Croquet Club

In 1988, Arthur Larcombe and Beryl Denham, the two people responsible for the running of the King George V Playing-Field in Uplyme, were anxious to see wider use made of its facilities. They decided that it might be appropriate to introduce croquet to the village's range of sporting activities. So it was that the Lym Valley CC came to be founded with Bill Simpson as its first secretary. With only meagre resources initially provided by generous donors, the first year was largely spent in becoming familiar with the complexities of what is, after all, quite a complicated game. During this time the late Frank Firth became the first treasurer of the club and is still remembered as the Frank Firth trophy continues to be awarded to the winner of the club's annual championship.

Under its first chairman, Tony Childs, in 1990 the club became affiliated to the Croquet Association and to the South West Federation of Croquet Clubs. Members regularly participate in the Federation's league games. Through the 1990s membership rose considerably but natural wastage means that the club

is always ready to accept new members and to provide free tuition if required. During the winter members are kept in contact by playing a miniature version of the game on a specially made tabletop croquet court, which, being a novelty and not seen since Victorian times, was actually featured in 1991 on South West Television.

In 1993 the Trustees of the playing-fields placed at the disposal of the club an enclosed area, which they could develop as a permanent croquet court. A special appeal for funds was made and the members themselves contributed something like £1,000 in order to have the area levelled and re-sown. This acquisition means that there is always an area available for members who wish to develop their skills with private practice.

In 1998, the founder, Bill Simpson (who was troubled by ill health) and Tony Childs felt that it was time they made way for younger blood. So Dave Freebody of Uplyme agreed to become the new chairman with Julian Twiston-Davies of Bridport as the new secretary. The two veterans, however, still continue to play regularly and even met in the final of the 2003 club championship. The result was the same as in 1990, when Bill and Tony first met in a final – a narrow win for Tony Childs.

Over the years the club has consistently played in the League of the South West Federation. It once reached the peak of its own division, only to be eliminated in the Federation semi-final by a much younger team of players from the Bristol Croquet Club. Nevertheless, looking back over the years, the club has had its successes, even against such powerful adversaries as Budleigh Salterton and East Dorset (Parkstone). Even in 2003 the club played the powerful Budleigh Salterton club and, thanks to the efforts of its secretary, Julian Twiston-Davies, and its veteran founder, Bill Simpson (coaxed from retirement!), Lym Valley CC managed to emerge victorious.

The club hopes that its endeavours will continue for many years to come to provide an outlet for local enthusiasts who feel that they would like to try their hand at the game.

Bill Simpson, Jean Potter, Vera Liddiard and Tony Childs ready for the fray.

Left and above: *The Whalley Lane
VE Day 50th anniversary street party in full flow on
8 May 1995.*

Below: *The magnificent iced cake made by Jan Fowler for the VE
Day 50th anniversary party in Whalley Lane takes pride of place
on the tables beside the rector, Stuart Worth. Mrs Rose
Honeybun is first on the right and then comes local historian,
Albert Manley.*

Chapter 18

HIGH DAYS & CELEBRATIONS

News that both Mafeking and Ladysmith had been relieved was the signal for the church bells to give a day-long demonstration of the patriotic fervour of an age when it was as strong in small, and at the time remote, country villages like Uplyme, as it was in London.

Although the Boer War ended in June 1902, it was not until towards the end of the year that the East Devon men who had served in South Africa came marching home. Among the first, we are told by *Pulman's Weekly News*, were Sergeant Harry Cleal of Rousdon and two (unnamed) Uplyme men. Sergeant Cleal was met at Seaton Station and pulled home to Rousdon in a carriage (up Bos Hill?) by his friends. That worthy newspaper does not record how Uplyme's two heroes reached the village but 'they were royally entertained at the Talbot Arms along with their families by the rector and others, the inn being brilliantly illuminated.'

East Devon's Mafeking and Boer War Victory bunting would have been used for the coronation of Edward VII (1901–10) that should have taken place on 26 June 1902. But he was taken ill with appendicitis a few days before the event and it was thought for a while that he would not survive the operation. But he did survive and was finally crowned the following year on Saturday, 9 August.

Obviously the national and local arrangements to celebrate what was the first crowning in the country for around 65 years were already completed and, although such things as mugs, flags and bunting could be put into storage, much of the food that had already been bought for celebratory meals would be wasted or, more likely, handed out by village charities to the poor.

Our Victorian and Edwardian forebears were particularly fond of erecting arches decorated with tree branches and flags, with patriotic mottoes on, at such occasions, and Uplyme had one at each end of the village – one at the Talbot Arms, the other at The Black Dog.

Among Lyme Regis' highlights were the presentation of a new chain of office to the Mayor of Lyme Regis and the fireworks display that was discharged on the north wall of the Cobb by the coastguards. Uplyme scored over its bigger neighbours as far as bonfires went. It was on the top of Knoll Hill and was easily seen at Lyme Regis – and as far away as Beer Head. Otherwise, Uplyme's day included the almost obligatory luncheons and teas, and sports and mugs for the children.

Unlike neighbouring Lyme Regis, Uplyme approached the coronation of George VI in 1937 determined to put on the best possible show. Not everyone in Lyme Regis wanted to celebrate the coming coronation, or, to be more exact, they did not want to spend the ratepayers' money on it. Objections to the elaborate celebrations planned at Lyme Regis were lodged at the January meeting of the Lyme Regis Town Council by Mr Owen who contended that the sum of £100 for the proposed civic parade and service, luncheon for the old folks, sports on the sands for the children followed by tea and dancing on the Marine Parade, the special illuminations of the Langmoor Gardens, a day's holiday for all council employees, and a memento for all the children, was too much. But, despite some murmurs of support during the meeting, when the matter was put to the vote, everyone, except Mr Owen, was in favour of the £100 being spent.

Uplyme, however, put on a first-class show, starting with a service in the church and ending, well past midnight, with dancing and singing in the Village Hall and on the cricket field. In between there had been a 'sumptuous dinner to which every one had been asked to bring their own knife, fork, spoon, cup and plate.' The three pubs, the Talbot Arms, the New Inn and The Black Dog, did a roaring trade, Uplyme's long arm of the law turning a blind eye to the blatant disregard of the hours laid down as desirable for grown-up people to have a drink – and probably even joining in that disregard. But it was, first and foremost, the children's day. Sports and games in the cricket field followed 'an excellent tea after which each and every child received a Coronation Mug.'

VE Day, Tuesday 8 May 1945, was not the end of the Second World War – that came later in August when Japan surrendered on VJ Day. It was celebrated in much the same way as the end of the European War had been some three months earlier.

Ever since the village had built its own Village Hall and opened it on 8 November 1923, Uplyme's big shindigs have been centred there and the next-door King George V Field. It was there that, on a Wednesday evening, after the news of the birth of the

The egg and spoon race at the 1908 Uplyme Fête on the cricket field. The odds-on favourite must be the little girl, unencumbered as she is by any magnificent hat.

Among the spectators were three little girls in white, the Irish sisters, Edith, May and Nellie.

The start of the men's race at the same fête. The favourite is not so obvious here. The contestant second from the left obviously means to keep a record of his time. The race is about to be started by 'Bumper' Morgan on the right, headmaster of Mrs Ethelston's School.

A 1950s Uplyme Fête with fancy-dress judging in progress.
Left to right: *Roger Mody, Katharine Allhusen and Roy Irish.*

Uplyme Men's Club in fancy dress in 1912.

Between the street party and evening entertainment at Whalley Lane on 8 May 1995 to mark the 50th anniversary of VE Day, a short service that included a minute's silence and the Last Post took place in the estate's car park. The standard party are, **left to right:** *Kevin Griffiths, Olive Cooper and Adrian Furzey. Behind Mrs Cooper is Jonathan White, the bugler.*

nuclear age and Japan's surrender had reached the village, that a grand dance was held. Mrs Sharman was at the piano, John Tasker the piano accordion, and Devereux Mence was on the drums, with several of the dancers giving him a hand. Uplyme's ladies (as always) were magnificent with refreshments for all at short notice and they were thanked, along with Mrs Marchant and Mr Lawes who were behind the organisation of the celebrations.

The following evening there was a dance for the children between the ages of 6 and 15 years with games also being played. It was a huge success, not least because the indefatigable Mrs Sharman was again at the piano. On the Friday 140 children sat down to a very fine tea, the refreshments being supplied by the local baker, Mr Matthews, and many local people. After the tea there were games in the cricket field with Donald and Diana Page, William Stone, Joy Sharman, Roy Crabbe, Tom Beavis, A. Austin, B. Larcombe, Roy Powell, P. Matthews, R. Beavis, Betty Farrant, Wendy Raymond, ? Fisher, Henry O'Mahoney, one of the four Castell children, two of the Bealch family (combining to win the under-tens wheelbarrow race) and Lily Farrant among the winners. The races were organised by Mr Freeman (headmaster at Mrs Ethelston's School), George Tucker (the verger) and Mr Baxter (a visitor), all of whom also gave prizes.

Two of the highlights of village life have been the annual flower show and the village fête. *Pulman's Weekly News* mentions the Lyme Regis and Uplyme Flower Show's AGM in 1910, saying that a Mr John Radford and a Mr F. Mathew had started the show several years earlier. That year the show had been cancelled as a mark of respect following the death of Mr Radford (secretary) shortly before the date of the show.

The committee lodged their cups with the Lyme Regis branch of the Wilts and Dorset Bank where they had a credit balance of £8.13s.3d. (£8.67). The cups in question had been one given by Colonel R.

The annual horticultural display in the big marquee is always one of the high spots of the social season. Here Philip Noakes, OBE, the president of the Lyme Regis and Uplyme Horticultural Society, is presenting one of the cups while Mary Frings, the secretary, looks on.

Jim Tasker, head gardener at Woodhouse, was a founder member of the Uplyme and Lyme Regis Horticultural Society that he served for many years including spells as both secretary and assistant secretary.

Williams (MP for West Dorset) and the Woodroffe Cup, given by Alban Woodroffe's father, the Hon. J.T. Woodroffe, a staunch supporter of the show.

Mr F. Britton and Mr P.A. Richards were elected as joint secretaries to follow Jon Radford, Alban Woodroffe suggesting that they needed only three officers to manage the affairs of the show, and this was accepted as being sound.

The Lyme Regis and Uplyme Flower and Vegetable Society went into abeyance in 1960 and it has not restarted. The Uplyme part of the name was dropped, possibly in 1929 when the Uplyme, Lyme Regis and District Horticultural Society was formed, although the District part of the newcomer's name was also dropped in time. It almost goes without saying that Alban Woodroffe took a great interest in the fledgling society and was its first president. The early shows were held in Cooks Mead, then without any housing and farmed by Charlie Hockey. Exhibitors were divided into three classes and, with the exception of the A class, which was 'open to all England', had to reside in the parishes of Uplyme, Lyme Regis, Rousdon or Combpyne. Division B was open to amateurs, their gardeners and market gardens; Division C was for cottagers who cultivated a garden or allotment for 'their own family suste-nance'. What happed if an amateur who lived in Uplyme employed a gardener who lived in Musbury was never explained.

The Uplyme and Lyme Regis Horticultural Society enjoyed the support of all of the owners of the 'big houses' – Ware House, Woodhouse, Rhode Hill, St Mary's etc – and among the founding fathers were Frank Hutchings, who was employed as a gardener at Rhode Hill from the age of 16, George Bastin and Jim Tasker, who was employed as head gardener at Woodhouse at a very young age. Jim is listed as assistant secretary to Mr C. Tucker on the 1931 sched-ule, the earliest one in the society's possession; 20 years later (1951 and 1952) he served as secretary and also gave many years of dedicated service on the committee. Both Jim and Frank Hutchings exhibited at the 1929 show with Frank exhibiting certainly until the society's 60th anniversary in 1969. Although he won hundreds of cups during those years, his name does not appear on them very often because, at the time, it was the owners of the 'big houses' who had their names engraved on the trophies and not their gardeners. At that 60th anniversary Frank recalled that, 'A working chap could pick up two or three weeks' wages in prize money, but now it would not keep you in beer money.'

In the early years the shows included classes for dead poultry and live rabbits, and schoolchildren were challenged to exhibit 'The Largest Collection of Queen Wasps'. What the animal rights lobby would say about it in today's world is open to conjecture. A live pig was the prize for those with the highest score during the skittle competition; by 1962 the pig had been substituted for a £5 Premium Bond.

In 1938 the show was held on the football field in Venlake Lane and included in the entertainment was a mounted games. After a five-year gap during the Second World War the society resumed activities in 1946, and some time between then and 1952 the show moved to its present home on the King George V Playing-Field. The actual date of the move is not known because no records exist of the society between 1947–52.

The evening entertainment at that 1952 show was a motorcycle rodeo, during which 'the daring leapt through a ring of fire'. What the cricketers said or thought when they saw them has not been recorded.

The following year the show was a much more muted, low-key affair, partly for financial reasons and partly because 'another fête would follow limply after the coronation festivities.' Only two classes were fitted into the Village Hall. In 1954 a small marquee was pitched outside to take the overflow and in 1957 there was another gymkhana. It was not until 1960 that the traditional big marquee returned to the cricket field with, for the first time since the war, the Comic Dog Show, which included a class for the fattest dog.

Miss M.E.M. Wilson became show director in 1978, soon after retiring as the village vet. The following year she organised the Golden Jubilee Summer Show and, ten years later, the Diamond Jubilee Show which would be her swansong. She remained on the committee, however, until 2003 when her resignation left Allan Booth as the longest-serving member.

Although the annual summer shows have always been the society's main focus of activity, at one time it ran two smaller shows. The Rose and Sweet Pea Show was discontinued in the 1980s due to lack of entries and the Autumn Show was introduced in its place. Then the Spring Flower Show was downgraded to a non-competitive display. At first everybody attending the meeting brought bunches of daffodils and other spring flowers but, after a few years, the only contributions were from one or two committee members and this too was abandoned.

During the early-twenty-first century the summer show has flourished with 700–800 entries and a varied programme of activities on the field. The cost of hiring a big marquee and 90 tables adds up to a huge loss. But this is generally met from members' subscriptions and the proceeds from the highly profitable plant sales.

In 2003 the wettest show day in memory led to all the outdoor activities having to be cancelled or moved into the Village Hall. There was a paddling-pool at the entrance to the marquee but over 300 supporters turned up and gave generous donations. It seems that the chairman's 'message' of 45 years earlier still holds good (although the membership has risen to £3):

By paying a membership fee of two shillings (10p) members have the satisfaction of knowing that they are helping to sustain a healthy and charming tradition of country life.

The year 2004 will see the society's 75th show. The practice of the Olympic Games, in which the games not held during the war years were still numbered, was adopted by the society (the shows which should have been held in 1940–45 were numbered as 11 to 16). There was a suggestion in 1956 that the two organisations should amalgamate but Uplyme rejected the idea although, four years later when the Lyme Regis Flower Show folded, it did inherit their cups.

Another attraction at many local events have been the Morris dancers. The dances are believed to have their origins in fertility rites, and were traditionally associated with special festivals. The name 'Morris' seems to be derived from 'Moorish' and it was fairly common for dancers to blacken their faces and resemble the Moors. The Uplyme Morris was formed in 1989 and first danced in public on 1 June 1991, and met at both the Lyme Leisure Centre and the Devon Hotel. There was no joining fee or subscription and any monies collected went towards expenses, with any profit going to the Lyme Regis Lifeboat. They were members of the Morris Ring, the national association of Morris Sides, and were a great favourite at all locals occasions, especially the annual fête. Other favourite and regular fixtures were the celebration of the sunrise at Lamberts Castle and the midwinter solstice sunrise at the Cobb in Lyme Regis. Sadly a declining membership led to the end of the Uplyme Morris in 1998.

Uplyme's memorable VE Day 50th anniversary street party came about because of a chance remark in the New Inn some four years before the anniversary. The idea lay dormant for some time until an ad-hoc committee was formed to mastermind the event. It was intended that the street party would be held in Whalley Lane and be for the children who lived there. But, long before the event, it was realised that the entire village intended to hijack the

The magnificent cake, baked by Jan Fowler, for the millennium party given to all the children of the village on 1 January 2000.

big day and the organisers upped their plans accordingly. In any case, many of the 'hijackers' supported the event with much of the sumptuous repast on the flag-decked tables that stretched from the telephone kiosk to almost the other end of the lane. It was not just the children. Invitations went out to the rector, Revd Stuart Worth, and many of that generation of the villagers who had lived through the Second World War.

The evening ended, after a ceremony in the car park that was headed by the local branch of the Women's Section of the Royal British Legion and included the playing of the Last Post, with a well-attended barbeque and bar.

Although there was never any intention of making a profit, when the committee wound up its affairs there was a balance of £300. And who better to give it to than the Uplyme branch of the Women's Royal British Legion?

One of the more amusing episodes of the fund-raising efforts, although the committee members concerned did not think so at the time, was the dispatch of a team to a quiz evening at West Hill near Ottery St Mary. The committee sent a tried and trusted local quiz team (who would go on to win the

local league eight years running) but, to their horror, there was not one question asked all night. The event might have been labelled as a quiz, but in fact it consisted of a series of competitions in which entrants tried to get blindfolded members to park a model radio-controlled car in a parking bay, shoot at moving targets, build things out of paper and rubber bands and so on. Our middle-aged (plus) team, let us call them Imogen, Ian, Charlie, Jack and Gerald, overcame their horror, finished third, and took home prize money of £125.

The same ad-hoc committee (by then the Uplyme 2000 committee) that had masterminded the VE Day 50th anniversary party was responsible for much of Uplyme's millennium celebrations. At midnight 2000 there was a service at St Peter and St Paul's, which was floodlit for the occasion. Later that morning two yew trees were planted in the churchyard, one by then 91-year-old Walter Keeley, the other by four-year-old Brett James, the youngest pupil at Mrs Ethleston's School.

Then came the highlight of the great day, the children's party in the Village Hall which ended with the presentation of a special commemorative mug from the Uplyme 2000 Committee to every child in the parish including, at that evening's adult party, one for a child who was not born until three or four days later. Jennie Pearson designed the mugs, which needed a second 'throwing' to meet the heavy demand throughout the village. They depicted features of Uplyme, including the school, church, cricket pavilion and viaduct.

That evening there were fireworks and a buffet party in the Village Hall for the grown-ups.

The hard work and the fund-raising of the Uplyme 2000 Committee, especially from the sale of mugs, meant that around £2,000 was shared out between the school, church, Village Hall and Uplyme Football Club, who still proudly wear shirts emblazoned with UPLYME 2000.

Uplyme Morris dancers at the Talbot Arms around 1990. Left to right: Matthew Wyon-Brown, ?, Ross Harding, Geoff Browne, Mick Birks.

Uplyme Morris dancers outside the New Inn around 1988. Among the dancers are: Jim Purvis (melodeon), John Wood, Geoff Browne, Jim McLachlan, Dave Burgess, Ross Harding, June and Mick Birks, Rosemary and Francis Lock.

IN MEMORIAM

1914–19	
Captain	*Valentine J. Jones*
Captain	*Stanley Jones*
Sgt	*Frank Stocker*
Bombadier	*Frederick Gale*
Private	*Percy Bate*
Private	*James Bate*
Private	*Edward Bowditch*
Private	*Enoch Bowditch*
Private	*Bert Cake*
Private	*Jack Champion*
Private	*James Finnemore*
Private	*Charles Gale*
Private	*Bert Gudge*
Private	*William Hooper*
Private	*Albert Samways*
Private	*William Smallshaw*
Private	*Sam Smith*
Private	*Harry Stocker*
Private	*Arthur Thornton*
Private	*Bertie Turle*
Private	*Clifford Wheadon*
Gunner	*Steve Stocker*
Guardsman	*Francis Marchant*
Gunner	*George Stocker DSM*
CPO	*Ernest Copp*
1st Class PO	*Arthur Curtis*
1st Class Stoker	*Joe Gudge*
1st Class Stoker	*Herbert Street*

1939–45	
L/SM	*Walter Austin RN*
AC2	*Richard Austin RAF*
PO	*Harry Copp RN*
CPO	*Sidney Furzey RN*
Sgt OB	*Arthur Hutchings RAF*
AC	*James Henderson RAF*
Sgt	*Gilbert Marks RAF*
LAC	*Thomas Reakes RAF*
Lt	*Leonard Saunders RNVR*
Ft/Lt	*Harold Stapleforth RAF*
GR	*Wilfred Tapper RA*

The West Kents in 1939, billeted at the Village Hall, marching towards the Talbot Arms. West Ley is on the right. The line of chestnut trees was chopped down to give access for the Talbot Arms car park.

The unveiling of the war memorial in 1921. Legend has it that the memorial was placed opposite the Rectory so that the rector would not have far to walk! The village has repulsed two attempts to have the memorial re-sited by the church. Shapwick Copse on the horizon has since been chopped down.

Chapter 19

WARTIME UPLYME

It is of more than passing interest that of the 11 men who died in action in the Second World War and are remembered on the war memorial, only one served with the Army. Six of the others served with the Royal Air Force and four with Royal Navy.

THE ROYAL BRITISH LEGION

The Uplyme branch of the British Legion (now Royal British Legion) was formed in around 1923 and has played a prominent part in the Armistice service of remembrance (later Remembrance Sunday) around the war memorial opposite the Devon Hotel. It was still very strong in the immediate aftermath of the Second World War but by the 1960s a falling membership was already giving cause for concern – so much so that towards the end of that decade the branch closed and its remaining members transferred to either the Lyme Regis or the Axminster branch.

In 1949 a Women's Section was formed with 104 members, which had risen to a peak of 129 by 1953 but in 2003 dropped down to about 50.

It has been, and still is, a very successful branch, having donated a sum of at least £14,500 to the head-quarters. This has only been possible through much hard work and, considering that in the early years annual subscriptions were only a matter of pennies (it is still only £3.30), this is quite an achievement. These efforts have played a large part in the branch being rewarded with 55 cups, awards and certificates, marking its various activities. In its 21st year it won the national cup for increased membership – 21 new members. It has added its voice to some matters of discussion in the village, such as the suggested moving of the war memorial to a site near the church, and many more mundane tasks – repairing the curtains in the Village Hall and knitting socks for troops during the Korean War, to mention only two.

The branch is fortunate to have a nucleus of long-standing and devoted members who have served on the committee, been standard bearers and have taken on the roles of chairman, vice-chairman, secretary and treasurer, sometimes managing two positions at the same time. The most outstanding member most certainly is Dracaena Allhusen, who was a founder member and the first vice-chairman, and has taken on the post of secretary, vice-chairman (again), and also

county vice-president, chairman and president, and is now the branch vice-chairman yet again. Many others have given devoted service in various capacities, including Susan Mence, Olive Cooper and Kate Cross, all as standard bearers, and the chairperson at the time of writing, Beryl Denham. Taking a very quiet back seat is the president Pat Day who, with her husband Fred, gives unstintingly of her time in so many ways. Her years of organising the annual Poppy Appeal were given public recognition at the 2002 Remembrance Service in Exeter. Thanks to all her hard work, the collections have gone up year by year, a very considerable achievement for a small village.

All of the branch's activities are based on raising funds for the Royal British Legion and its myriad good works. It takes part in many of the village occasions – the annual fête, the Horticultural Society's annual show, as well as its own monthly meetings, which sometimes raise quite small sums of money, but which add up during the year. Whist drives, jumble sales and wine-and-cheese evenings are also held to enhance funds that can be sent to help wives, widows and dependants of service personnel, a worthwhile charity making life a little easier for some ex-servicemen and women and their families.

WARTIME MEMORIES
By Violet Gosling

Our (Raymond) family came to live in Uplyme in the autumn of 1938 from London and settled into Quest Cottage in Cathole Lane, where my mother lived until the mid-1980s. I can still remember the long, cramped journey in a small Morris 8 car, into which my father had packed himself, our mother, myself and my four younger sisters – Ray, Yvette, Wendy and seven-month-old Jill, for a journey that, at that time, took nearly all day.

Even more I can remember my mother's relief when she found that the removal men had not only been thoughtful enough to light a welcoming fire, but that we could use it for a much-needed hot drink before falling into bed.

A few days later my sister Ray and I were taken along to Uplyme's Mrs Ethelston's School where we joined the other pupils in Miss Westcott's class. She was affectionately known as Miss Waistcoats, but not to her face. I was placed beside a rather small girl called Pat Norris, a great wriggler and one who was often reprimanded for not paying attention. We became great friends and are still in Christmas-card contact.

Not long after I arrived at Uplyme, Rousdon school closed and its pupils were transferred to Uplyme. There was a family called Brooks who had two children, June and Jimmy, and, through my father's work as an insurance agent, we became quite friendly with them all, resulting in Sunday afternoon visits between the two families for some time.

At that time, along with other pupils, I had been moved to the middle class where we came under the guidance of Miss Wannell and, later, Mrs Paul. I strongly suspected that, although Miss Wannell was equally fair to all her charges, she did have a few favourites. One was a cheeky little boy named Micky James who used to wave his arm in the air and, whether he knew the answer or not, call out, 'Miss! Miss!' Her face visibly softened when she looked at him.

The other favourite child was I; once I told her that my favourite book was *Little Women* and that the only time I could read it was when I visited my grandparents at South Petherton. I was completely overwhelmed when, on the last day of term, she presented me with my very own copy.

By now the Second World War had started and my father was becoming increasingly frail from the illness that he had been fighting for some years. It finally claimed him on 8 March 1942. However, from the time that war had started, we were in no doubt that we were living in perilous times. Young as we were, we had to sit and respectfully listen when it was time for the news on the BBC. Maps of Europe had been purchased and pinned to the sitting-room walls and we followed the unfolding of the great events on them.

Everybody had been issued with gas masks and gas-mask practice was carried out at school under the guidance of the headmaster, Mr Freeman. These practices were held twice a week in the playground and we were shown how to take the masks out of their cardboard boxes and fit them over our faces as quickly as possible. Naturally we had to remember to take the masks to school every day and on any other occasions that we left home. Happily the occasion when they had to be used in earnest never arrived.

We often heard the throbbing engines of enemy planes and, on one occasion, when we were walking home after school, there was a loud zooming noise. Two planes appeared and started circling each other in the sky. The eldest boy in our group was sure they were German planes and ordered us all to crouch down in a nearby ditch. Before we had time to take out our gas masks, however, the planes had disappeared.

There were some bombs dropped in Uplyme, probably by planes that were jettisoning their loads as soon as they reached the English coast. Some were dropped on Woodhouse and the craters among the fern and bracken could be seen from our home in Cathole Lane for many years afterwards.

At school we played the usual games of the time during our break periods. One was Statues in which everyone ran around and, at the cry of 'Stop,' would strike up as elegant a pose as was possible for little girls in thick, knitted socks and worn-out, scuffed shoes. The first child to tremble or lose her pose was out of the game and it went on until one, the winner, was left. Of course there were the usual skipping games. 'All in together Girls, this fine weather Girls, when I say your birthday Girls, please jump out!' What with the walk to and from school, the games and the entire PT that we did, it meant that we were all lean and (hopefully) healthy.

Most of the children took food to school for their midday lunches. We also had a daily, half-pint bottle of milk that was delivered to the school by Mr Tom Mead who farmed at Lane End Farm. If my memory serves me correctly, the milk cost a halfpenny a day but later was free. That is until Mrs Thatcher (Milk Snatcher) arrived on the scene in the 1970s and decided children no longer needed the milk.

During the winter months (I am sure they were colder then than they are today) we were all glad to be able to huddle around the big, black stoves (complete with their guards) that were in each class-room. Coke-fired, they were kept going by Mr George Tucker, the caretaker at the school and also the verger of the church next door.

The pupils at Mrs Ethelston's School did their best to help the war effort; a patch of ground at the side of the school was dug over and turned into allotments, where the boys grew vegetables including potatoes. I do not recall seeing any of them staggering into the school with their arms full of fresh vegetables – but the thought was there. In addition to working in the allotments the boys were taught to make little V-shaped signs that were sold for a very modest price and displayed around the village.

The girls were taught to knit and sew by Miss Westcott. I remember losing a sewing needle in a ball of wool and taking the rest of the lesson to unwind the wool, find the needle, and wind the wool up again. Miss Westcott was not amused.

From 1939 Mrs Ethelston's School had been over-crowded with evacuees from the London area and other large towns. Accommodation had to be found for them and the mothers who accompanied the very young children. One of the evacuee families, Mrs Harniman and her children Ernest and Margaret, was still living in Whalley Lane as late as the 1950s. There was also Mrs Castell and her children, Harry, Wilfred, Henry and Dorothy

Marian Hellier (née Mitchell) tells me that some of the evacuees still come back to the area and that one of them has been a life-long friend of hers. Among the names she could remember were Donald, David and Diana Page (all ginger-haired and liberally freckled), Marjorie and Eileen Spendley, Sylvia and Dennis Hobden, May and June Taylor, Heather Lock, Sylvia and Mary Moore, Lizzie Todd, Phyllis Hill, June Steel, Yvonne Verity and Dennis Taylor.

We must not forget the native Uplyme pupils during the war. Among them were: Alan Batten, Stanley Hansford, Pat and Shirley Norris, Frances Ryder, Dennis Peach, Marian Mitchell, my sisters Ray and Yvette, Harold Lanfear, Barbara Larcombe, Tony Harris, David and Patricia Slade, Horace and Mary Wraxall, Pete Rutherford, Donald Hoare, Terry and Michael Street, Arthur Stamp, Jimmy and June Brooks, David and Peter Matthews, June Cawley, Kenny Bowditch, Roger Wood, Rita Stocker and Emily and Lily Farrant.

Lily would become a very close friend of mine, remaining so throughout our schooldays at Uplyme and, later, at Axminster. She lived at 2 Whalley Lane and, like myself, was a great bookworm. Our joint ambition was to go to a boarding-school and have midnight feasts and the adventures that the children had in the Angela Brazil type of books that we loved to read.

After one summer holiday Lily and I, along with the other pupils of our age (nine), were moved up into Mr Freeman's class. This was definitely a downside to our school life. He was the headmaster and, I am sorry to say, a bully. One of my duties was to take two of my sisters, Ray and Yvette, to school and, trying to move them along, we were often five minutes or so late. The cross examination from Mr Freeman would follow: Why were we late? Why did we not go to bed earlier and get up earlier? He would go on and on and on and all this from a man who lived almost opposite the school. Thankfully he did not cane the girls but he certainly used the cane freely on most of the boys, particularly poor Arthur Stamp who seemed to be caned every other day, often for no apparent reason. I was more than happy to escape to Axminster Secondary School after the 1943 summer holidays when I was 12.

Obviously we travelled to Axminster School by bus. At Axminster school dinners (a main course and a pudding) were available at two shillings (10p) a week. Some of the pupils pretended to turn their noses up at what they called stodgy food. But I always enjoyed mine and hoped for second helpings, especially of pudding. One odd point was that Mr Ted Denham, who became headmaster at Mrs Ethelston's School in Uplyme and taught my children there, taught me at Axminster.

One person we were always glad to see at Uplyme school was Mr Bestic, the rector of Uplyme during the war. He used to visit the school most Thursdays and give us lessons on the Bible. He was much liked and respected by the entire village. The more daring of the pupils, which grew to be just about all of us in

time, would, when we met him in the road, say, 'Good Morning Mr Biscuit', and then giggle at our wit. He would doff his hat and smile benignly at us all. He was a handsome man who always dressed in black and had a shock of very thick, white hair that was well swept-back. He was equally courteous to everyone, whether old or young, rich or poor.

Life was not dreary and deprived all the time during the war. In the run-up to Christmas the members of the Mothers' Union managed to collect enough food from among the villagers to put on a party for the school-children. It was quite an accomplishment with the strict food rationing in force at the time. The party was held in the Village Hall and was followed by games and dancing. One year I remember there was a slide show. Mrs Matthews, who lived in Church Street, added to the occasion by playing the piano. At the time I was impressed by the fact that instead of looking at the keys she watched us enjoying ourselves. She also played the piano at the Saturday Evening Social that was held both before, during, and after the war. Those evenings invariably ended with the National Anthem and, during the war, the American Anthem.

Quite often we would attend the Saturday matinée at the Regent cinema in Lyme Regis. It seemed that cowboy films were the commonest, which was all right for the boys, but, naturally enough, we little girls much preferred the likes of Judy Garland and Betty Grable singing and dancing for our pleasure.

During the summer months there was the lure of the beach at Lyme Regis, paddling and turning over stones to see what was hiding beneath them. But because my sisters and I were all fair-skinned, we had to cover our backs and arms after half an hour in the sunshine; and then a long happy trudge back to Yawl at the end of the afternoon. I do not remember having an ice-cream, another wartime shortage I suppose.

There were a surprising number of small businesses in Uplyme at the time. Opposite the Village Hall was a tailor's shop run by Mr Brewer; the house still retains the name of Stanbury in 2003. There was Gracie Brewer who ran a little shop in which she sold various odds and ends (this is the doll's house shop in 2003). There were two butchers' shops, one run by Mr Wheadon, which was on the corner opposite Church Street. The other was run by Mr Irish and was next to the Devon Hotel (converted to flats in 2003).

Mr Bealch, universally known as Billy, was a character and ran the village stores. At that time the Post Office was a separate business, to be found in the house behind the telephone box opposite the Talbot Arms. Before the Post Office moved back to the village it was housed for many years in Venlake Lane and opposite Mr Matthews' bakery. At Venlake Cross Mr and Mrs Lawes had a small sweet shop in their private house. Sadly, of course, sweets were rationed during the war and, if my memory serves me correctly, it ran to one bar of chocolate or the same weight in sweets a week.

Below: *Sergeant Observer Arthur John Hutchings, who died on 12 April 1944 while on active duty in the Middle East.*

Above: *Private Roy Wiscombe 1916, former patrol leader in the 1st Uplyme Scout Troop, served in the Devonshire Regiment during the First World War. In later years he farmed at Hill Farm.*

Above: *Gilbert Marks, lost in a Lancaster bomber over Germany in the Second World War.*

During the Second World War Uplyme man Bill Finnemore served in India where he met and married Thelma Roots at St Teresa's Church in Calcutta in September 1945. He brought his bride back to Uplyme where the happy couple lived until Bill's death in 1996.

Harold Stapleforth, pictured here in his policeman's uniform, was lost while flying a Spitfire out of Gibraltar in the Second World War.

There were three inns in the village, four if you count the Hunters Lodge. During the war the landlord of the Talbot Arms was Tom Sloman; the New Inn's landlord was Mr Lawes, the brother of the man at the sweet shop; and The Black Dog was owned by the Stapleforth family who also ran a taxi business from their pub.

The Devon Hotel, a very fine building that was once the rectory, had an immaculate garden and I remember the monkey-puzzle tree that was growing there. Captain Wales owned the hotel – he was a rather distinguished-looking man, whose wife was addressed as 'Madam' by the staff. For quite a while I thought that she was French.

In the early years of the war we had our groceries delivered from the Co-op stores in Lyme Regis. After a while this service was stopped because of the rationing of petrol, and my mother and I had to go to Lyme Regis, usually on a Saturday, to do the shopping. We almost always walked to Lyme Regis but, because of the hills, caught the bus home. My mother would stop for refreshment before catching the bus. It was either at the Tudor Café (long-since closed) or the Mad Hatters for tea and a scone. I suspected my mother and Mrs Ada Cummings, the evacuee staying at our home, were not getting on too well, probably due to the worries, rationing and conditions of the war, and Mum was only too pleased to get out of the house from time to time. Presumably, so was 'Auntie' Ada, a former friend of my mother's who, with her two small children, came to stay with us for about two years. Her name was Ada Cummings and her children were Geoffrey and Vida. We then had a teenage relative for another two years who was called Betty. She had long, auburn hair and loved to dance. I had to be her partner when she practised her waltzes and quick steps. I must have learnt quite a bit from her and, when I went to dances in later years with my friends, my male partners often told me that I would be quite a good dancer if I did not try to lead.

Standing side by side, Court Hall Farm and the church are the two oldest buildings in Uplyme. Below them is Knapp House where the schoolmasters once lived. In the foreground is an Army hut put up in the First World War and used throughout the Second World War, after which it was burnt down.

Uplyme's Home Guard in the old Village Hall before they were stood down on 31 December 1944.

My father's death led to my mother taking over his job as an insurance agent. He was aware of his impending demise and had wisely, and with the approval of the Co-operative Insurance Company, taken the steps that meant she knew most of the basics. Mother being away from the house so often meant that we had a 15-year-old 'childminder' called Mary looking after the children. Mother also took over my father's car after learning to drive (although she never took a test). It was on its last legs – or should it be its last wheels?

Quest Cottage belonged to the Moss family who farmed at Cathole Farm. They were excellent and kindly landlords from whom we bought all our milk and eggs. We children were always made welcome there and were allowed to ride a docile, white horse known as Molly. Molly's main purpose in life was hauling the milk churns up to the collection stand at the bus stop opposite the top of Cathole Lane. Mr Moss dreaded the arrival of the farm inspector who called monthly with seemingly never-ending reams of forms to be filled in. Mr Moss was not a modern farmer but, just in time to save his sanity, a Land Girl, another Mary, arrived; not only did she pull her weight around the farm, she also did all the paperwork for him as well.

One of my chores was collecting the milk each evening and I remember spilling the can on one occasion. I went back to the farm and, no explanation needed, no questions or charges, the can was refilled.

My mother's youngest brother Leslie had joined the Royal Navy at the age of 17 and I can well remember her baking fruit cakes to send to him, and also myself and my sisters drawing pictures and writing letters to him throughout the war during which he served all through on HMS *Warspite*. Sometimes he would visit us when on shore leave and he always seemed to have a good supply of chocolate bars. He kept a mouth organ in his pocket and would play any tune we requested. Quite often the neighbours would drop in and join the fun. Chief among them was Jean Moss, the daughter of Mr Moss who farmed at Cathole Lane. She was a very good friend of ours and obviously had a very soft spot for Uncle Les. Sadly, she became engaged to a rather handsome, dark-haired soldier who was killed in northern Italy. Later she married Jimmy Pike and lived in Whalley Lane.

In 1943 British soldiers became increasingly rare in the area, their places being taken by the Yanks during the run-up to the D-day invasion of Normandy. They were soon handing out sweets, chocolate and comics to all the local children. Yawl House had been requisitioned at the start of the war and the Americans had taken it over. They liked our company and mimicked our accent – and we mimicked theirs back. One American soldier in particular remains in my memory; he was called Benny Marriotti and was 20 years old. He was one of the cooks at Yawl House and was soon bringing spaghetti, something we had not even heard of before, and a packet of butter to cook it over the fire at Quest Cottage. He was convinced that we British were half starved. He had three younger sisters and suggested that I became a pen pal to one of them who was the same age as me; her name was Shirley. I wrote her a letter and she replied with a much shorter letter than mine. I did not really know what else I could write about and the hands across the sea quickly foundered. In June 1944 we awoke to find that our friends at Yawl House had all been spirited away. It was almost like a bereavement. But, after the end of the war, we received a letter from Benny, now back in America, thanking us for our friendship during his few months at Yawl and saying that we would all meet again one day. Of course we never did.

One GI who did visit us was Richard who married our 'childminder' Mary Trenchard from Axminster. Her parents were unhappy at the time, thinking they would never see her again, but she came home on a few occasions and always added our family to the friends that she visited on such visits.

Returning to the evacuees. I can honestly say that I do not recall the names of those who came singly and found homes in the village. But I do remember a Mrs Harniman and her children, Ernest and Margaret, who were still living in Uplyme as late as the 1950s. But, most of all, I remember a Mrs Castell and her family, Harry, Wilfred, Dorothy and Henry. Mrs Castell became quite friendly with my mother and I have never known anyone, before or since, who moved house in one small village as often as she did. First she rented a bungalow at Woodhouse, then a cottage in Church Lane. After that she moved to Rosemary in Whalley Lane and then to one of the new council-houses at the far end of Whalley Lane, before she finally went back to London. I little dreamt at the time that, over 50 years later, I would write such notes as these in the front room of that council-house in Whalley Lane.

One great benefit that Uplyme had at that time was a resident doctor, Doctor Cook, and Miss Newton the district nurse. She lived in a house called Hygeia (for obvious reasons) almost on the Venlake crossroads; later, and for many years until the 1980s, Hygeia became the doctor's surgery.

We also had our village 'bobby', PC Street, who, by that time, was living in the Police House just below Yawl. He was seen regularly during the daytime going about his duties and checking the local inns at night. It was rumoured, probably falsely, that he liked a little 'refreshment' himself before retiring for the night.

There was a frequent and crowded bus service that continued to be much used for many years after the war. It was due to the considerable number of passengers that both a driver and a conductor were needed.

Above: *Mrs Elsie Raymond (later Humphrey) with her brother Lesley Lee in 1942.*

June Cawley (later Mrs Moulding) inspecting the damage caused by a bomb which fell on Woolcombe Cottage in 1941. Frank Hutchings, who lived there, slept peacefully throughout the night!

Chapter 20

SPECIAL ARTICLES

KILLED BY THE FALL OF HIS AEROPLANE

The year of 1912 had not been good for Great Britain. There had been a crippling coal strike, Captain Scott had died at the South Pole and over everything loomed the gathering war clouds. Indeed, conflict had already broken out in the Balkans. But above all, the unspeakable and unthinkable had happened. Off Cape Race on 14 April the pride of the White Star Line, the unsinkable RMS *Titanic*, had struck an iceberg and gone to the bottom with terrible loss of life. It was the end of an era.

Uplyme too had suffered a tragedy. The rector of Uplyme was Revd Alfred Parke, grandson of the great Revd Charles Wickstead Ethelston. The pride and joy of Alfred and Winifred Parke's lives was their second son, Wilfred, born in April, 1889. In 1912, aged 24, he was a skilled and daring pilot. Lt Wilfred Parke, RN, served in the Naval wing of the Royal Flying Corps (this was long before the creation of the RAF on 1 April 1918). Wilfred had started flying in 1911. He was instructed at Brooklands where he gained his pilot's certificate from the Royal Aero Club on 11 April. In May of 1911, he was appointed to Actaeon as a Lieutenant of the RFC. The future looked rosy, the sky was the limit.

As a pilot he rapidly acquired a reputation for being skilled, enthusiastic and fearless. He was also extremely versatile, being equally at home flying hydroplanes, monoplanes or biplanes. But his flying career was not without its adventures and hazards. In May 1912, flying from Brooklands to Hendon, he had crashed an Avro monoplane, happily without incurring serious injuries. Then again, in August during Army manoeuvres on Salisbury Plain, he put his Avro into a death-defying vertical dive of 600 feet. At the very last moment he managed to bring the head of the plane up and level off. 'Parke's Dive', as it became known, was famous and widely discussed at the Royal Aero Club and in aeronautical circles.

The weather forecast for Sunday 15 December 1912 was not good. 'Strong winds are predicted for the south of England.' Nevertheless, Wilfred was determined to fly. It was not only the winds that were headstrong on that Sunday. He was at London Airport, then located at Hendon. He wanted to spend his Christmas leave at Oxford. Mr A. Hardwicke, the manager of the Handley Page Company, also wished to go. The two men took off on their fatal flight at noon, just as Wilfred's father was finishing his sermon in Uplyme church.

The plane that Wilfred chose to fly was a Handley Page monoplane with a 70hp engine. It was equipped with the latest safety device, a gadget designed to assist in keeping the plane evenly balanced. In theory the plane could not turn over. In theory the *Titanic* could not sink.

At Hendon the winds were gusting up to Force 6 and Wilfred was strongly advised not to fly. He chose to ignore the meteorological report. After all, he was a skilled pilot who could look after himself and handle any eventuality. Chocks away, he took off and his 70hp enabled him to climb rapidly up to 150 feet. But at that height he immediately found that the wind was exceptionally strong. It was obvious even to him that he would have to turn back.

He turned the joystick and, as the machine responded, a fierce gust of wind struck the tail of the plane. At once it was flipped upside down to plunge headlong out of control to the ground. The plane hit a portion of Wembley golf course, not far from Wembley Park Station. Both occupants were killed instantly. Dr Goddard who examined the bodies found appalling injuries, including fractures of the legs and skulls. The cause of death was given as shock.

Lt Wilfred Parke RN was the first Royal Naval Officer to die in service and the eighth serving officer to be killed in a flying accident. *The Times* carried a full account of the event the next day, Monday 16 December, devoting several columns to it.

A year later, Alfred and Winifred Parke gave a fine stained-glass window in Uplyme church in memory of their son, Wilfred. The triptych depicts the empty tomb with Mary confronting the angels. The text reads, 'He is not here but risen.' Underneath the window is a brass plaque recording briefly the details of the tragedy. Air flight was so new in 1912 that the word 'crash' had not been coined. Instead the plaque says simply that Lt W. Parke RN, son of the rector, was killed at Wembley on Sunday 15 December 1912, 'by the fall of his aeroplane'.

The Devon Hotel in 1940 with Church Street on the left. In the background is Knoll Hill, Uplyme's most prominent feature.

Prudence Jane Davie, 1831–83, who lived in Ware Cottage and is buried in Uplyme churchyard.

Colonel Percy Harrison Fawcett in 1911.

FROM UPLYME TO CHRISTCHURCH, NEW ZEALAND

Cyrus Davie (1786–1846) and Jane Eveleigh, both of Uplyme parish, were married by licence in the parish of Lyme Regis on 4 February 1819 in the presence of Mary Ann James and James Blackmore. Their marriage was blessed with seven children. Their eldest child, named after his father, was Cyrus, born in 1821. Then came John Eveleigh who became a Comptroller of Her Majesty's Customs, Gloucester. The third child was a girl christened Hannah Eveleigh, the fourth was called Frances. There followed William Petersen (named after a William Petersen of Lyme) who lived to the ripe old age of 85. Prudence Jane, who was born in 1831, died tragically in 1883, aged 51. Last of all was Mary Anne who died in 1874, aged 40.

Cyrus, the eldest, was named after his father. The second son, John Eveleigh of the Royal Navy, was probably named in memory of his mother's brother, who was killed in action in 1814. William, the third son, is named after a prominent Lyme citizen and friend of the family. As for the girls, Hannah Eveleigh is named after her maternal grandmother; Prudence Jane for her paternal grandmother, an aunt and her mother; and Mary Anne is named after her mother's best friend and bridesmaid, Mary Anne James, who married Robert Bourchier Wrey of Ware House in 1820. The Wreys were very much landed gentry, tracing their ancestry back to the time of William the Conqueror. They could include in their family tree such aristocratic names as Plantagenet, Neville and Mortimer (the Earls of March), all of whom feature in Shakespeare's history plays.

The Land Tax records for Uplyme at that time reveal that Syris Davie (sic) is recorded as the occupier of a property known as 'late Harris's', owned by Whiting and on which tax of 5 shillings was due. This is almost certainly Hill Farm at the top of Gore Lane.

By the time of the 1841 census, the Davie family had scattered. Cyrus senr was 60 years old and Comptroller of Customs in Gloucester, where he died on 10 July 1846 from an enlarged prostate and inflamed bladder. Jane, his widow, was living in Uplyme in that part of the parish which lies to the south of Woodhouse Road from Myrtle Cottage to West Coombe. What of the children? Cyrus, by now aged 20, was a land surveyor. Hannah had emigrated to the United States where she became a governess in Cambridge, Massachusetts, to the children of Mary Appleton Macintosh, sister of Fanny Longfellow and of Henry Wadsworth Longfellow, the distinguished poet. The 1851 census reveals that Hannah Davie was also a governess to the Longfellows.

What of Cyrus, the eldest boy, 29 years old in 1850? He decided to emigrate to New Zealand to become a Canterbury Colonial, as the first settlers were known. Four ships were scheduled to sail to New Zealand. Cyrus chose the *Randolph* of 761 tons. Together with the *Sir George Seymour*, the *Charlotte,* and the *Jane and the Cressy,* the four ships carried 791 emigrants to the antipodes. On board each ship was a chaplain and a schoolmaster. The cargo included a printing press, 2,000 books presented by Oxford University, a church organ and a church bell.

A week before the sailing Cyrus attended a service at St Paul's Cathedral. Cyrus should have embarked on the *Randolph* at Gravesend; he had already loaded all his luggage, including his bed and furniture for the cabin. At the last minute he suddenly decided to go over land to Plymouth where he could join the ship as she stopped there to pick up a few passengers – the rail link from London to Plymouth having been completed in 1848, Cyrus would have gone down to Plymouth by train. For some inexplicable reason, Cyrus missed his ship. He embarked, however, on the *Sir George Seymour*, recording laconically in his diary:

Sunday 8 September, 1850, Embarked from the Barbican, Plymouth, and arrived on board about 7am. Weighed anchor at 10am. We lost sight of Old England with the closing day.

About a month later on the voyage they sighted the *Randolph* and in mid-ocean Cyrus was transferred by boat to her and his own possessions to the chief cabin, much to the commotion and amusement of all the passengers. He arrived in Lyttelton, the port of Christchurch, on 16 December 1850, a glorious New Zealand summer morning, to be greeted by vociferous cheers. They were welcoming the arrival of an Uplyme man who had the unique experience of coming out in two ships, starting from Plymouth in one and arriving in New Zealand in another, without having been shipwrecked.

Cyrus became the chief surveyor of the province of Canterbury, working on maps for £300 a year. He married, had children and died in 1871. After a distinguished career in Christchurch he is still remembered with pride and affection by his descendants who live there.

So what has happened to all his sisters who stayed in Uplyme? Well, Prudence Jane was living in Ware Cottage. She was returning from church in Uplyme when her horse shied, throwing her from her trap and killing her. She died in 1883, the last survivor of the Davie family to be living in Uplyme. Their fine memorial, recently restored, in Uplyme churchyard, commemorates Jane the mother who died aged 85 on 4 April 1878; Hannah Eveleigh who died on 20 November 1878 aged 54; Prudence Jane who died aged 52 on 25 April, 1883; Mary Anne who died aged 40 on 28 May 1874; and surprisingly, a fifth name on the tablets, Esther Alice Fisher, who probably paid for the memorial. Alice Fisher was the granddaughter of Jane and the daughter of William, who also emigrated to New Zealand.

The Davie family are lovingly remembered both in Uplyme churchyard and in the antipodes at Christchurch.

FROM UPLYME TO THE JUNGLE
By Imogen Thomas

Uplyme has been home to few men of international stature and fame, but Lt Col P.H. Fawcett, explorer and map-maker, is one. In the early part of the twentieth century, Col Fawcett rented Waterside in Mill Lane.

A military man with a passion for exploration and adventure, Fawcett spent more than ten years deep in the jungles of South America, exploring and mapping the inhospitable and dangerous boundary lines between Peru, Bolivia and Brazil. The year 1906 saw Fawcett's first foray. At the request of the Royal Geographical Society, he set off along a succession of rivers which were dangerous and unmapped. They contained electric eels, stingrays, piranhas, crocodiles and disease-carrying insects. At night jaguars invaded the campsite. One man was squeezed to death in his hammock by an anaconda. Fawcett himself shot one anaconda which measured 60 feet long. The inhabitants of the jungle were not any less dangerous – some were cannibals and all existed in unhealthy conditions. Life was nasty, brutish and short. At camp one day a native was moaning on his bed. Fawcett's Indian host said, 'You've got to die in about half an hour, so why all this palaver? It spoils the breakfast of the senhores.' Sure enough, the man died soon after.

Fawcett returned to Uplyme in 1910 to visit his wife and children at Waterside. He wrote:

How incredibly neat and secure the Devonshire lanes and meadows seem to me after the vast expanses of forest and plains. How far removed from those sordid outposts where a man's life is not worth the flip of a finger. After a few months of this sheltered existence in the park-like scenery of Uplyme, my imagination comes to regard it as a prison gate slowly but surely shutting me in. Even Waterside, the big house with its extensive garden, is menacing in its snugness. Or should I say smugness?

So back he went to South America. Having dined with the President of Bolivia in La Paz, soon he was off again up the river. Confronted by hostile Chincho Indians, he and his companions resorted to song. They had worked their way through 'A Bicycle Made For Two', 'Swanee River' and 'Onward Christian Soldiers' before the intrigued Indians stopped shooting at them with their bows and arrows and made friends.

As they searched for the lost city of Eldorado, discomfort was acute. Temperatures oscillated between 22 degrees Fahrenheit on Mount Altoplano and a sizzling 112 degrees in the jungle.

By 1924 he was back in England where he recruited his son Jack, aged 22, and a friend, Raleigh Rimell, son of a Seaton doctor, to accompany him on a big treasure-hunting expedition to the poisoned hell of the Mato Grosso. Off they went in 1925, full of optimism. But the mosquitoes soon gorged themselves on Raleigh's limbs, the wounds turning bad and festering. On 30 May 1925 Col Fawcett, Jack and Raleigh left their Indian village and walked into the jungle. With his heavily bandaged legs Raleigh trailed after the other two. For a few days smoke from their camp-fires was noticed, then all trace of them vanished – they were never seen again.

Back in Uplyme, for some time Mrs Fawcett was not worried by the lack of news. Her husband had warned her, 'You need have no fear of any future.' Gradually people became anxious. For the next 20 years stories of what might have happened continued to appear in the British press. Travellers brought back tales of aged white men held prisoner in Indian villages. Objects that had belonged to Col Fawcett were found. There was even found a boy who claimed that he was Jack's son, but turned out to be an albino Indian. Expeditions were mounted but failed to find anything. The most notable of these was that led in 1932 by Peter Fleming (brother of James Bond's creator), who subsequently wrote a description of the experience in a best-selling travel book, *Brazilian Adventure.*

To this day the fate of Col Fawcett who found Uplyme too tame for comfort has never been resolved. The jungle has kept its secrets.

THE UPLYME HELP SCHEME
By Fred Day

The Uplyme Help Scheme started in 1973, following a meeting between the organiser of a Portsmouth community-care scheme and Peter Ransford, the secretary of the Uplyme PCC. With the support of the rector, Revd W.C. Wordsell, he recruited five parish councillors and the village postmistress, Mrs Stevens. After careful consideration the group decided that a help scheme, although ambitious, was both needed and feasible.

Leaflets were distributed to every household. The scheme received a very positive response with over 100 people offering their services. To make the scheme operational the committee was enlarged and also became independent of the PCC. The rector, however, continued as a source of advice. A packet of information was delivered to every household. Included was a letter from the voluntary body explaining its aims, which were:

1. *To visit the elderly, distressed, lonely and sick at home or in hospital.*
2. *To supply transport in an emergency.*
3. *To deliver prescriptions, pensions, paraffin and shopping.*
4. *To contact doctors, relatives, neighbours, welfare and social services.*
5. *To supply 'H' cards (Help Signs) to be placed in front windows to attract attention for those requiring help.*
6. *To lend basic home-nursing equipment.*

With the letter were supplied cards with emergency telephone numbers and an information sheet about village activities. A box , checked daily, was placed in the Post Office in which written requests could be left. The scheme got off to an excellent start with a committee of eight people who met three times a year. The home-nursing equipment required storage, distribution and recovery. Fred and Pat Day, responsible for this busy section, became the longest-serving committee members, making hundreds of trips over the course of the years with the equipment. The teams visiting the elderly, sick and lonely were the largest to cope with the demand. The chairman normally dealt with outside bodies such as welfare and social services, Age Concern, doctors, relatives and other factors. But the largest group were the drivers, who made regular journeys to Axminster and Seaton, as well as the main hospitals in Exeter, Dorchester, Taunton or Yeovil.

Almost all of the helpers declined to accept any recompense for their services as a way of making their contribution to the welfare of the village. The many donations received created a fund which enabled the scheme to widen its ability to support the village. Nursing-aid equipment, zimmer frames, flexible leg/foot stools, medical-bed tables, commodes, back rests, rubber rings, a child's cot, a highchair and a pushchair all became available. Surplus funds were used to purchase a hardwood seat for donation to the Village Hall patio and a picnic table for the playing-field.

Every newcomer to the village receives information about the Help Scheme which has been a tremendous success and a lasting reward for all who have taken part. Of course conditions have changed considerably since 1973. Now there is a modern medical centre accessible to all, and most people have a telephone and even a car. Whilst there is still a very small requirement for transport and home-nursing equipment, the need for the scheme is steadily declining. It will cease altogether in the not too distant future.

What is certain is that throughout the 30 years of dedicated and devoted service by the volunteers operating the Uplyme Help Scheme, everyone involved has felt a strong, underlying awareness that informal care by families, friends and neighbours has been and is still a powerful force. It will surely continue as a force long after the Uplyme Help Scheme, which has played such a commendable and beneficial part in the village's welfare, has ceased its operations.

The Davie grave in Uplyme churchyard.

The report of Revd Ethelston's funeral in Pulman's Weekly News *of 10 December 1872.*

UPLYME.—The funeral of the late Rev. C. W. Ethelstone took place on Friday at twelve o'clock, and was numerously attended by his family, friends, parishioners, and inhabitants of Uplyme and Lyme, by all of whom the deceased was held in high esteem. He had been rector of the parish for nearly half a century, and his kindness to the poor was almost proverbial. His doors were always open to relieve the wants of the sick and needy, and, at this season, in addition to other comforts, he bountifully distributed blankets and warm clothing. His loss will be sorely felt. The funeral procession moved from the rectory in the following order :—

The Rev. Foster Lewis.   The Rev. J. B. M. Camm.
Gentlemen.
Servants of the Family.
Mr Sellers (undertaker)   Mr Brown (lead coffin maker)
Mr Hoare (coffin maker).   Mr Miller (hearse proprietor).   Mr Taylor (vault maker).

Four bearers   HEARSE   Four bearers

FIRST MOURNING COACH
— Speke, Esq., Mrs Speke, Edmund Peel, Esq., R. Peel Ethelston, Esq.
SECOND MOURNING COACH
C. J. Parke, Esq.,   Mrs Parke,   Perry Watlington, Esq., Mrs Watlington
THIRD MOURNING COACH
Miss Parke   Ethelston Parke, Esq.,   Miss Charlotte Parke, Edmund Ethelston, Esq.
FOURTH MOURNING COACH
Miss Mildred Parke   Edmund Parke, Esq.   Mr Alfred Parke
FIFTH MOURNING COACH
Sir Edmund Prideaux   Charles Gordon, Esq.   Dr. Skinner
Close carriage of H. F. Ingram, Esq., E. L. Ames, Esq.

The burial service was impressively read by the Rev. Mr. Rawlinson, of Symondsbury, and whilst the corpse was in the church a beautiful cross, composed of white camellias and violets, was placed upon the coffin by an affectionate daughter of deceased. At the close of the service a muffled peal was rung upon the church bells. The coffin, made by Mr. Hoare, of Uplyme, was of polished oak, with silver plated furniture. On the breast plate was inscribed —"Charles Wicksted Ethelstone, died November 30th, 1872, aged 72." The lead coffin was supplied by Mr. C. Brown, and Mrs. Sellers and Sons were the undertakers. all the arrangements were ably and most satisfactorily carried out. On Sunday morning the Rev. Mr. Rawlinson preached an eloquent funeral sermon from the 2nd book of Corinthians, 6th chapter, 10th verse.

Undercliff Farm and Ware Cliffs in 1904. From this farm John Fowles, who lived here 1967–69, could see the end of the Cobb, featured in arguably the most famous scene of The French Lieutenant's Woman. *On the left is Chimney Rock.*

Meryl Streep dressed as Sarah Woodruff, the part she played in The French Lieutenant's Woman, *in 1981. Meryl is standing in front of Pinhay House which is just outside the boundary of Uplyme. Some of the film was shot in the part of the Landslip which lies in Uplyme.*

Chapter 21

UPLYME'S WORTHIES

SARAH ANDREW

Sarah Andrew was the granddaughter of Solomon Andrew, a rich Lyme Regis merchant and a gentleman of extensive property who purchased Shapwick in 1670. Henry Fielding (1707–54), father of the English novel and author of *Joseph Andrews*, *Tom Jones* and *Amelia*, attempted to elope with Sarah. He is said to have based the divine Sophia Western in *Tom Jones* (1749) on Sarah Andrew. Tom Jones, the eponymous hero, pursues Sophia unsuccessfully from Somerset along the Bath road all the way to London before marrying her in the last chapter. According to George Roberts in his *History of Lyme Regis*, Sophy Western was supposed to portray the excellences of Miss Andrew.

LAURENCE AND CATHERINE ANHOLT

Laurence Anholt and his wife Catherine who live on Woodhouse Hill are two of Britain's top children's authors and illustrators. Laurence has written four enchanting books about children involved with famous painters. First he wrote and illustrated *Camille and the Sunflowers*, a story about Vincent Van Gogh, which was short-listed for the 'Waterstone Book of the Month'. Next came *Degas and the Little Dancer*, then *Picasso and the Girl with the Ponytail*. Finally he wrote *Leonardo and the Flying Machine*. He has won the Nestlé Smarties prize. With his wife he has produced over 70 highly successful children's books, published in 23 countries around the world.

NATHANAEL CARPENTER

Nathanael Carpenter (1589–1628), who was born in Uplyme, was the son of Revd John Carpenter, rector of Northleigh, near Colyton. Educated at St Edmund Hall, Oxford, he was a fellow of Exeter College, by mandate of James I. He became a Doctor of Divinity and a schoolmaster of the King's Wards in Dublin. He was a skilful geographer who published several learned works on geography and philosophy, the latter directed against Aristotelianism.

PETER COOK

The parents of the comedian Peter Cook lived at Knollside where Peter also lived for some time. He was a founder member of 'Beyond the Fringe' and 'Not Only But Also' with Dudley Moore.

OLIVER FORD DAVIES

Oliver Ford Davies who lives in Venlake is an Olivier-award-winning actor. He has been working in the theatre, films and television since the 1970s. He played Count Shabielski in the acclaimed production of *Ivanov* at the Almeida Theatre. At the Royal National Theatre he acted in David Hare's *Racing Demon*, as well as *The Shaughraun* and *Hamlet*. From 1975–86 he was with the RSC at Stratford acting in 25 productions. Films he has made include Emma Thompson's *Sense and Sensibility*, *Mrs Dalloway*, *Defence of the Realm*, and *Paper Mask*. In television he has acted in numerous productions including 'Kavanagh QC' and 'Inspector Morse'.

JOHN CHURCHILL, DUKE OF MARLBOROUGH

The Churchill family first came to Ashe, between Axminster and Musbury, when Elizabeth Drake, the great-granddaughter of John Drake, who bought the estate in 1526, married a Dorset knight called Winston Churchill. Oddly enough the Churchills were Royalists and the Drakes Parliamentarians.

The happy couple had 12 children but only five survived into adolescence. One was Arabella, born on 23 February 1647 and baptised at Ashe the following month. She grew up to become the favourite mistress of the Duke of York (later James II). Again, oddly enough, her son Berwick followed James into exile in 1688 and fought for France against his uncle Marlborough. Arabella died in 1730 having lived through two protectors' and seven monarchs' reigns, eight if you count William and Mary as two.

John Churchill was born in 1650. There is some confusion over both the date and place. That Ashe had been almost completely burnt down during the Civil War led some authorities to claim that Churchill was born at Trill, a farmhouse barely a mile away.

His baptism was recorded in the parish registers at St Mary's Church in Axminster as: 'John, the sonne of Mr Winston Spencer Churchill was baptised at Aish, ye 26 day of Jun.' The actual page

General Sir David Mostyn.

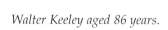

Walter Keeley aged 86 years.

has since been removed, more than likely stolen. A later Winston Spencer Churchill mistakenly gives this date as his birthday in his book *Marlborough*; later he is less certain and contents himself with saying in his *History of the English Speaking People* that Marlborough was born in May or June. Even Hoskins (*Devon*) claims that he was born at Trill. The truth can be seen in St Michael's Church in Musbury where a facsimile copy of the entry in that village's parish register is displayed. The date given is 26 May and the place as Musbury. Ashe is in Musbury and Trill is in Axminster.

Churchill was educated at first in Dublin and later at St Paul's. Like that later Winston Churchill he was never much of a scholar and, also like the great Premier, he opted for a life in the Army where, by 1667, he had been commissioned in the King's Own Company in Colonel Russell's Regiment of Foot Guards.

He may have been a good soldier but he was never much of a politician and was unable to hide his mistrust of William III (1689–1702) whom he suspected, with good reason, of using England to further the interest of the Dutch in helping him in his French wars. Such thoughts led him to hanker after the return of James or the succession of Anne. When Anne became Queen in 1702, she created him a Knight of the Garter and elevated him to a Dukedom (Marlborough).

The names of his battles roll off the tongue like an ancient litany; chief among them during the War of the Spanish Succession were Blenheim (1704), Oudenarde (1706) and Malplaquet (1708).

Sadly, his wife fell out with Queen Anne and the shock waves led to Marlborough's disgrace and to his spending his last years in retirement. But, when he died in 1722, he was Duke of Marlborough, Marquis of Blandford, Baron Churchill of Aymouth in Scotland, Prince of the Holy Roman Empire and Knight of the Most Ancient Order of the Garter, and still described as England's finest soldier; all in all a long way from humble Ashe.

The Churchill family were patrons of St Peter and St Paul's Church at Uplyme for 500 years.

THE RIGHT HONOURABLE JOHN DENHAM PC, MP

The Right Honourable John Denham MP was appointed Minister of State for the Home Office on 11 June 2001.

He was born in Uplyme where his father Ted was headmaster of Mrs Ethelston's School for 20 years and his mother Beryl a parish councillor, becoming chairman in 1977. John was educated at Mrs Ethelston's School, Woodroffe Comprehensive School, Lyme Regis, and Southampton University where he became president of the Students' Union. He was Head of Youth Affairs at the British Council from 1979 until 1983, and was responsible for public education and advocacy for War on Want from 1984

until 1988. He subsequently worked for Christian Aid, Oxfam and other development agencies.

He was a Hampshire County Councillor from 1981 until 1989, where he was spokesman on education. From 1989 until 1993 he served as a Southampton City Councillor and as chair of its housing department.

He was elected to Parliament in April 1992 as Member for Southampton Itchen. John was appointed as Parliamentary Under-Secretary of State at the Department of Social Security in May 1997 and was made a Minister of State at the DSS in July 1998. He then served as Minister of State for Health from December 1998 until his new appointment. In June 2000 the Queen appointed him a Privy Councillor.

In March 2003 John Denham resigned from the Government when he was unable to support the decision that led to Anglo-American forces invading Iraq.

John is married to Ruth Dixon and they live at their home in Itchen with their daughter Rosie who is 16 and their son Edward (aged 14).

As a young man John, along with his brother Michael, joined his father as a member of the Uplyme and Lyme Regis Cricket Club, and later played cricket for Axminster.

REVD CHARLES WICKSTEAD ETHELSTON

Revd Charles Wickstead Ethelston (1799–1872) was curate and then rector of Uplyme for 47 years. He extensively restored the Rectory (now the Devon Hotel) in 1838 and Uplyme church with his own money in 1876. He died in office on 30 November 1872. His tombstone and cross in the south-west corner is the largest in the churchyard.

COLONEL PERCY HARRISON FAWCETT

Colonel Percy Harrison Fawcett (1867–1925) lived at Waterside in Springhead Road, Uplyme. Born in Torquay, he was an inveterate and fearless explorer. After service in the Army in the Far East, Colonel Fawcett was given a border delimitation assignment on behalf of the Bolivian Government. This led to several hazardous expeditions in the Mato Grosso area in search of ancient civilisations. In 1925 he disappeared with his eldest son near the Xingu River.

A keen cricketer, during his time at Uplyme he turned out for the village side, as well as guesting for the Axminster, Lyme Regis and Seaton clubs.

JOHN FOWLES

John Fowles, the author of *The Collector*, *The Magus*, *Daniel Martin* and many more distinguished books, lived for three years at Undercliff Farm in Uplyme from where he could see the Cobb, the setting of his book, *The French Lieutenant's Woman*, published in 1969 and turned into a film in 1981.

Sandra Furzey

SANDRA MAUREEN FURZEY

Sandra Key was born at Bodmin in Cornwall in 1944, moving to Axmouth when her father took up a post as manager of the Stedcombe estate. She moved to Uplyme after her marriage to Joe Furzey in 1978.

Her interest in local affairs started in the early 1980s when she was press-ganged into attending Village Hall committee meetings 'to take notes'. It was a short step to becoming a member of that committee. Around the same time her interest in the local Cub pack was nourished when her second son Adrian joined. She also joined and was soon a Beaver Leader.

She was always ready to do anything for either organisation. But it was her awesome (there is no other word) reputation with the draw book for which people will always remember her. In this she was well supported by Charlie Bachelor, an old friend of her father's who moved to Uplyme to retire and become an honorary member of the Furzey family, and who was also press-ganged into the noble art of selling draw tickets.

Lots of people helped with the building of the new Village Hall, and many have helped with the raising of money for the refurbishment of the Scout Hut. Sandra would be the first to play down her own, immense contribution. But let her have the last word – 'Whenever I pass the Village Hall I think to myself that I helped with that.' Was there ever a bigger understatement?

NEIL INNES

Neil Innes (1903–89) was educated at the Royal Naval College, Dartmouth, Haileybury College and Trinity Hall, Cambridge. He was in the Sudan Political Service and became Foreign Minister to the Sultan of Muscat and Oman. After retirement in 1958 he was at various times chairman of the Uplyme Parish Council, the Uplyme Horticultural Society, the King George V Playing-Field Committee and the Uplyme Conservative Association, and a vice-president of the local cricket club. He was a governor of Allhallows School and Northbrook Approved

School in Exeter. He always regarded Uplyme as his home, living at The Orchard and later at Thursater, both in Rhode Lane.

WALTER KEELEY

Walter Keeley (1908–2002) was a much-loved and respected citizen of Uplyme. Born in Worcester in 1908, he came to Uplyme in 1919 where he lived for 85 years until his untimely death in 2002. Walter was one of nine children – six boys and three girls. In the batting order he was in the middle.

Walter worked for Roy, his son and Anne in their nursery business at Blossom Hill. He calculated that he had potted, in the last 15 years, 25,000 plants a year. That makes half a million busy lizzies and fuchsias that have felt the loving fingers of Walter carefully kneading them down into fresh compost.

Walter's long life was one of service to the community. During the vicious winter of 1962 Walter was a postman who regularly walked the 12 miles from Venlake up to Woodhouse Hill, over to Shapwick, back to Cuckoo Hill and Venlake. Despite the blizzards, the mail always got through.

In his youth Walter was captain of the Uplyme football team. He was also a fireman and a nurseryman who worked for 36 years at Charmouth House where he proudly says, 'I never had a day off.' During the war he dug for victory and went haymaking on Fern Hill, loading the wagons until midnight.

But that's not all. When Walter arrived in Uplyme, the churchyard was a wilderness. Walter decided to do something about it. Under his tender care, the graves and grass around the church were restored to the pristine condition they enjoy today. The turf is shorn, the gravestones are (mostly) erect, the wild flowers flourish, the birds find a haven and all is peace and serenity, thanks in no small part to Walter.

Afflicted with a bad back in 1969, he was discharged from hospital where he had lain in bed with a rack and pinion to stretch him; the doctor told him that he should give up work and just sit in a chair and pass the time. Walter's response was typical. He said, 'I might as well be dead as do that.' He got out his bicycle and cycled over to Beaminster. He told that doctor that he would have made a better vet than a doctor!

Nothing would stop him. One day he was cycling to Exeter to see his father who was in hospital. He got as far as Rockbeare when his bicycle broke down. Undeterred, Walter walked into Exeter, saw his dad and then proceeded to walk back to Uplyme, a distance of some 35 miles.

In 1988 at the age of 80 Walter dug half an acre of vegetable garden in Rhode Lane all by himself, such was the strength of the man.

He attended church regularly where he sang the hymns and psalm lustily at evensong. Before the service he used to toll the bell for ten minutes. Probably at the age of 92 he was the oldest bell-ringer in Devon.

For 50 years he was married to Gladys with whom he had three children – Mary, George and Roy, all of whom still live in Uplyme in 2003.

Young in heart, youthful in appearance, cheerful in adversity and strong in faith, Walter Keeley was an inspiration to all who had the privilege of knowing him.

The Right Honourable John Denham PC, MP.

LAURENCE ARNOLD AND JEAN MARGARET MASTERS

Laurence Masters was born in Winchester in 1924, moving to Uplyme in 1933 when he was nine years old. He attended Mrs Ethelston's School but spent the last few weeks of his schooldays at the newly opened Axminster Secondary Modern School, where Uplyme children began attending when they reached the age of 11. Laurence, being a few weeks short of his 14th birthday at the time, the age at which children then left state schools, was soon working at Burrowshot Farm, near Hunters Lodge. From there he moved to R.J. Luff, the Axminster coal and builders merchants, before joining the Royal Air Force as a mechanic and fitter in 1942. He served in India and Burma.

After demobilisation he worked at Tytherleigh Garage between Axminster and Chard, before starting out on his own in 1951 at Masters Garage just above the Hunters Lodge on what is now the main A35 trunk road. Two years earlier he had married Jean Wiscombe, a Lyme Regis girl, at that town's St Michael's Church. They sold the business in 1965 and moved to Combehayes Farm in Uplyme where they applied for change of business planning permission to operate four motor caravans out of there. It was a badly needed facility locally, the nearest such business being in Taunton. Almost unbelievably some local opposition led to permission being refused and Laurence went into farming, almost by accident you might say.

Starting with his 25 years of support for the local Scouts, for which he was awarded the Chief Scout's Commendation for Good Services, he has done so much for Uplyme that most people would agree that he is the most worthy of Uplyme's 'worthies'. He has served on the village committee and its fund-raising committee and, with Jean, organised the regular dances in the hall for many years, and behind the scenes is an outstanding supporter of Uplyme football club.

In a different, and more important, direction his many gifts to the village include the land for the old hall's car park, the new hall and its car park and, more recently, the newer overflow car park to the rear of the hall. Add to that land off Venlake Lane for cheap starter homes for locals, and the refusal to sell for a sizable sum to developers the land that he later sold to the football club (at a far from sizeable sum)

to give them a permanent home. And, when the National Playing Fields Society, or their local branch, stopped the footballers from using the 'path' through the hedge behind the old cricket pavilion, he gave the footballers a strip of land on a neighbouring field to guarantee access to their pitch. Uplyme is lucky to have two such friends.

BISHOP HENRY MORGAN

Henry Morgan, Bishop of St David's, Pembroke, was rector of Uplyme 1528–50. He was a Prebendary of Exeter Cathedral.

GENERAL SIR DAVID MOSTYN KCB, CBE

General Sir David Mostyn KCB, CBE, was Adjutant General and ADC (Gen) to the Queen 1986–89. As Adjutant General he was the Army board member responsible for all personnel matters and second in seniority to the Chief of the General Staff. He was GOC and British Commandant, Berlin, 1980–83, where he was inter alia in charge of Rudolf Hess, the last prisoner in Spandau Prison whom he found overly intelligent, extremely keen on football (Bayern Munich was his favourite team) and the sky at night.

Sir David is married with four sons and two daughters, some of whom live in Uplyme. He was educated at Downside and RMA Sandhurst. He has been president of the Devon Royal British Legion and the Uplyme and Lym Valley Society.

ADRIAN FRANCIS PEARSON

Adrian Pearson was born in Lyme Regis on 1 August 1953 and educated at Mrs Ethelston's School in Uplyme, the Woodroffe School, and Bristol University where he studied music, a life-long love, and then took a teaching course at Reading University.

For three years he taught at Totton on the edge of the New Forest before taking a four-year sabbatical to visit Australia. He took a year reaching Oz before spending two years at Perth where he met Jennie, who accompanied him back to England, another 12-month journey.

They had never made any plans to marry but, on

Laurence and Jean Masters pictured at the official opening of Uplyme's new Village Hall on 1 October 1994.

Below: *Mr and Mrs George Furzey at their Thirty Acres home in Yawl Hill Lane in the 1930s.*

arrival in England, Jennie had trouble in getting past the steely eye of the immigration people. 'How will you support yourself?' seemed to be their chief worry – or excuse. In the end she was give permission to stay for one or two months to get a job. So they got married – the impetus being the Immigration Office rather than Cupid's bow – and, certainly, have lived happily ever after since.

The first year of their marriage was spent in Bristol where Adrian earned a living playing the piano in restaurants and Jennie, with his help, started a screen-printing business making tea towels, T-shirts, curtaining etc.

Although that was not the reason, the village of Uplyme benefited immensely when Adrian's mother decided to move out of her Haven home in Harcombe. The couple moved back to Uplyme and, after family calls began to put an end to the screen-printing business, Adrian took a teaching post at Manor House School, Honiton, in 1984, where he is the deputy headmaster in 2003.

The decision to build a new Village Hall in Uplyme had been taken in 1984. Progress at first was, of necessity, slow. In all such projects money, in the shape of interest, tends to flow in much quicker when the foundations of a substantial bank balance have been laid.

Towards the end of 1987 Adrian was approached by Lexie Sumner and the hall chairman, Doug Emmett, and asked to chair the fund-raising committee. He did so, but preferred to look upon himself as 'an enabler' who brought the main committee and the fund-raising committee together as a team. 'I just had the job of welding them,' he claims. That bald statement does not even begin to cover the immense amount of work that he, and a lot of other people, put in to raise over a quarter of a million pounds for the new hall. The rest is history.

BRIAN RAWLINSON

Brian Rawlinson who lived in Harcombe was an actor with a distinguished career in theatre, television, films and radio. He was probably best remembered for his playing of Robert Onedin in the long-running TV drama 'The Onedin Line', much of which was filmed in Exeter and other places in Devon. He made over 300 appearances in 'Dixon of Dock Green' and numerous parts in the 'Carry On' films. He was an actor of distinction.

PRINCE MAURICE

Prince Maurice (1620–52) served during the Civil War as an English cavalry officer. He was the third son of the Elector Palatine Frederick V and Elizabeth, daughter of King James VI and I of Scotland and England, and commanded the Royalist army at the Siege of Lyme in 1644. Numbering between 2,500 and 4,000 men, his army arrived on the high ground above Lyme on 20 April 1644. They were first sighted on Rhode Hill by scouts from the Lyme garrison. From here the Royalists advanced to Uplyme Hill where, by means of a trumpeter, Prince Maurice summoned the town to surrender. When they peremptorily refused, the siege of Lyme began.

ADMIRAL THE HONOURABLE SIR JOHN TALBOT GCB

Admiral the Honourable Sir John Talbot GCB (1768–1851) was born at Malahide Castle in County Dublin in either 1768 or 1769. He joined the Royal Navy on 24 March 1784 as a captain's servant on board the frigate *Boreas*. His captain's name was Horatio Nelson. By 1790 Talbot had been promoted to Lieutenant and in 1795 on board the *Astrafa* fought a glorious battle with the French ship *Gloire*, in which she forced the *Gloire* to strike her flag after an hour's fierce fighting at 'half pistol shot' range. Lieutenant Talbot was the officer who went aboard the *Gloire* and sailed her into Portsmouth. His captain said of him, 'I must not omit to mention the just sense I entertain of his Service and good Conduct upon this occasion.' Promotion followed rapidly, first to commander, then captain of the *Eurydice*, in which he captured three French privateers and enjoyed a distinguished naval career. By 1808 Talbot was given command of the 74-gun brand-new *Victorious* that in 1812 fought a very hard but successful battle with the *Rivoli* and three French frigates who were defeated. In the course of the action Talbot was severely wounded in the head by a splinter. The Admiralty rewarded him with a Gold Medal. He finished his active career in 1814. The following October he married 24-year-old Juliana Arundell, third daughter of the 9th Lord Arundell, who presented her husband with two sons and five daughters before her death in late 1843. John Talbot was promoted through the ranks to full admiral on 23 November 1841. In 1847 he achieved his final promotion, Admiral of the Red. He bought Rhode Hill House, a Georgian stuccoed house, in 1815 with his accumulated prize money. It comprised about 1,000 acres. In the 1840s he bought another 500 acres from the Henleys who were the lords of the manor of Lyme (a great gambling family who sold Sandringham to Queen Victoria to pay off a gambling debt). He died on 7 July 1851, aged 82, at Rhode Hill, and is buried under the aisle below the Sanctuary in the Catholic Church of St Michael and St George in Silver Street, Lyme Regis.

ERIK WEST, MVO

Erik West, who lives in the centre of Uplyme in 2003, is by Royal Warrant the Queen's Heraldic Artist. He is responsible for all the royal coats of arms on the Queen's carriages, her 20 royal Phantom Rolls Royces and even her helicopter. For 20 years Erik has been the

Head Carriage Restorer. He has restored and maintained the Gold State Coach, better known as the Coronation Coach, on which he used over 1,000 books of gold leaf. The Queen owns over 100 coaches, all of which Erik supervises and maintains in pristine condition. The Irish State Coach in which the Queen drives to Westminster for the State Opening of Parliament took Erik 18 painstaking months to repaint, refurbish and overhaul. The Queen and the Duke of Edinburgh appreciate all the work Erik has done. In his sitting-room, there is a framed photograph of the Queen and Prince Philip, which they have both signed. In the 2004 New Year's Honours he was awarded the MVO.

THOMAS WHITTY

Thomas Whitty, the undoubted father of Axminster Carpets or, to some extent, modern carpets with a small c, came from middle-class Devonian stock and a family that had settled in and around the town of Axminster in the middle of the sixteenth century when John Whittey (Thomas's great-, great-, great-, great-grandfather) moved from Wells to Kilmington where his son, another John, was born in 1555.

The second John's great-grandson, the second Thomas Whitty (1694–1756), married Sarah Braddick, a mercer's daughter from nearby Lyme Regis. Together they had nine children, our Thomas Whitty and eight daughters, none of the latter seeming to have had children of their own.

All the Whittys from John Whittey (1581–1634) down to Thomas Rampson Whitty (1846–1912) had a son called Thomas – the last being killed on the Somme in 1916. This tends to make the family history hard to follow at times. To help our readers, and starting with the founder of the carpet industry in Axminster, we have named the four Thomases who ran the family business as Thomas I, Thomas II, Thomas III and Thomas IV.

In the sixteenth century the most dangerous period of life was early childhood. Thomas I would have 12 children, six sons and six daughters, out of which only two sons, another Thomas (II) and Samuel, survived infancy, and Samuel's family died out in 1820. Some of Thomas I's children died very early, even stillborn, because, in his *Axminster Carpets (Hand Made) 1755–1957*, Bertram Jacobs gives him as having 12 children in the Whitty family tree on page 19; two pages earlier he states that 'he married Sarah Rampson at Axminster... and raised a family of five daughters and two sons... .' Thomas IV, the son of Samuel Rampson Whitty and a nephew of Thomas III, who died without issue at the age of 35 in 1810, was one of 14 children and the only one of the 14 to continue that particular line of the family.

Thomas I was born into a family of tanners and mercers, his father one of the former and his father-in-law one of the latter, and, as far as is known, he joined his father's business. But, aged 24, left to start

his own cloth-weaving firm in 1737. For 13 years he went quietly about his life doing well enough to have to employ several weavers. Unfortunately for him, or so it seemed at the time, the competition of the Huguenot weavers, who were fleeing religious persecution on the Continent, played havoc with the traditional English styles with their new textures. Some of the Wilton weavers adapted their horizontal looms to make carpets and, by the mid-eighteenth century, they were successfully producing loop-pile Brussels and velvet-pile Wiltons.

As we would say today, Thomas I was forced to diversify and tried his hand with some large seamless carpets of a type that he spotted in a friend's house in London, where a large bale of imported Turkish carpets included some as big as 36ft by 24ft. Carpets of this type were also made in London by Pierre Norbet from Lorraine. Rather out of character for a staunch son of Axminster's Congregational church, Thomas I took advantage of Norbet's absence and, posing as a relative, was taken on a guided tour of the factory. A shrewd businessman, he soon spotted that Norbet's methods were too slow and that he was employing too many people to produce any real profit. He was also well versed in his trade and quickly realised that Norbet's horizontal looms were far too narrow.

Returning to Axminster he designed and built a new loom with a perpendicular frame on which he quietly trained his five daughters and Elizabeth, a sister, to work. On midsummer day 1755, when the factory was empty, Whitty and his family workforce produced the very first Axminster (knotted) carpet. This carpet was obtained by a Mr Cook of Slape Manor, Netherbury, on behalf of Mr Twynihowe, steward to the Earl of Shaftesbury, who was so impressed that he promised to give Whitty all the support that he could. The first service, and the best as it happened, was that he mentioned the carpet to Lady Shaftesbury who promptly obtained the carpet from Mr Cook because 'she wanted to have the first carpet of that manufactory.' It was, of course, for Thomas I, a foot in the door of the best market in England – the gentry, landed or otherwise, who were the people with the money. The Shaftesburys would become regular patrons of Axminster Carpets.

Whitty's factory was in Silver Street on the site of what later became the first Axminster hospital and, fittingly, it is now in the hands of Axminster Carpets Limited. The family dwelling-place, now the Law Chambers, was adjoining, and both, seemingly, were cramped enough to force Thomas I to look elsewhere for a showroom when his business flourished enough to make one necessary. For this purpose he rented a site in South Street from his father-in-law Samuel Rampson. When, in 1828, the Silver Street factory was destroyed by fire, it was rebuilt on the same site, although not necessarily along the same lines.

Thomas Whitty I's connection with Uplyme stems from his use of dyes prepared from land that he owned in Uplyme on what is now known as Whitty Down at the head of Rocombe Bottom.

ALBAN WOODROFFE, MBE, JP, CA

Alban Woodroffe, MBE, JP, CA (1875–1964) was the son of James Tisdall Woodroffe, Advocate General of Bengal who converted to Catholicism. Born in London, Alban was educated at the Oratory school. In 1893 he was sent to Argentina to study farm management on an estanzia there. Subsequently, his father bought the El Mirador Estanzia for him. In 1903 he married Laura Talbot of Rhode Hill, sister of General Mostyn's grandmother. At the same time Alban bought the Ware estate. He was twice Mayor of Lyme Regis (1910–12 and 1914–19). Among the more important works of his mayoralty were the building of the first set of houses for working people in Corporation Terrace, the widening of Bridge Street, the purchase of Langmoor Gardens for the town, the rebuilding of the sea groynes and the introduction of electric light to the town. In 1912 Alban bought the Rhode Hill estate to keep it in the family. Between 1912 and 1915 Laura and he completed the redesigning of Rhode Hill House, a process that the Talbots had begun, converting it from a Georgian to an Edwardian house. From 1916 to 1919 Rhode Hill House became a VAD hospital for convalescent wounded soldiers. Local GPs and VAD nurses staffed it with Alban as the commandant. During the First World War he was responsible for coast watching by Boy Scouts from Exmouth to Poole. He was a County Councillor and later Alderman of Dorset. As chairman of the Dorset Education Authority in the 1930s, he bought the land and built the school that now bears his name, laying the foundation-stone on 29 April 1929. In November 1932 he became an Honorary Freeman of the Borough of Lyme Regis. He was County Commissioner of Scouts in Dorset for seven years, a personal friend of Baden-Powell and founder Scoutmaster of the 1st Uplyme Troop. He was chairman of the Lyme Regis Cottage Hospital for 23 years and a great supporter and benefactor of the Catholic church in Lyme Regis. He was for several years the president of the Uplyme (later Uplyme and Lyme Regis) cricket and football clubs. In 1960 Alban looked around for another Talbot descendant with children to make his heir and the lucky recipient was General Sir David Mostyn. He died, aged 88, in 1964 and is buried in Uplyme Cemetery.

Alban J. Woodroffe, MBE, JP. Born on 6 June 1875, the son of a former Attorney-General of Bengal, he was a considerable benefactor both to Uplyme and Lyme Regis. He was mayor of Lyme Regis for seven years, chairman of the Dorset Education Authority, County Councillor and Alderman of both Devon and Dorset, a Justice of the Peace and a director of the Lyme Regis branch line. His name is remembered in Woodroffe School, formerly Lyme Regis Grammar School. He bought the site where the school stands, employing the same architect who had modernised his home at Rhode Hill which he bought in 1912 from the Talbots. He died, aged 88, on 1 June 1964 and is buried in Uplyme Cemetery.

Admiral Sir John Talbot.

THE FUTURE OF UPLYME

As the year 2003 closes, the centre of Uplyme looks like a bombsite. More than 50 houses are being built, the Devon Hotel is closed and being developed, and the butcher's shop next door has been demolished. Attempts to calm any traffic that speeds through the village have so far proved not entirely successful. It is tempting to say 'change and decay in all around we see'. But we remain buoyant. Uplyme is full of nice people and set in countryside that is too beautiful to be spoilt. In our book we have looked at the past. What of the future?

An Uplyme Parish Plan Group has been formed to prepare a draft Parish Plan that looks at where the village may go. There will be a design appraisal to help developers and residents fit into the ambience of the village within the East Devon planning constraints.

The village does not want to be seen to be sitting still. Nor does it seek to be overwhelmed by our next-door neighbours Lyme Regis. Rather, Uplyme wishes to keep and improve on its past. We would endorse the words on the plaque in the foyer of our magnificent new Village Hall.

'This hall is dedicated to future generations in the belief that there is good in all people.'

So is this book.

The war memorial now sits in splendid isolation alonside the main road through the village, with the Barnes Meadow development behind.

BIBLIOGRAPHY

Berry, Les, and Gosling, Gerald, *Around Uplyme and Lyme Regis*, The Chalford Publishing Company, Stroud, 1995

Bickley, Francis, illustrated by J.W. King, *Where Dorset Meets Devon*, 1911

Bird, Sheila, *Lyme Regis, Uplyme & Charmouth Companion*, Creeds

Bridport News, East Street, Bridport, various editions, 1890–2003

Cherry, Bridget and Pevsner, Nikolaus, *The Buildings of England – Devon*, Penguin, 1981

Cresswell, Beatrix F., *Notes on Devon Churches, Volume 1, 1906–17*, Devon Family History Society

Gosling, Gerald, *Exe To Axe, The Story of East Devon*, Sutton Publishing Company, Stroud, 1994

Fleming, Peter, *Brazilian Adventure.*

Matthews, C.M., *English Surnames*, Scribner, 1967

Matthews, C.M., *Place Names of the English-Speaking World*, Scribner, 1972

National Census, Uplyme, West of England Records Office, 1851

Pearson, Adrian, *A Brief History of Uplyme Village Hall*, 1994

Parliamentary Return, 1818, 1833

Pulman's Weekly News, South Street, Axminster, various editions 1890–2003

Roberts, *History of Lyme*, 1834

Roberts, *Social History of the Southern Counties*, 1856

Seale, Revd Robert Lionel, *Uplyme Parish Church*

Sellman, Roger R., *Devon Village Schools in the Nineteenth Century*, 1967

Sellman, Roger R., *Early Devon Schools*, 1984

Smith, Margaret, *Emily Smith Goes to Lyme Regis*, Margaret Smith, 2000

Thomas, Jack and Imogen, *St Peter and St Paul, Uplyme*, Creeds, 1991

Uplyme Burials and Marriages, 1813–37

Uplyme Churchwardens' Rate 1830–68

Uplyme Minutes of Vestry 1857–1965

Uplyme Women's Institute, *The Story of Uplyme*, 1956

Wanklyn, C., *Lyme Regis, A Retrospect*, 1922

White, *Directory of Devonshire*, 1850

Subscribers

George and Frances Allhusen, Whitlands
Marion E. Anderson, Uplyme
Catherine and Laurence Anholt, Uplyme
Robert Ashley-Jones, Lyme Regis, Dorset
Mr and Mrs R. Bean and daughters, Uplyme
Mr and Mrs D. Booth, Uplyme, Devon
Mrs W. Borland, Wimbledon
Mr and Mrs F.W. Broad, Uplyme, Devon
Richard and Barbara Bull, Uplyme
K.J. Burrow, Bucks Cross, Devon
Peter H.F. Burton O.B.E., Uplyme, Devon
Daphne and David Clarke, Lyme Regis
Vivien Cleal (Cross), East Coker, Somerset
Mrs Jean Cook, Uplyme, Devon
Kate Cross, Uplyme, Devon
Charles F. Day, Uplyme, Devon
Mr and Mrs James Delaney, Church Street, Uplyme
Beryl Denham, Uplyme, Devon
John Denham, Southampton
Michael Denham, Broadmayne
Derek and Sheila Denning, Uplyme
Gerald Denning, Holcombe, Uplyme
Dan and Anne Docherty, Uplyme
Herr Und Frau Drescher, Bergneustadt, Germany
John and Rosamund Duffin, Uplyme, Devon
Kathy Elliott, Uplyme
Alan Ellis, Lyme Regis, Dorset
Colin and Paul Ellis, Australia
Derek and Rita Ellis, Lyme Regis, Dorset
Jeffrey Ellwood and Toni Delaney-Ellwood, Uplyme House, Uplyme
Allan Emmett, Whalley Lane, Uplyme
Melinda Ennis, London
Michael and Ann Evans, Chetnole, Dorset
Keith and Wendy Fountaine